Foreword

Olav Fykse Tveit, General Secretary

The International Ecumenical Peace Convocation (IEPC), held in May 2011 in Kingston Jamaica, was a remarkable and historic ecumenical event and the biggest since the Ninth WCC Assembly in 2006. Inspired by sharing the experiences of the churches around the world and their commitment to justice and peace, more than one thousand participants at the IEPC were nourished and enriched by a renewed theological, moral and spiritual incitement to unite in the call to build a culture of justice and peace. Nurturing peace involves developing and nurturing positive attitudes toward fullness of life, inspired by the ethos of justice. The IEPC made every effort to lift up the spirit of justice and peace.

The Convocation provided us with a platform for the work for justice and peace that is now of great significance in the context of the Tenth Assembly and its theme, "God of Life, Lead Us to Justice and Peace." In its manifold events, deliberations and reflections, the IEPC emphasized the importance of confirming and even celebrating the work for justice and peace as belonging not only to the core business of the WCC but to the heart of our calling to follow Christ and carry our cross together as churches and disciples. The Convocation also saw the need for common platforms for the many initiatives and institutions that promote peace with justice locally, nationally and globally and recognized that the WCC offers a unique opportunity for this. We learned that the common manifestation of the church as a fellowship of peace-makers and of the ecumenical movement as one body uniting different peace initiatives is of vital importance.

Our efforts to organize this complex event yielded much precious fruit. We gained sincere and clear expressions of commitment from our constituencies and promises that the work for justice and peace in the world would be pursued as a priority. The IEPC was not a decision-making body, but we did learn about the challenges and confirm the existence of a solid platform for the further involvement of our constituencies and networks in reflection and action for justice and peace.

The IEPC follow-up reference group has categorically emphasized the need to consider the outcome of the IEPC and its various elements as contributions to the Assembly theme. They should, in fact, be considered as enriching the lifeblood that will flow through the different Assembly components – an understanding that will underlie all our Assembly preparations.

We still aim for an ecumenical declaration on just peace. The emphasis should now be on reflecting the relevance of and the challenges to this concept in different contexts, as I did in my report to the Central Committee 2012 in Crete. More work related to the Assembly is being done that we must harvest and bring into a definition on what just peace is, or should be. The reflection on the theme of the Tenth Assembly should be seen as a process and discussion to develop the concept of Just Peace. The harvest of our consistent efforts throughout the Decade to Overcome Violence and the hard labour centred on the culmination of decade-long programmes in the IEPC have built a solid base on which to develop profound ecumenical thought on peace with justice in the 21st century.

The wider understanding of peace, which builds on the rich legacy of WCC work ever since its inception and over the past several decades, has been clearly expressed through the IEPC focus on the four thematic foci: peace in the community, peace with the earth, peace in the marketplace and peace among the peoples. The sum and substance of this report thus provide us with new insights that will help us to build a culture of Justice and Peace.

This report attempts to weave together various insights gained at different stages of the convocation. A new ecumenical agenda for peace in the conflicts of our time is needed. Thus, in our efforts to develop and shape our journey toward building a culture of peace with justice, I am sure that this publication will be an extremely useful resource.

BUILDING PEACE ON EARTH

BUILDING
PEACE ON EARTH

*Report of the
International Ecumenical
Peace Convocation*

Edited by
Mathews George Chunakara

**World Council
of Churches**
Publications

BUILDING PEACE ON EARTH
Report of the International Ecumenical Peace Convocation
Edited by Mathews George Chunakara

WCC Publications is the book publishing programme of the World Council of Churches. Founded in 1948, the WCC promotes Christian unity in faith, witness and service for a just and peaceful world. A global fellowship, the WCC brings together more than 349 Protestant, Orthodox, Anglican and other churches representing more than 560 million Christians in 110 countries and works cooperatively with the Roman Catholic Church.

Opinions expressed in WCC Publications are those of the authors.

Cover image: Deborah Stockdale, "Journey to Peace," quilt commissioned for the IEPC

Cover and book design and typesetting: 4 Seasons Book Design/ Michelle Cook

Photo credits: WCC/Peter Williams

ISBN: 978-2-8254-1591-7

World Council of Churches
150 route de Ferney, P.O. Box 2100
1211 Geneva 2, Switzerland
http://publications.oikoumene.org

Contents

Editor's Preface

In ecumenical history, every event is unique and important. Every ecumenical event and gathering is a convergence point where various dimensions of people's experiences and ideas meet. They germinate new ideas, vision and enthusiasm. The International Ecumenical Peace Convocation (IEPC) that we have experienced in Kingston, Jamaica, the first such major international ecumenical event held in the Caribbean region, became another such unique ecumenical experience in its context, content, deliberations and the presence of a wide range of participants.

The long-standing policies and programmes of the global ecumenical movement concerning justice and peace as well as the Christian response to violence were emphasized in the content of the IEPC and reflected throughout its deliberations. The 9th Assembly of the World Council of Churches (WCC) at Porto Alegre, Brazil in 2006 recommended an international ecumenical peace convocation to commemorate the end of the Decade to Overcome Violence (DOV) programme which was launched in 2001. It was difficult to measure the impacts of the work related to DOV. However, the IEPC was described by many as a "harvest festival" celebrating the achievements, especially the increased awareness among churches and the ecumenical movement that peace is a gift of God.

The final report of the IEPC brings together various resources, especially the thematic contents. The narrative report gives an overview of the entire proceedings of the IEPC in different segments – from opening plenary, thematic plenaries, workshops and side events. Most presentations or summaries of presentations from the four thematic plenary sessions are included in the report. In addition to these, several other related documents and substantial inputs have been included. This report will remain as a record of the events of the IEPC and at the same time a helpful tool to understand and reflect on the issues and themes related to the forthcoming WCC Assembly theme: "God of life, lead us to justice and peace." In this sense, the IEPC and the follow-up programmes should also be seen as a contribution toward enriching the thematic focus of the Assembly.

The IEPC became an impetus for churches all around the world seeking reconciliation and peace. It encouraged individuals and churches to renew their commitment to nonviolence, peace and justice. Many have laboured for the success of the IEPC, from the Geneva staff to the local host committee

and members of the IEPC Planning Committee, the Message Committee, DOV Reference Group, Spiritual Life Working Group, stewards, participants, resource persons and numerous others. We must also remember
the efforts of and challenges to the host committee under the leadership of
the Jamaican Council of Churches. Almost all our colleagues in the WCC
worked day and night for days and weeks to make the IEPC a success.

All of those who participated, and who became part of the planning and
preparatory process from the beginning till the end may be proud of their
contributions to enhancing the richness and traditions of another saga in
the ecumenical journey.

IEPC Participants

Kingston, Jamaica, May 22, 2011. International Ecumenical Peace Convocation "Glory to God and Peace on Earth". Ecumenical Worship & Celebration, University of the West-Indies, Kingston

Opening Plenary

Keynote speaker Canon Dr Paul Oestreicher

Metropolitan Hilarion

The Rev. Dr Margot Kässmann

Rev. Dr Paul Gardner

Opening prayer with Prof Dr Nancy Cardoso, Brazil

Mr Gerard Grenado, CCC

Rev. Dr Olav Fykse Tveit, WCC Gen. Secretary

Opening prayer with Rev. Dr Ofelia Ortega, Cuba

Ms Jenitha Abela Kameli and Dr Fulate Mbano-Moyo during the opening prayer

In Worship

Plenary on Peace in the Marketplace

Call to worship

Opening prayer

Plenary on Peace in the Community

Dr Martin Luther King III, USA

Martin Luther King III, USA

Dr Muna Mushahwar, Palestine

Prof. Ram Puniyani, India

Dr Deborah Weissman, Israel

Plenary on Peace with the Earth

The choir of the Global Network of Religions for Children sang about respect

Speaker Fr Dr Kondothra M. George, India

Speaker Rev. Tofiga Falani, Tuvalu

Speaker Ms Ernestina Lopez Bac, Guatemala

As a symbolic act a number of trees were planted at the end of the morning's Bible studies

Plenary on Peace in the Marketplace

Plenary on Peace in the Marketplace

Archbishop Valentine Mokiwa, Tanzania

Rev. Garnett Roper, Jamaica

Rev. Dr Roderick Hewitt, Jamaica

Ecumenical Prayer Service for Peace

Ecumenical Worship and Celebration, University of the West-Indies, Kingston

Opening prayer

Bethel Steel Orchestra

Ecumenical Prayer Service for Peace

Congregation listens to Ecumenical Patriarch H.A.H. Bartholomew's message

Rev. Dr Ralph Hoyte, United Church Minister, Jamaica

Rev. Dr Burchell K. Taylor preached the sermon

I.
Report of the IEPC

A Search for Peace on Earth

Mathews George Chunakara

Introduction

When one thousand participants from different parts of the world gathered in Kingston, Jamaica as part of the International Ecumenical Peace Convocation (IEPC), it became another milestone in the history of the ecumenical movement. Organized by the World Council of Churches from 17 to 25 May 2011, the IEPC gave an impetus for the wider ecumenical family and its related constituencies to pursue their search for the way toward building peace. For more than a week, the participants from every continent worshipped and prayed together in the mornings and evenings; listened and discussed the IEPC themes in formal sessions; talked in informal encounters; interacted formally and informally on various occasions and shared their experiences of peace-building in local, national, regional and global contexts.

Many formal components of the IEPC, including the plenary sessions on each of the themes, workshops ("Reasoning"), seminars ("Innerstandings"), Bible studies, spiritual life, as well as informal meetings and sharing, helped participants from all over the world to deepen their search for and sharpen the focus of their journey toward justice and peace.

The event was much more than the sum of its formal sessions. The IEPC took on a true character of celebration and sharing through the many other diverse offerings, experiences and encounters that made it a life-changing experience for many.

The formal components of the IEPC programmes outlined in this section provide a panorama of this historical ecumenical event.

Opening Plenary

Moderated by the World Council of Churches (WCC) General Secretary Rev. Dr Olav Fykse Tveit, the opening plenary session of the International Ecumenical Peace Convocation (IEPC) brought greetings and words of welcome, stories of churches seeking peace and reconciliation, words of inspiration for the pursuit of peace with justice as well as music and images.

The plenary session launched the "weaving together" of prayer, testimony, celebration, dialogue and sharing that characterized the life of the Convocation and was facilitated throughout the IEPC by one of the presidents of the Caribbean Conference of Churches, Rev. Dr Lesley Anderson.

As the participants entered the plenary hall for the opening, they watched a "procession" of video images from the "Stitching Peace" quilts exhibition that was on show throughout the event. Setting the scene for the participants' common "journey" over the coming days, Rev. Dr Tveit explained that "The pilgrimage to Just Peace demands that we seek peace in all ways: peace in the community, with the earth, in the marketplace and among the peoples," and that "in this time together in Jamaica, we will commit ourselves to drawing these four threads together."

IEPC participants were formally welcomed to the country by Jamaica Council of Churches President, Rev. Dr Paul Gardner, who noted that the IEPC was the end of a decade-long process and, at the same time, the beginning of recommitment to creating a just and peaceful society. Gardner affirmed that in Jamaica, "ecumenism is [...] lived out in the daily encounters and interactions among the different churches and people of other faiths who are our neighbours and friends."

"The pilgrimage to Just Peace demands that we seek peace in all ways: peace in the community, with the earth, in the marketplace and among the peoples," and "in this time together in Jamaica, we will commit ourselves to drawing these four threads together."

Welcoming the participants to the region, WCC President representing Latin America and the Caribbean, Rev. Dr Ofelia Ortega noted that "the life of this people has been founded on its spiritual resilience and resistance."

In his role as "weaver of thought," Rev. Dr Lesley Anderson suggested that "Our stories, our testimonies, our conversations, our prayer and our songs are like threads of many colours that will be woven together during our time in Kingston."

The "Stitching Peace" exhibition on display during the IEPC was a concrete illustration of the "weaving" together concept; curator Roberta Bacic explained that all the exhibition tapestries addressed issues related to violent conflict – issues like poverty, hunger, displacement, unemployment, environmental degradation, domestic violence, migration and debt – but also the use of non-violent action to address urgent social issues.

Singing by a children's choir under the auspices of the Jamaica chapter of the Global Network of Religions for Children, a video celebrating the Decade to Overcome Violence, and an exchange with the co-winners of a youth essay competition organized by the World Council of Churches (WCC) Commission on Youth in the Ecumenical Movement (Echos) on the IEPC motto, "Glory to God, Peace on Earth" were other components of the opening plenary. This was followed by three presentations highlighting voices from the churches, an overview on the Decade to Overcome Violence and a keynote address featuring the theme of the IEPC.

Voices from the Churches

For the plenary's first speaker, Metropolitan Hilarion of Volokolamsk of the Russian Orthodox Church, "The principle question we have to answer is what we as Christians can do together in the face of growing violence, aggression, exploitation and terror."

While a "peace-loving rhetoric has prevailed in international organizations and at an intergovernmental level," the media "send us a daily torrent of what could be called a systematic estheticisation of violence." Furthermore, violence in the form of exploitation and injustice "has acquired a structural and systemic character," Metropolitan Hilarion said. That being the case, "We ought to expose the injustice of modern society without fear of tarnishing our reputation in the eyes of the powers that be and the mass media… Our task is to identify the cause of this evil and to overcome not the consequences but the causes." Denouncing the "open persecution of Christians" in Egypt, Iraq, India, Pakistan and Indonesia "and a number of other countries," Metropolitan Hilarion emphasized the need to organize a system of protecting Christians in their minority situations. This requires setting up information structures to monitor crimes caused by religious hatred.

Citing the work of Russia's Interreligious Council and the Russian Federation's Council for Cooperation with Religious Organizations, "People in our country have been able to find a language of mutual understanding, friendship and good-neighborliness despite their differences in faith, culture and ways of life," Metropolitan Hilarion affirmed.

The Decade to Overcome Violence: An Overview

The origins of the 2001-2010 Decade to Overcome Violence (DOV), the churches' involvement in the DOV and what can help the churches to continue the journey were the focus of a plenary intervention by Rev. Dr Margot Kässmann from the Evangelical Church in Germany (EKD).

After watching a DOV video, plenary participants listened as Kässmann traced the history of the Decade starting with the Amsterdam founding assembly of the WCC in 1948 and the 1968 Uppsala Assembly (where Martin Luther King Jr. was to talk about the power of nonviolence), through the 1983-1990 Conciliar Process for Justice, Peace and the Integrity of Creation, the 1988-98 Decade of Churches in Solidarity with Women, Bishop Mogoba's call at the WCC Central Committee meeting in South Africa in 1994 for a programme to combat violence, the 1994-1998 Programme to Overcome Violence and the Seven-City Campaign, and culminating with the motion at the 1998 Harare Assembly to prepare a Decade to Overcome Violence.

"But the past ten years have not turned the world into a peaceful place. Very far from it! Since September 11 2001, terrorism and the so-called 'war against terrorism' have caused nameless suffering," Kässmann declared. Quoting Roman Catholic theologian Hans Küng, Kässmann affirmed that history has shown that that there is no peace between nations without peace among religions, and that there is no just war, only just peace – "which needs creativity, time, engagement and financing."

"We believe in God who is not almighty but comes as an infant, dies under torture and, thus nonviolent and powerless, challenges violence and power. That is the point of reference for Christians. They and the church have always gone astray in history when that was forgotten and violence and destructive power were legitimated," she said.

"Here in Kingston, we are not at the end of a journey," Kässmann concluded. As they continue the journey, churches will do well to be guided by clear theological convictions that violence is in no way to be legitimized by religion, and by the understanding that "There is no way to peace; peace *is* the way." On that basis, churches should offer spiritual and financial support to peace-makers, and challenge their governments to stop producing, financing and purchasing weapons.

A New World Is Possible!

In his keynote address to the opening plenary, peace-builder Rev. Dr Paul Oestreicher of the British Yearly Meeting, Religious Society of Friends identified possibilities and what needs to be done if they are to become realities, while warning that there are no quick fixes. An Anglican priest, Oestreicher criticized Christians' "pact with Caesar" and insisted on the need to say no to war: "Until we throw this [...] 'just war' theology into the dustbin of history, [...] we will have thrown away the one unique ethical contribution that the teaching of Jesus could make both to the survival of humanity and to the triumph of compassion."

Saying no to war means withdrawing all support from the "military-industrial complex, Oestreicher said. "Jesus was not an idealistic dreamer. He was and remains the ultimate realist. The survival of our planet demands nothing less than the abolition of war." As the former Chair of Amnesty International (British Section) and Director of the Coventry Cathedral Centre for International Reconciliation, Oestreicher affirmed that the abolition of war is possible in the same way as was the abolition of slavery.

Although exploitation and human trafficking still exist, they are universally recognized as both morally wrong and illegal, Oestreicher said. Moreover, without immediately eliminating armed violence, passing legislation to abolish war will bring offenders before the International Court of Justice.

"The struggle for greater justice will remain a task for every generation, for as long as human society exists ... Non-violent resistance to evil will never be a quick fix. It will call for long suffering and patience. It will be a living expression now of the new world that is not yet."

At the same time, he continued, we need to learn to resolve our conflicts without militarized violence. "Love of those who threaten us and care for the welfare of those whom we fear is not only a sign of spiritual maturity but also of worldly wisdom. It is enlightened self-interest." Oestreicher suggested that while the IEPC was about the world's need for a just peace, "to speak of a *more* just peace would be nearer the truth. The struggle for greater justice will remain a task for every generation, for as long as human society exists [...] Non-violent resistance to evil will never be a quick fix. It will call for long suffering and patience. It will be a living expression now of the new world that is not yet." What *was* happening now, he said, was that international law was paving the way for genuine alternatives to violence by trying not only crimes committed in war but the crime of war itself. And the laws of peace were being enforced by soldiers trained under UN command to prevent or end violent conflicts. In conclusion, Oestreicher gave a moving account of two "humble men who simply said no," in the context of the First and Second World War, respectively.

Thematic Plenary Sessions

Peace in the Community

As people walked into the plenary tent to attend this session, they were given coloured ribbons with the slogans "Justice for all for Peace in the Community" and "Dignity for all for Peace in the Community." The beating of drums recalled resistance struggles against slavery as well as the struggles of those who still suffer from modern forms of slavery.

The Convocation's "weaver of thought," Dr Leslie Anderson, highlighted the significance of Peace in the Community within the overall framework of the Convocation. Session facilitator Rev. Karen Georgia Thompson, Minister for Ecumenical and Interfaith Relations for the United Church of Christ (USA), reminded the audience to reflect on the images of violence presented in a video, and invited them to prepare themselves for a vocation of peace with justice: "Peace is not a mere feeling of togetherness but a lived-out ethic informed by the values of dignity, respect, hospitality and justice. The challenge, therefore, is to determine what we, as churches, peace activists and movements, have to offer as alternative models of community."

Challenges

First of the thematic plenary's presenters, Dr Muna Mushahwar, a young Palestinian Christian medical doctor from Jerusalem, gave a moving account of the combination of factors – the 63-year-long occupation and patriarchy – that make the life of Palestinian women utterly miserable. She also threw light on the torture, harassment, verbal and physical abuse, medical negligence and poor living conditions suffered by Palestinian women detained by the Israeli government. As regards discrimination, abuse and exploitation caused by patriarchal culture, she emphasized that there is hardly any difference between the experience of Muslim and Christian women, and called on the church to stop misinterpreting the Scriptures and tacitly justifying the current historical injustice against the Palestinian people and against women in general.

Ms Asha Kowtal, a young woman Dalit activist from India, presented an account of violence experienced by nearly 260 million Dalits in South Asian countries who are the worst victims of the caste system considered as the world's most massive and systemic violation of human rights. The cruelty of a culture that holds some as inferior by birth and denies their dignity and rights from their birth to death was described by Ms Kowtal. She emphasized the need to explore ways of teaching nonviolence to the powerful instead of preaching peace and forgiveness to the victims.

Prof. Ram Puniyani, a well-known scholar, writer and social activist against religious fundamentalism in India, spoke on the "violence caused by excessive and irresponsible assertion of religious identities." He cited situations of growing religious fundamentalism and the divisive role of certain Hindu extremist groups that are spreading religious hatred and violence against minority religious communities in India. Although these groups use religion to spread hatred, there is nothing religious about their ideologies, Puniyani stated. He described them as agents of the existing powers that thrive by encouraging and legitimizing dehumanization.

Reflecting on the theme from her context in Israel, Dr Deborah Weissman, president of the International Council of Christians and Jews, acknowledged the unfortunate reality of religions as perpetrators of or partners in violence. "But our religions also offer powerful tools for alternate interpretations as well as spiritual and cultural resources for developing more positive approaches toward the Other," she suggested. According to Dr Weissman, a strange fascination with violence makes us more receptive to hearing the negative; she called on the participants of the Convocation to nurture a culture of peace by making the vocation of peace interesting and attractive.

Buzz groups reflected together for a short while on the questions: What do these challenges mean to you? What are the other challenges? How can you make a difference?

"The oppressed have the moral stamina to effect positive change. When oppressed people get organized and practice disciplined nonviolence, they can produce far-reaching social change."

Possibilities for Peace in the Community

In a powerful message during the first plenary, Dr Martin Luther King III, Executive Director of the King Center for Nonviolent Social Change, USA, suggested that "affirming the human dignity and rights of all and nurturing values of mutuality and interdependence" are important ways of ensuring peace in the community. Recalling the non-violent struggles of African Americans for their right to live with dignity and rights, Dr King elaborated on the Jesus values – also common to most religious traditions – of unconditional love and forgiveness, treating the poor and oppressed with kindness and generosity.

The oppressed have the moral stamina to effect positive change, stated Dr King. "When oppressed people get organized and practice disciplined nonviolence, they can produce far-reaching social change."

He recalled that his father Dr Martin Luther King Jr. saw mutuality and interdependence as an inescapable part of the human condition and lamented that instead of celebrating this mutuality, we spend so much time, money and effort in conflicts. Dr King called on the Convocation to affirm the bonds of mutuality and interdependence that unite freedom and justice-loving people everywhere.

Dr Tania Mari Viera Sampaio, from the Catholic University of Brasilia, Brazil, offered a theological reflection and called the gathering to feel their oneness with the earth, fire, air, water and wind, insisting on the need to understand the interconnectedness of all life. Having worked with poor communities in Brazil, she suggested that churches, institutions and universities can learn much from their analysis of society and the world that has the capacity to ensure emancipation, empowerment and participation for all in the community.

Churches could make a difference, she said, by seeing the ecosystem as interdependent and complex and human beings as different rather than superior. For Sampaio, this "theory of complexity" promotes relations of connectivity between different living beings while the "theory of gender" shows that there is no single universal human being but only heterogeneity or plurality; an ethic of solidarity that accepts the differences and promotes fair and inclusive communities.

Toward the end of the plenary, the participants tied the ribbons they had received at the beginning to themselves or to their neighbours as a sign of solidarity and commitment to strive together for justice and dignity for all for the sake of peace in the community.

Peace with the Earth

As humanity continues on its reckless path of overexploitation and destruction, violence is perpetrated against the earth and creation is neglected. The present dominant civilization treats the whole creation in a violent way. Extracting, modifying, deforesting and expanding monocultures are changing the environment in order to produce more, to consume more. Climate change and water crises – "groaning creation" - are expressions of this earth crisis. These were some of the affirmations made at the plenary on "Peace with the Earth."

The session opened with songs on care for creation and peace sung by the Jamaican section of the Global Network of Religion for Children's choir. The Convocation's "weaver of thought," Dr Leslie Anderson, recalled the previous plenary on "Peace in the Community" and stated that violence against women, children, racism, casteism and religiously motivated violence are related to violence against the earth, against the whole creation.

"The creation is groaning! Can we hear its groans? Do we listen attentively? Are we responsible stewards of God's good creation?" Dr Anderson asked.

A Cry from Tuvalu

The plenary audience watched a video evoking the fears and hopes of the people of Tuvalu in relation to climate change. A Polynesian island nation in the Pacific Ocean between Hawaii and Australia that is home to 11,000 people, Tuvalu's life at one time was tied to the ocean and its bounty. Today, its very existence is threatened by rising ocean water levels.

Rev. Tafue M. Lusama, the General Secretary of the Congregational Christian Church of Tuvalu and Chairperson of the Tuvalu Climate Action Network (CAN), who described the plight of the people of Tuvalu, said his country is now facing longer droughts, and saltwater has invaded the underground water table. "Now we depend on rainwater only, and we are facing unpredictable weather patterns." The people's once-sustainable existence is endangered by forces beyond their control and they are unable to use their traditional survival skills. The cause of the rising waters finds its roots far from this south Pacific paradise in the industrial heartlands of the northern hemisphere Rev. Lusama affirmed, calling on the churches to respond to the challenges faced by creation today.

Buzz groups identified challenges related to Peace with the Earth in their own countries, churches and communities and discussed how they have been addressing them.

Prophetic Witness of the Churches

Elias Crisóstomo Abramides, a Greek Orthodox layman from Argentina, shared examples of prophetic witness of the churches. The role the Ecumenical Patriarchate was playing by creating increasing environmental awareness, caring for God's creation in an environment at peace with its Creator was a specific example. A long-time WCC delegate to UN conferences on the environment and climate change, Abramides reported that among other contributions, the late Ecumenical Patriarch Dimitrios had established 1 September as a Day for the Protection of the Natural Environment as well as a *Time for Creation* (1 September to 4 October) in the churches' calendar.

Other events initiated by the Patriarch included annual summer seminars stressing the connections between environmental issues and education, ethics, communication, justice and poverty, and biannual international symposia on the impact of wasteful lifestyles on the waters of the Aegean,

Black, Adriatic, Baltic and Arctic Seas as well as on the Amazon, Danube and Mississippi Rivers.

"Our natural environment is beautiful. It still keeps a lot of peace and the perfect balance of the original good creation of God," Abramides said. "However, it faces challenges and aggressions. Greed and pride and an exacerbated consumerism imposed by the established economic order have discarded the role of human beings as stewards of creation, turning them into its exploiters and abusers, treating everything, including human beings as commodities."

Abramides also reminded the audience of the various side events, ecumenical and interfaith celebrations and statements presented on behalf of the WCC at the Conference of Parties (COP) of the UN Framework Convention on Climate Change (UNFCCC) as concrete ways of doing ecumenical advocacy at the UN level.

"Greed and pride and an exacerbated consumerism imposed by the established economic order have discarded the role of human beings as stewards of creation, turning them into its exploiters and abusers, treating everything, including human beings as commodities."

Wisdom from the Heart

Sr. Ernestina López Bac, a Kaqchiquel Indigenous theologian from Guatemala, reflected in her presentation on the spirituality, theology and worldview of the Indigenous Peoples of Central America, the Mayas. A member of the National Commission of Indigenous Pastoral Ministries of the Guatemalan Roman Catholic Bishops Conference, López Bac evoked the "heart and energy" of Maya thought and wisdom, the set of values that constitute their social identity and relationship with nature. At the core of this set of values lies the sacredness of Nature, of God as the centre and energy of the universe. Everything is alive and the presence of God is in everything, hence the value of protecting everything.

Fr. Kondothra M. George, a prominent Asian theologian from the Malankara Orthodox Syrian Church in India, opined that IEPC participants had gathered in Jamaica to express their deep distress because of the fatal divorce between earth and life. "We are threatened in our very existence. The crisis of our times is precisely that the earth is being emptied of all life, that life is being uprooted from its ground," Fr. George warned. "Peace and justice are not simply human issues to be debated. They are integrally related to respect and compassion for the myriad forms of created existence that God saw as good. All carry the stamp of God's Will and Love. All life is hatched in the uterine warmth of the Holy Spirit, the Life-Giving Breath of God."

"Peace and justice are not simply human issues to be debated. They are integrally related to respect and compassion for the myriad forms of created existence that God saw as good. All carry the stamp of God's Will and Love. All life is hatched in the uterine warmth of the Holy Spirit, the Life-Giving Breath of God."

The great Cappadocian Fathers saw the human body and soul as "fellow servants yoked together" in the quest for *theosis* or divinization. The whole creation has a profound share in our body and the divine right to be tenderly cared for in view of its participation in God's glory. Justice is essentially loving care to a member of our own body, Fr. George said.

Quoting Mahatma Gandhi – there is enough in our world for everybody's *need* but not for everybody's *greed* – Fr. George concluded that our total inability today to see the difference between need and greed is at the root of all violence.

What Can Churches Do?

Mr Adrian Shaw, a member of the Church and Society Team of the Church of Scotland dealing with environmental issues, made a strong call to churches to be more environmentally friendly.

Churches worldwide must begin to lead the fight against climate change. But to do so in a credible way, there is a need for a big change within parishes and congregations. Eco-congregations, he said, is a movement that has been spreading for some years in Scotland. Today more than 270 congregations have pledged to become informed about their carbon footprint and have taken steps to reduce it. Responding to global warming and expressing stewardship for creation, the movement has also developed in other countries in Europe.

Winding up the session, "weaver of thought" Dr Anderson referred to the need for a profound change. As Christians, we are called to *metanoia*, to repentance and to change: change of mind, change of paradigm, change of lifestyles and attitudes and change of international legal instruments. Perhaps very timidly, churches and individual Christians are already involved in this process of change. However, much more is needed from Christians and churches all over the world. Seminars and workshops, Dr Anderson concluded, offer the opportunity to learn more and share other experiences, challenges and wisdom.

The plenary closed with music, lyrics and dance performed by the Jamaica section of the Global Network of Religions for Children's choir and evoking some of the challenges to Peace with the Earth.

Peace in the Marketplace

The plenary session on "Peace in the Marketplace" analyzed the links between economic justice and violence based on biblical and current examples; took stock of economically related violence, particularly against vulnerable groups such as women, youth, Indigenous People and persons with disabilities, and of how peace and justice can be forged in the marketplace by sharing good practices; and proposed an ecumenical way forward for promoting peace based on economic justice.

On the morning of the plenary and in line with these aims, breakfast was served to only a few participants. Morning prayers thus provoked an initial reflection on the global paradox of deepening poverty amidst unprecedented wealth; on empty stomachs, lines from the Lord's Prayer – "Give us this day our daily bread" – could not but resonate with greater meaning.

The "weaver of thought" reminded participants of the previous plenary sessions. Issues raised at the "Peace in the Community" and "Peace with the Earth" sessions were intimately related to "Peace in the Marketplace" because poverty, economic injustice and market rules have a strong impact in communities and on the environment, he suggested. To analyze how wealth is produced and distributed, to see the links between economic injustice and violence and, at the same time, recognize the signs of emerging alternatives were important components of what the Peace in the Marketplace plenary would address.

No Peace without Economic Justice

The plenary opened with a skit performed by young people. Their message was clear: there can be no peace without economic justice. The skit sought to illustrate two main points. Firstly, that hunger, joblessness (especially among youth) and the lack of access to social services such as education and health (which in a market economy are available only to a privileged minority who can afford them) undermine community and are key ingredients for violence. Secondly, that despite differences in race, gender and class, the foundations of a long and lasting peace are based on genuine care and attentiveness to each other's wellbeing and to the equitable sharing of the Earth's fruits so that all may live fully.

The skit was followed by a panel of four presenters who offered compelling stories and analyses of how different situations of economic injustice pose a threat to peace and how it leads to violence.

Bishop Valentine Mokiwa, President of the All Africa Conference of Churches, gave an example of how the multinational gold mining industry in Tanzania intensifies economic violence. The industry continues to reap and repatriate tremendous wealth to its corporate headquarters abroad while at the same time contributing minimally to Tanzanian government revenues, displacing small miners, evicting entire communities from their ancestral land and polluting the earth. Mokiwa called on churches to stand with and advocate for those adversely affected by extractive companies.

Ms Omega Bula from the United Church of Canada brought the story of women, especially women of colour, who suffer from the collusion between globalization, patriarchy and racism and are pushed to poverty despite the fact that they are the main producers in the economy.

Rev. Prof. Dr Emmanuel Clapsis from the Ecumenical Patriarchate painted a picture of a global economic system that is devoid of morals and ethics and hence results in structural violence. He called for radical spiritual renewal in response to the violence of market globalization.

Rev. Dr Roderick Hewitt from the UK-based Council for World Mission reminded participants that the University of the West Indies, the venue for the IEPC, stands on what was formerly a sugarcane plantation in colonial times where hundreds of slaves toiled to death for the financial gain of a few. The system of slavery and colonialism continues to be mirrored in the current market-based capitalist economy whereby countries and peoples of the South are exploited through unequal and unjust structures of global trade and finance, he said.

While attempting to understand the logic of wars and terrorism in various forms, it has become more and more apparent that, in part, violence stems from the infliction of misery on others by depriving them of material goods and dignity. It is structural violence embedded in the market that brings death instead of life. In this context, there is growing recognition that God's vision of peace is imperiled by the massive socio-economic inequalities – among and within nations – characterizing our world today. The political and economic crises of the early 21st century thus compel Christians to take a critical look at our core assumptions about wealth and poverty, growth and sustainability and how these might be obstacles to justice and generate violence. As structures for exchanging goods, services and information between buyers and sellers, markets – in particular, increasingly liberalized and globalized markets – no doubt play an important role in these dynamics.

As an instrument for expanding choices, promoting economic interdependencies and creating and diffusing prosperity, can markets sow peace and security? If so, under what conditions can markets aid nonviolence? Put the other way around, is there no way for markets to promote peace? Do they inherently exclude the poor and inevitably widen inequities between the haves and have-nots? Are markets imbued with values? And if so, do these values support or undermine peace-building? Finally, what is the role of Christians and churches in the world's markets, both as participants and in their witness and ministry for justice and reconciliation? These are questions that churches were encouraged to raise back home as well.

In his closing remarks, the "weaver of thought" evoked the topic of the next day's plenary – Peace among the Peoples. Peace in the Marketplace, he suggested, is related not only to Peace in the Community and Peace with the Earth but also to Peace among the Peoples. Confrontations between states have a strong economic component as a root cause, sometimes hidden by propaganda.

Peace among the Peoples

An increasingly inter-dependent world challenges Christians in all parts of the world to work in new ways to build "peace among the peoples." This thematic plenary explored the nature of "just peace"; presenters from different walks of life shared their commitment and knowledge and portrayed peace-making as a calling that is widely shared within the church – and well beyond it.

Plenary participants took part in small "buzz" groups followed by a public forum to discuss and amplify the plenary topics. Panelists answered key questions raised by the "Ecumenical Call to Just Peace." These related to the importance of the rule of law in international affairs, including human rights and humanitarian law, the necessity of strengthening mechanisms for accountability over the use of armed force, the need to eliminate the most indiscriminate and destructive weapons, and the Christian pursuit of conflict resolution and reconciliation across all barriers and borders.

Panelists debated the churches' role in generating dialogue and action on governments that invest heavily in *national security* via military power while investing relatively little in *human security* via commitments such as the Millennium Development Goals. The debate on this and other topics is summarized below.

How Do Churches Define Security?

"Jesus does not use the word security. He is often telling us to give our own lives in the service of others. So the language of the church is much more about justice and peace than security," said Eastern Mennonite University (USA) professor of peace-building Dr Lisa Schirch.

Schirch compared governments which "tend to speak of security in narrow terms of national security, which is very often expensive security for some at the expense of others," to the church, which "may speak of safety for peoples around the world."

Describing the church's vision of peace, Schirch said that "When God tells us to love our enemies and to do good to those who hurt us, this is not just moral advice, it is strategic advice…. If we would approach Iraq and Afghanistan and Pakistan with generosity… as partners, not as patrons, then we would actually see a warming and a transforming of hearts."

Women as Peace-Makers

"Women are often among those who suffer most deeply during armed violence. Despite their commitment to solving conflict, they are given practically no role afterwards in the negotiation process," said Ms Christiane Agboton-Johnson, a former leader of women's initiatives in peace-making, peace-building, armed violence reduction and peace education for young people in West Africa.

"I want to see women at the negotiating table in all conflicts, [in all regions of the world] and I want to see them at the negotiating table on nuclear weapons," said Dr Patricia Lewis, a researcher/analyst for the UN and various governments and universities. Church women could play a critical role in providing early warnings on emerging conflicts, Lewis said, noting that "One of our research findings is that when you don't ask the women in a conflict area, you don't know what is happening."

Love of God and the Search for Peace in Iraq

In the face of the mass violence and displacement under the US occupation of Iraq, Archbishop Avak Asadourian, the Armenian Orthodox Archbishop of Baghdad and General Secretary of the Council of Christian Church Leaders in Iraq, has played a key role in bringing long-divided churches together and reaching out to Muslim leaders.

"As Christians in Iraq, we are part of Iraqi society and do everything we can for the cause of peace... God came to bring us peace…and by peace I mean more than the absence of war, I mean equality." Whatever the laws of a particular country, all are equal under a loving God and are saved by a saving God, Asadourian emphasized.

Most Muslims in Iraq appreciate the role of Christians in the country – church schools and hospitals serve society without discrimination – as well as their ancient roots there, and attacks against Christians are the work of a small, militant minority, he said.

Hiroshima 1945: The Meaning of Survival

Addressing the IEPC by video, Setsuko Thurlow, who survived the atomic bombing of Hiroshima as a 13-year-old schoolgirl, described in tragic detail her own experiences on that morning 66 years ago: Most of her classmates were burned alive. A few years later, she heard that an organization called the World Council of Churches had declared that war was contrary to the will of God. This helped her to become a lifelong advocate so that no one else should ever have to suffer the fate of the half-million casualties of Hiroshima and Nagasaki, Thurlow said.

> bleeding, ghostly figures … naked and battered, blackened and swollen… flesh and skin dangling from their bones, some with their eyeballs hanging in their hands… There was deathly silence, only broken by the moans of the injured: …'Water, water, please give me water.' But we had no containers to carry water. We went to a nearby stream … tore off our blouses, soaked them with water and hurried back to hold them to the mouths of the dying who desperately sucked in the moisture. …

Yet, "In spite of the effects of the atomic bombing, the unimaginable defeat of Japan, and the humiliation of occupation by foreign troops, we survivors were able to begin to see the meaning of our survival…and transcend our personal tragedies. We became convinced that no human being should ever have to repeat our experience of inhumanity, illegality, immorality and cruelty of atomic warfare," Thurlow declared.

"We identified our mission as warning the world of the danger of nuclear weapons. Convinced that humanity and nuclear weapons cannot co-exist… we have been speaking out around the world for the total abolition of nuclear weapons."

The 21st Century Less Lethal than the 20th Century?

At least 160 million people died in armed conflicts in the 20th century, with the causes ranging from dehumanization to nuclear bombing, said Dr Patricia Lewis, Deputy Director at the Monterey Institute of International Studies (USA). Was that due to an inability to address conflict early, to share resources equitably, to see others as our equals, or "Are we not wise enough as a species?" she asked.

"We need to understand that we can prevent man-made deaths in the 21st century," Lewis stated. Military leaders increasingly recognize that nuclear weapons have no military use at all, and that their magical symbolism rests on the willingness to use them. "That is the essence of nuclear deterrence; it no longer exists, if it ever did." "We can say the same thing to war. Why can't we look to abolish war? Where is our faith? … We, particularly in the West, need to take the planks out of our own eyes and apply conflict prevention strategies to all of our countries," she argued.

"We need to understand that we can prevent man-made deaths in the 21st century."

Lewis wondered what nuclear weapons were doing to the souls of people who use them in the name of their own security. In nuclear powers and countries sheltering under the nuclear umbrella, "we are all prepared to exterminate whole cities, to exterminate whole civilizations in the name of our security," Lewis said. Is the ability to think about killing so many other people in the name of our security was not "part of the fundamental malaise that we see throughout the world today?" she asked.

Agboton-Johnson reported that Africa had recently become a Nuclear-Weapon-Free Zone, that the WCC had helped bring this about, and that these zones now covered more than half the world.

Participants formed small groups with leaders of ecumenical peace networks to discuss the key challenges related to "Peace among the Peoples." Comments were then shared in a plenary forum whose final remarks spoke primarily to peace-making as a call to discipleship. The cross of Christ points us outward to other people, upward to God, and into the earth and all of creation. It is a guide to our efforts at peace and reconciliation, the forum observed. Further, Christians must become suffering servants in order to bring about real peace, and churches must free themselves from fear in order to free others from fear. It is good to walk in the realm of ideas, but we also need a strong voice in the corridors of power to make peace real in our communities and the world.

Spiritual Life during the IEPC

Providing the environment and means with which a meeting, conference or consultation may develop its own spiritual life is not a simple task. Enabling a spirituality that can inspire and lament, praise and hope and allow for the unresolved and irresolvable is more difficult. And the task is even harder when participants from diverse traditions bring often opposite understandings of prayer, spiritual life, the way the Bible might be read and used, the purpose of symbols, liturgy, song and colour to such a meeting. Add to this WCC member churches' different theologies of peace and justice and the enormity of the task that faced the Spiritual Life group in planning for the

International Ecumenical Peace Convocation was evident. Not surprising, therefore, that it took four years of work to create an IEPC Spiritual Life programme, but in the end it all worked out very well and that was evident throughout the IEPC.

Preparing for the Spiritual Life programme at the IEPC was a journey in several stages. The group first met together in Baar, Switzerland in early December 2007. Maintaining a constancy of ethos and purpose in spite of changes in its composition over the four years, the group began to explore the possible shape and sense of the Convocation's spiritual life. There was passion in the discussions, a passion for justice brought from Palestine and Scotland, Argentina and Tanzania; there was a gentleness of spirit from East and West, North and South. And as group members prayed together, there were tears of grief. For spiritual life comes from the depths of our being and is created out of the ways in which God holds us and hollows out hospitality of spirit.

The second meeting of the planning process of the spiritual life group in Damascus, Syria in December 2008 gave opportunities to walk through the streets and the hills and to hear Iraqi refugees' stories. Deeply affected ("What have we done, what have we done?") the group prayed, worked on Bible studies, tried out ideas and struggled with difficult Bible texts that seem to sanction honour killings of women, texts about rape... The texts they would recommend should not exclude those that present disturbing visions of justice and peace, the group resolved. New songs were composed and shared both during the group's formal work sessions and in the evenings sitting together with guitars – a sign of the group's vitality and own emergent spiritual life. By the time it met in Hildesheim, Germany in August 2009 and in Geneva, Switzerland in September 2010, the group's work was well underway. Its musicians were selecting songs and words were being written and tested. The IEPC sending prayer was a great "catch," with all the joy of carrying nets loaded with goodness, commitment and hope!

A collection of liturgical resources for the four Sundays of Advent prepared during a workshop in Matanzas, Cuba, in July 2008, *Imagine Peace* was the fruit of collaboration with musicians and liturgists from the Latin American liturgical network "Red Create." The workshop also provided space for developing an excellent model for creative spiritual work that could ensure a lively and generative fountain of resources and experience and training in this field in the future.

In her reflections on the spiritual life at the IEPC, Alison Phipps, from the Iona Community in Scotland, observes that "when our prayer is carefully, respectfully and hopefully crafted as a sign that, for all our extraordinary differences in doctrine and understanding of spiritual life, liturgy and worship, we can bring our offerings to God together in common prayer, then our prayer for Just Peace is the very heartbeat of the ecumenical movement."

Prayer

Throughout the Convocation, morning worship took the theme of the day as its central focus. The prayer for "Peace in the Community" focused on children. Children around the world had been asked to draw pictures of conflict and their hope for peace. The pictures were projected onto the central screen during the time of prayer. Persuasive and poetic, the images offered a challenge and inspired hope. Stronger than words, they spoke about the central hope for peace in the future – the peace longed for in each generation and seen with such clarity by children all over the world. The songs for peace included *Miren que bueno* and *Bwana utupe Amani*, a song written especially for the IEPC by ethnomusicologist Jenitha Kameli from Tanzania, which she led with her drum.

Morning worship on the second day reflected on the theme of the day "Peace with the Earth." In a strong symbolic action, participants were given a dead battery to hold. Images of batteries were projected alongside a video of the Convocation's midday tree-planting prayer, and members of the worship congregation were invited to hang the dead batteries on a huge dead tree on the university campus. A mood of lament was at the heart of this prayer. The prayer leader explained that "Every day millions of batteries are thrown away in the world, and many of these are then transported thousands of kilometers by a hidden recycling trade to parts of the world where they are dumped for cash. The dead battery in your hand represents one of the many insoluble problems facing the earth and humanity." After a song from the Pacific, the congregation heard words of assurance which yet conveyed a strong sense of the need of grace, and that what participants held in their hands – dead, unrecyclable batteries – were a sign of our brokenness.

"When our prayer is carefully, respectfully and hopefully crafted as a sign that, for all our extraordinary differences in doctrine and understanding of spiritual life, liturgy and worship, we can bring our offerings to God together in common prayer, then our prayer for Just Peace is the very heartbeat of the ecumenical movement."

The prayer for "Peace in the Marketplace" had participants up extra early so that some could receive breakfast packages during the worship, while the majority would receive nothing. The packages arrived late, adding to the sense of worry about not being able to feed anyone! Finally, however, food packages were distributed to about one in ten members of the congregation. This created feelings of confusion, lack of worth, desire to share and many, many conversations. The simple enactment of the reality of the unjust distribution of wealth was felt right through the prayer for mercy and for forgiveness. "Until all are fed we cry out; until all on earth are fed; like the one who loves us each and every one, we serve until all are fed," the congregation sang.

The prayer for "Peace to the Peoples" also contained a strong symbolic action. Up nearly all night making signs in the WCC's official languages, Convocation stewards then divided the tent into seven regions. During the prayer, the congregation was divided according to their regions. As people moved to be with those from their region, all kinds of realities were made visible: the large contingent from Europe, especially Germany; the one person from the Middle East on her own; very few from the Global South regions.

Midday prayer and tree-planting were a strong affirmation of solidarity in the local context. Many trees were lost to Jamaica in hurricanes and because of deforestation. Despite difficulties of communication and logistics, all the Convocation participants were able to take part in a tree-planting, with Psalm 1 being recited in a wide variety of languages. And around midday, they paused and committed themselves to pray that they might be like "a tree planted by water."

Bible Study

During the week-long IEPC, participants met in small groups for Bible study each morning immediately after the morning prayers. Each Bible Study text corresponded to the theme of the day, later discussed in the morning's plenary session.

The passages studied were:

2 Samuel 13:1-22	The rape of Tamar, in relation to "Peace in the Community"
Isaiah 11:6-9	The wolf and the lamb, the leopard and the kid together, in relation to "Peace with the Earth"
Matthew 20:1-16	Labourers in the vineyard, in relation to "Peace in the Marketplace"
Ephesians 2:11-22	He is our peace, he has abolished the wall, in relation to "Peace among the Peoples"
2 Kings 6:8-23	Fear is transformed in peace, was the concluding theme for peace and nonviolence.

Forty-seven Bible study leaders were selected from the general list of IEPC participants and invited to undertake the role of facilitators of the Bible studies at the Convocation; a good number were members of the Ecumenical Disabilities Advocacy Network (EDAN). Most of the Bible study groups worked in English, but two worked in German, two in French and three in Spanish. Facilities in some of the University of the West Indies locations did not allow for the use of planned methodological tools like, for example, a power-point presentation for the story of Tamar's Rape (2 Samuel 13:1-22). In spite of this, the Bible studies were positively evaluated throughout the Convocation and especially so at the end. While each group was planned for a maximum capacity of twenty persons, in reality numbers varied between five and twenty. Although the number varied, the Bible study groups worked in a very participatory way which developed a real *esprit de corps* while the members' consistent attendance indicated the level of both their engagement and enjoyment.

Bible study group reports ended with powerful messages, for example:

- "The church must address and bring to light that which destroys life."
- "The Good News is that peace will come through God's divine action, in and through humanity."
- "In the face of violence, God will act to bring wholeness, protection and peace."
- "In order to keep going in our commitment for peace in the community, peace with the earth, peace with the marketplace and peace among the peoples, we need to continue to be sustained and empowered by the stories of good practices, the beauty of creation and the communion of saints."

World Day of Peace/Caribbean Day

The observance of a World Day of Peace on Sunday 22 May 2011 was an important feature of the week-long IEPC. The Day began with an ecumenical worship service with a Caribbean flavour. The liturgy, developed by the Jamaica Council of Churches' Caribbean partners, was a dynamic and spirited experience that celebrated the foci of the Convocation and provided opportunities for the participation of children, youth, women and men.

Revelling in an atmosphere that reverberated with the rhythms and tongues of the Caribbean, IEPC participants were particularly moved and inspired by the Bethel Baptist Church Steel Band, the University Singers and the sermon delivered by the pastor of the Bethel Baptist Church, Rev. Dr Burchell Taylor.

The celebration included a special video-recorded "peace message" from Ecumenical Patriarch His All Holiness Bartholomew.

Message from Patriarch Bartholomew, Archbishop of Constantinople-New Rome and Ecumenical Patriarch

✠ BARTHOLOMEW, BY THE MERCY OF GOD, ARCHBISHOP OF CONSTANTINOPLE-NEW ROME AND ECUMENICAL PATRIARCH

To the Plenitude of the Church:
Grace, Mercy and Peace from our Saviour the Lord of Peace

Sunday, May 22, 2011

Beloved brothers and children in Christ,

At the celebration of each Divine Liturgy, after glorifying the divine name and blessing the heavenly kingdom, we offer three petitions "to the Lord" "for peace," "for the peace from above," and "for the peace of the whole world." It is our passionate yearning that our world may reflect the kingdom of God, that the God's love may reign "on earth as it is in heaven."

Nevertheless, while such peace is foremost in our prayer, it is not always central in our practice. As faithful disciples of the Lord of peace, we must constantly pursue and persistently proclaim alternative ways that reject violence and war. Human conflict may well be inevitable in our world; but war and violence are certainly not. If this century will be remembered at all, it may be for "the pursuit of what makes for peace." (Rom. 14. 19)

The pursuit of peace has always proved challenging. Yet, our present situation is in at least two ways quite unprecedented. First, never before has it been possible for one group of human beings to eradicate as many people simultaneously; second, never before has humanity been in a position to destroy so much of the planet environmentally. We are faced with radically new circumstances, which demand of us an equally radical commitment to peace.

This is why we welcome with great joy the WCC/International Ecumenical Peace Convocation to be held on May 17-25, 2011, in Kingston, Jamaica, as a fitting conclusion and continuation of the World Council of Churches decade to overcome violence, a global inter-church initiative to strengthen existing efforts and networks for preventing violence and to inspire the creation of new ones.

Now, the pursuit of peace calls for a radical reversal of what has become the normative way of survival in our world. Peace requires a sense of conversion or metanoia; it requires commitment and courage. Moreover, peacemaking is a matter of individual and institutional choice. We have it in our power either to increase the hurt inflicted on our world or to contribute toward its healing. Once again, it is a matter of choice.

Justice and peace are central themes in Scripture. However, as Orthodox Christians, we also recall the profound tradition of the Philokalia, which emphasizes that peace always ~ and ultimately - starts in the heart. In the words of St, Isaac the Syrian in the 7th century, "if you make peace with yourself: then heaven and earth will make peace with you." Nonetheless, this inner peace must be manifest in every aspect of our life and world. This is what the Jamaica Convocation underlines with its four sub-themes: peace in the community, with the earth, in the marketplace, and among peoples.

In an increasingly complex and violent world, Christian churches have come to recognize that working for peace constitutes a primary expression of their responsibility for the life of the world. They are challenged to move beyond mere rhetorical denunciations of violence, oppression and injustice, and incarnate their ethical judgments into actions that contribute to a culture of peace. This responsibility is grounded on the essential goodness of all human beings by virtue of being in God's image and the goodness of all that God has created.

Peace is inextricably related to the notion of justice and freedom that God has granted to all human beings through Christ and the work of the Holy Spirit as a gift and vocation. It constitutes a pattern of life that reflects human participation in God's love for the world. The dynamic nature of peace as gift and vocation does not deny the existence of tensions, which form an intrinsic element of human relationships, but can alleviate their destructive force by bringing justice and reconciliation.

The Church understands peace and peacemaking as an indispensable aspect of its life and mission to the world. It grounds this faith conviction upon the wholeness of the biblical tradition as it is properly interpreted through the Church's liturgical experience and practice.

The Eucharist provides the space in which one discerns and experiences the fullness of the Christian faith in the history of God's revelation. It reflects the image of God's Trinitarian life in human beings and relates in love with the totality of the created world.

This eschatological experience of being in communion with God and participating in God's love for the created world provides the hermeneutical key by which the community existentially interprets the fullness of Christian tradition, including Scripture, and structures the Church's life and mission to the world. Love is the core of God's revelation as it is revealed in Jesus Christ. Thus, in the Patristic tradition the violent texts of Scripture were understood to refer to the spiritual struggle of the believer against the devil, evil and sin.

This interpretation implies that in their view the God of Jesus Christ and the Christian faith cannot be identified with violence.

Paradoxically, however, we can only become aware of the impact of our attitudes and actions on other people and on the natural environment, when we are prepared sacrifice some of the things we have learned to hold most dear. Many of our efforts for peace are futile because we are unwilling to forgo established ways of wasting and wanting. We refuse to relinquish wasteful consumerism and prideful nationalism. In peacemaking, then, it is critical that we perceive the impact of our practices on other people (especially the poor) as well as on the environment. This is precisely why there cannot be peace without justice.

"Blessed, then, are the peacemakers; for they shall be called children of God" (Matt. 5.9).

To become and be called children of God is to move away from what we want to what God wants, and from what serves our own interests to what respects the rights of others. We must recognize that all human beings, and not only the few, deserve to share the resources of this world.

This is the peace that our Risen Lord offered to His disciples and the hope of our Lord for all of His children. It is also this same peace, which "surpasses all understanding" (Phil, 4.7) that, from the martyred Throne and Mother Church of Constantinople, we invoke upon all of you.

The offertory taken during the service was dedicated to the "100 Lane/Park Lane After-school and Training Centre," a peace initiative of the Jamaica Baptist Union and the Jamaica Council of Churches.

Following the ecumenical service, participants moved outside the tent to an open-day offering of Caribbean music and a tent-city of cultural displays.

Special Events and Exhibitions

The Assembly Hall of the University of the West Indies served as the main hub for the participants, the place where they registered for the event and the site of the information desk. It was the space in which many groups and initiatives shared their stories of seeking peace and overcoming violence. It was also the venue of Exhibits and Encounters.

Stitching Together the Fabric of Just Peace in our World

"Stitching Peace," the main exhibition in the centre of the UWI Assembly Hall, was a selection of *arpilleras* (appliqué collages from Latin America) and quilts from Africa, Latin America and Europe. The *arpilleras* illustrated some of the focal points for discussion on the topic of a peaceful society. The curator of the exhibition, Roberta Bacic, a former member of Chile's truth and reconciliation commission who now lives in Northern Ireland, uses the arts as a way for people to tell their stories and build peace. At the exhibition's centre was a work by quilt-maker Deborah Stockdale specially commissioned by the WCC and entitled "Journey to Peace." Also central were three new and never before displayed works on the exhibition theme that had been specially made at the invitation of the curator.

The collages speak to the social justice concerns that underlie and result from violent conflict, such as poverty, hunger, displacement and unemployment. Alongside these were quilts that juxtapose the chaos of conflict with the ordinariness of daily life, but also reveal the hope that is sustained during times of war.

The collection as a whole draws on a concept of peace that calls attention to the "bigger picture" of all that stands in the way of a peaceful society. It raises quality of life issues such as domestic violence, structural issues like migration, economic violence and debt as well as the theme of environmental degradation. The use of non-violent actions as a way to address urgent social issues is also depicted in some works. Many of the stories told in thread and fabric were created in the midst of conflict. They express the biblical vision of resisting injustice and working for peace with justice, of piecing together relationships that have been torn. For their creators, the themes represented were not abstract concepts but realities rooted in the life of their peoples and communities.

The Chilean folk craft that produced the *arpilleras* became an act of resistance to the Pinochet dictatorship. This act of resistance to injustice has since become an inspiration for many and, in the case of this collection, offered the contributors an opportunity "to begin to stitch together the fabric of just peace in our world." The exhibition's visitors' book was a significant record of the thoughts, emotions and reflections evoked. After the IEPC, the "Journey to Peace" quilt was put on display in the chapel of the WCC headquarters in Geneva.

"Hands Together"

Churches and specialized ministries are witnessing the human impact of unlawful, armed violence at the grassroots, in their communities and at the national level. It was therefore important that churches bring their stories and concerns about human protection into the UN global Arms Trade Treaty (ATT) negotiation process.

During the IEPC, the Norwegian participants organized a "Hands Together" stand, and invited the Convocation participants to make their handprints on a petition for just peace and to spread it around the world. Responding to the slogan "Give your hand and name for peace by joining the hand-print petition for a strong and robust Arms Trade Treaty at the Hands Together stand," signatories thus joined their hand-prints to other "Hands that drop the gun," "Hands that greet neighbours with peace" and "Handshakes for commitment to a strong treaty." The stand also called for use of the petition as "inspiration or model to mobilize church leaders as well as ordinary people in your country to demand a strong stand on the ATT from your government."

Many people participated in the action, and about 300 handprints were collected. Among the signatories were the WCC General Secretary Olav Fykse Tveit, and the Moderator of the WCC Commission of the Churches on International Affairs (CCIA) Rev. Kjell Magne Bondevik.

An event launching an ATT campaign by churches and specialized ministries during the IEPC provided a platform to discuss common strategies for the ecumenical family. The discussions were moderated by Eilert Rostrup of the Karibu Foundation, Norway. Representatives of the Church of Uganda, the All Africa Conference of Churches, the United Methodist Church, the Action Network on Small Arms in Sierra Leone, Project Ploughshares, Canada and the Church of Sweden took part in the panel discussion. The networks represented were an indication of church commitment to these questions. The message of the "Hands Together" stand would thus be carried forward in many ways.

The "Essen Banners"

On 16 May 2012, three people with bulky luggage travelled together from Düsseldorf, Germany to Kingston, Jamaica. Along with their personal luggage, they brought with them a snowboard bag packed with eight large banners. Measuring 100cm x 280cm and made of ecologically friendly stinging nettle fibre, the banners told stories about several very concrete peace-building issues including:

- Namibia's Basic Income Grant
- Fair trade
- HIV and AIDS prevention work
- Empowerment of women
- Gender sensitivity, and
- Spiritual life (with prayers and biblical verses in various languages).

The banners became known as the "Essen Banners" in Kingston.

Designated by the European Union as the European Capital of Culture in 2010, the town of Essen had organized a series of cultural events during that year. Within this framework and eager to demonstrate its commitment, the Essen branch of the Evangelical Church in Germany (EKD) had invited its local ecumenical partners to participate in this cultural endeavour. The result, after two years of planning and preparation, was an intercultural programme and a partnership conference on the subject of "Overcoming violence – for a culture of reconciliation."

Essen congregations invited ecumenical partners from all over the world to participate in the programme. Twenty-six international guests from nine countries, more than half of them women working in the fields of education, shelter, health services and church work, travelled to Essen, with an additional 16 guests from four other countries attending a separate youth programme.

The guests came from the Evangelical-Lutheran Church in Namibia, the Community of Disciples of Christ in Congo (DRC), the Mar Thoma Syrian Church of Malabar (India), the Czechoslovak Hussite Church and a Roman Catholic congregation in El Salvador, as well as from the "Hope for the Needy" programme (Uganda), the SERPAF Education centre for families in Sete Lagoas (Brazil), a youth project in Chile, and the "Putevi Mira" project in Bosnia-Herzegovina.

The conference focused on the reality of violence as well as on positive examples of how to overcome it and work for reconciliation. It addressed such issues as domestic violence, structural violence, HIV/AIDS and violence, men and violence, children and violence and religion and violence. Intercultural, international groups working with an artist and the teachers and students of a vocational school of design created the peace banners at the end of the conference. Each group designed a banner around a particular theme; each banner featured a related biblical passage. The banners were carried from one church to another in a peace procession through the town, and were presented in a special service to celebrate the end of Decade to Overcome Violence.

In Kingston, the day-long process of hanging up the banners was an event in itself, attracting much interest. A DVD about the partnership project was shown, and cards with the banner designs were produced and widely distributed for use as greeting cards or for worship projects. The organizers found it most encouraging to talk with people from Kingston who came as daily visitors to the Convocation and to share their experiences about the importance of intercultural communication for peace-making.

Back in Essen after the IEPC, the banners continued to be used for services on topics such as a partnership service or to mark the International Day of Human Rights. Worship material and material for Christian education and confirmation classes on the concept of just peace were also produced.

Remembering the Forerunners of the IEPC

A special booth offered reports and informative documents about the various annual foci during the Decade as well as material relating to the "Peace to the City Campaign" organized in the context of the Programme to Overcome Violence (POV). This booth was presented jointly by participants who had been actively involved in the WCC Decade to Overcome Violence: Churches Seeking Reconciliation and Peace (DOV) along with WCC staff involved in the "Living Letters" visits and the expert consultations related to the IEPC themes.

A "Living Letters" corner with illustrated flyers sharing testimonies of participants and photographs of delegations encountering local communities conveyed a sense of the meaning and purpose of the visits. Tables surrounding the booth carried copies of reports from the expert consultations and "Living Letters" visits, IEPC flyers, as well as "Imagine Peace" and "Telling Peace" booklets in various languages. At the end of the Convocation, a large number of the reports, flyers and stickers as well as DOV T-shirts had been shared with the IEPC participants.

The Ecumenical Accompaniment Programme for Palestine and Israel (EAPPI) booth, situated next to the POV-DOV booth, demonstrated the linkages between the two activities: EAPPI emanated from the first DOV annual initiative (2002) focusing on Palestine and Israel under the theme: "End the Illegal Occupation of Palestine: Support a Just Peace in the Middle East."

The EAPPI stand attracted the attention of many participants and visitors who could share their own experiences with the members of the EAPPI delegation. An "outpost" stand set up in the main tent where the plenary sessions were held also distributed printed materials and other resources. During one of the IEPC plenary sessions, a "check-point" was set up at the tent exit, forcing people who were leaving the session to "experience" the reality of a check-point in occupied Palestine.

EAPPI workshops reported that despite all efforts by the international community, particularly the UN General Assembly and Security Council resolutions, Israel had adamantly pursued its policy of colonization of the occupied territories, creating some "facts on the ground" that actually made a Palestinian state non-viable.

They testified that most churches were not well aware of the situation of Palestinians under occupation and were doing very little to address it in their own and in the international context. They also argued that the ecumenical movement and organizations like the WCC should be more intentionally engaged in awareness-raising and advocacy for a just solution to the conflict rather than holding the "moral high ground" as was sometimes the case.

Networking with some peace movements and organizations like the Iona Community or the Inter-religion Network for Peace Education, and contacts with individuals and church leaders interested in participating in the programme made this a very worthwhile initiative.

Eco-Booth: "Tread Lightly on the Earth"

Much attention had been paid in the planning and implementation of the IEPC to ensure that the event would "tread lightly on the earth." Efforts were made to manage and minimize the environmental impact by addressing the areas of travel, food and water, paper usage, energy use and waste disposal.

To this end, an eco-booth was mounted to help sensitize participants to the issues, share stories and ideas or simply to learn and talk about WCC's environmental work on ecology, climate change and water. The booth operated an initiative to off-set the environmental impact of the air travel that allowed most of the participants to reach the IEPC venue. With more than 1,000 participants, the IEPC's air travel carbon footprint was a deep one, but participants were encouraged to voluntarily offset their emissions by donating to "Hear the Children's Cry: National Youth Help Paper Recycling Project" – a Jamaican environmental stewardship project.

An estimation of the amount participants should donate was calculated according to the region from which they had come, using a Lutheran World Federation carbon offsetting instrument. Participants were invited to donate this amount or more to the environmental stewardship project. The contributions were generous, and many participants had already taken the initiative to pay an off-setting contribution back at their home bases.

"Rose Alley 76"

"Rose Alley 76" is an exhibition based on an initiative of Brot fuer die Welt in Germany. It presents a home interior with furniture and objects that make visitors feel they have stepped into a normal family residence. The unwanted but entrenched family member in that home, however, is violence. The facts about why this happens, who is responsible, what can be done, when this may happen and where to get help are written on cards on the objects, furniture and walls. Visitors can read them and experience "the thorns in family happiness."

A smaller version of the exhibition was brought to the IEPC by a representative of the Young Women's Christian Association (YWCA) of Finland. The concept and ethos of the exhibition were shared with participants via a display of leaflets and photographs, giving them an opportunity for further reflection on the issue of domestic violence as evoked through deliberations on the IEPC theme of "Peace in the Community."

Pray the Devil Back to Hell

Pray the Devil Back to Hell is the title of an extraordinary film screened at the IEPC. It tells the moving story of the women's peace movement in Liberia over more than a decade of war, dictatorship and oppression. It shows women in the churches coming together to pray for peace ... and Muslim women joining them. The film contains powerful footage of the women dressing in white to go on their first demonstration at the same time as warlords are preparing their weaponry. The women sing, dance and go on a sex strike to get the men to join with them. These were women who knew only too well what they wanted: they wanted their husbands, sons and brothers back. And only peace could secure a future for each family and the whole country. "We want peace, no more war. Liberia is our home."

The women showed enormous tenacity as well as the capacity for creative organization. Their campaign began at the grassroots, moved on to international peace talks in Ghana and developed into involvement in the detailed implementation of the peace agreement and helping to build a democratic culture and institutions after the war. The film brought together many elements that had been shared, discussed, sung about and prayed for during the Convocation. It was a powerful illustration of IEPC plenary keynote speaker Rev. Dr Paul Oestreicher's call for the abolition of war and his affirmation that "without peace, there is no hope for any kind of a future."

Rev. Dr Angelique Walker-Smith of the National Baptist Convention USA, who had had first-hand experience of the situation in Liberia, introduced the film and animated a lively debate after the screening.

Peace Concert

A highlight of the Convocation, the Peace Concert was a public event that gave IEPC participants the opportunity to meet local people. The site chosen for the concert was a beautiful New Kingston park created as a memorial to Jamaica's liberation from institutionalized slavery. Since the latter is considered one of the worst forms of violence ever meted out to humanity, it was an appropriate choice.

Each performance by group after group of some of the most gifted Jamaican singers and dancers, drummers and violinists, bands and choirs was somehow more exciting than the one before.

The stark beauty of a ballet duet performed by two members of the National Dance Theatre Company, and an impassioned rendition of "Let There Be Peace on Earth" by violinist Paulette Bellamy were just two examples of the exceptional quality of the performances, bringing home the fact that the IEPC was taking place in a country rich in cultural treasures.

The selection of performers and music also made it clear that the concert organizers from the Jamaican Council of Churches had intended the event to be as much about faith as about the arts. Outstanding local church choirs and youth dance groups were interspersed with popular musicians like saxophonist Dean Fraser, reggae/soul singer Tarrus Riley, Christian rap poet Nana Moses, the Fab 5 Inc. and Jamaican singer-songwriter Grub Cooper.

The climax of the concert was a performance of the IEPC theme song, written by Cooper and commissioned by the WCC. The Grace Thrillers, a gospel group that Cooper has produced for some 20 years, sang the brand-new peace anthem, "Glory to God and Peace on Earth" and the evening ended as participants danced to the Jamaican rhythm in celebration of peace. Presenting the CD to the WCC General Secretary, Cooper announced his intention to give the rights to the Council for use for the ecumenical movement.

Youth Evening

At the request of the WCC youth commission ECHOS, a slot on the IEPC evening sessions' agenda was specifically reserved for youth. Meeting before the start of the IEPC, youth participants and stewards worked together to produce an exciting and inspiring evening event that included songs and a thought-provoking interactive session on the use of creative arts, such as dance, to effectively raise awareness and address stigma on HIV and AIDS in Uganda.

Young people from Africa, Latin America, Asia and the Caribbean offered testimony on their understanding of peace in their contexts, sometimes challenging the audience to more deliberately involve youth – in their dual roles of victims and perpetuators of violence and exclusion.

At the end of the session, the audience joined the dancing and evangelical singing, expressing both their spirituality and their empathy with the youth concerns they had heard and seen expressed during the evening.

"Streetlight"

"Streetlight" is a musical in hip-hop, drama, song, music and rhythm that tells the story of Charles Moats, a young African-American who lived in a ghetto in Chicago.

During the IEPC, 50 students from St Andrews Technical High in Trench Town, Kingston, were coached by the 'Gen Rosso' band in two afternoon workshops. After rehearsing the musical, they performed on stage side by side with Gen Rosso in front of more than 700 people in the IEPC tent. The original play relates strongly to the realities and lifestyle of the areas that the young performers came from. It featured students from Trench Town and Denham Town High Schools and St Andrews Technical High school.

"Gen Rosso", an international performing arts group based in Italy comprising 19 people from nine different nations – Brazil, Kenya, Tanzania, Argentina, Spain, Italy, Switzerland, Philippines, and Poland – was born in 1966 in Loppiano, Florence when Chiara Lubich, the founder of the Focolare Movement, gave a red drum-set to a group of young people so that they could communicate Christian values and contribute to the realization of a more united world through music. Since then, more than 200 artists have participated in Gen Rosso, performing all over the world in theatres, squares, sport-palaces, jails, gymnasiums and convention halls. "Streetlight," concerts, workshops and performances come from the diverse artistic cultural heritage of Gen Rosso's members, as well as from their personal commitment to witness the Christian message in their daily lives.

Workshops have also become a part of Gen Rosso's educational projects for violence prevention and initiation to social dialogue. The workshops help young people to become protagonists and ambassadors of positive impulses in their own social contexts.

Seminarians Joining the Peace Harvest

Graduate study in peace-making and offering academic credits was an important feature of the IEPC. It consisted of a course for seminarians and other graduate students on "Overcoming Violence: An Engagement with the International Ecumenical Peace Convocation."

Responding to an invitation posted on the WCC Website to "Join in the Harvest! Participate in an IEPC Course for Seminarians!," a total of 42 persons participated as mentors or students in a course jointly offered by Boston University School of Theology, the United Theological College of the West Indies and supported by the Interdenominational Theological Center in Atlanta, Georgia.

The course "tracked" the IEPC as both a "harvest festival" celebrating the achievements of the Decade to Overcome Violence (DOV), and as the precursor to the next WCC Assembly in 2013 whose theme is "God of life, lead us to justice and peace."

The DOV was designed to call attention to the ways communities of faith are implicated in violence as well as to their unique resources for overcoming violence. Both the Convocation and the course provided an opportunity for ecumenical formation and encouraged individuals and churches to renew their commitment to nonviolence, peace and justice.

Students for whom the DOV and IEPC materials were new greatly valued their unique melding of biblical material with cutting-edge social thinking. The seminarians participated fully in all the elements of the Convocation through daily Bible studies, worship, plenaries, "Reasoning" workshops, *"Innerstandings"* panels and evening cultural events. The course aimed at carrying the DOV and Convocation work forward by surveying forms of violence which confront the churches in areas of concern to students; acquiring skills as peace-makers with respect to IEPC themes; and fostering learning in the context of ecumenical formation.

The project was the dream of DOV Reference Group member Rev. Dr Rodney Petersen from the Boston Theological Institute who brought it to fruition and was also co-facilitator with Rev. Glenroy Lalor of the United Theological College of the West Indies.

Closing Plenary

The last day's final sessions, moderated by WCC Vice-Moderator, His Eminence Metropolitan Gennadios of Sassima, were devoted mainly to discussion and adoption of an IEPC Convocation Message.

A ten-member team appointed by the WCC General Secretary had been meeting from the beginning of the IEPC to prepare a draft of the Message. The draft message was presented at the morning plenary.

Metropolitan Gennadios handled the delicate task of facilitating the discussions on the content of the draft message where more than a hundred participants were given the opportunity to comment and respond. The moderator received comments and reflections with a sense of humour and profoundly thoughtful comments.

The drafting committee then reviewed the draft Message in the context of the participants' input. While they were not able to incorporate all input, conscious of the need to keep the message succinct, the final version presented at the beginning of the afternoon plenary was unanimously adopted with joyous acclamation.

Address by WCC Moderator on reception of the IEPC message

It is with a feeling of joy and a deep sense of gratitude that I receive the IEPC Message on behalf of the WCC Central Committee and also on behalf of the 349 WCC member churches. It will be shared with the churches and the world. Each of us set out on a journey to come to Kingston, Jamaica to this truly historic event. We brought the voices of our churches here, as we begin the return journey to our churches, and we go with a common voice.

As we return, each of us becomes a living message of the International Ecumenical Peace Convocation. What the churches throughout the world have achieved here has been through your committed participation. You brought with you not simply your personal convictions but above all the experiences, the insights and the commitments of your churches and organizations. Here we have interacted with one another and now we go back to our countries, our churches and organizations. You take with you much more than a text. You take with you a profound ecumenical experience.

The text of the Message sums up what it is that brought us together and what it is that takes us forwards on the path of peace, justice and care for the whole of creation. As a text, it cannot convey all of the meanings and all the calls. It may have limitations, as is often the case with our human endeavours. The complexity of the issues we have addressed here certainly requires further work in reflection and in action. Our struggle for just peace has by no means come to an end here. We have celebrated the end of the Decade to Overcome Violence, but our commitment and our struggle have been further strengthened. In this ending is a new beginning.

So as we all go back, let us persevere in the commitment we have celebrated in our services of common prayer, rejoicing and singing. Always mindful that "Faith, hope and love abide. But the greatest of these is love." (1 Cor. 13:13). Let us go, then, confident in the peace of our Lord to be living letters of faith, love and hope.

Metropolitan Gennadios then invited Rev. Dr Walter Altmann, Moderator of the WCC Central Committee to receive the Convocation Message on behalf of the Central Committee and the Council's 349 member churches.

Accepting the Message, Dr Altmann addressed the participants that "You brought with you not simply your personal convictions but above all the experiences, the insights and the commitments of your churches and organizations. Here we have interacted with one another, and now we go back to our countries, our churches and organizations. You take with you much more than a text. You take with you a profound ecumenical experience." Noting that "Our struggle for just peace has by no means come to an end here," Altman added that "We have celebrated the end of the Decade to Overcome Violence, but our commitment and our struggle have been further strengthened. In this ending is a new beginning."

The two closing plenaries were also an opportunity to look back over the week's experiences. "Thought weaver" of the closing session, Ms Adele Halliday of the United Church of Canada, focused in turn on each of the four IEPC themes. For each theme, she recalled significant points that had emerged during the week and asked the participants "What threads will you take home?"

Looking back at the IEPC experience, Rev. Dr Hyunju Bae of the Busan Presbyterian University, South Korea, summarized what she had learned about the marketplace, recalled some of the stories of suffering and the inspiring stories of good practices she would take home to Korea with her, and expressed her hopes for the WCC Assembly in Busan on the theme "God of Life, Lead Us into Justice and Peace."

Statement from the Youth Participants at the International Ecumenical Peace Convocation

Glory to God and Peace on Earth!

Two days before many of you arrived in Kingston, 95 youth met together for networking, community-building, Bible study, prayer and reflection on the DOV and Convocation themes of peace in the community, with the earth, in the marketplace and among the peoples.

We have all come together and participated in the different elements of the IEPC. This reflection and our recommendations are expressions of the many discussions throughout the week by youth. We share this message with you, our fellow peace-makers, and we invite you to continue the conversation with the youth here and beyond – in your congregations and in your communities.

Youth Participation and Inter-generational Dialogue

Just Peace can only be achieved when we all work together. Here at the IEPC, we have worked together between different generations. We have thoroughly enjoyed the interactions with our brothers and sisters. In the future, we would like even more opportunities to share our insights and interact with one another.

We rejoice that young people participated in this meeting in a wide variety of roles. 12% of the participants here were young people. We thank those churches and organizations who have sent young people as their representatives and encourage all churches to meet the recommended 25% youth participation rate in the future. We are looking forward to also seeing young people as keynote speakers and panelists – sharing their experiences and expertise. We wish to journey toward Busan together, and greatly value the inter-generational dialogue which enables us to learn from each other and be creative.

Foundations

Churches provide a unique contribution to the work of Just Peace. We strive to follow in the footsteps of Jesus Christ. We affirm that God's word speaks to us and challenges us on the journey of peace-making. We wish that our work of peace and justice will be deeply rooted in the Scriptures and in theological reflection. We want to commit to a continued reflection on the concept of Shalom.

Partnership

Youth organizations within the ecumenical movement share the vision for Christian unity. Relationships and partnerships make up the foundation of our common work. Therefore, we believe that it is imperative for the WCC, member churches and ecumenical youth organizations to deepen their partnerships and co-operation. Not only do we want to continue such togetherness, but we also want to develop a strategic way to take action in our local and global contexts.

We need strong support from our churches.
We need each other.
We must pray and work together.

Personal Recommitment
After our time together, we are deeply inspired by the many stories that have been shared, such as the moving testimony of the situation of the Dalits given by Asha Kowtal. As this meeting is coming to an end, we find that we are deeply grateful for the sharing and learning that will equip us to face challenges ahead. We encourage each other to continue with concrete actions for peace back home.
God of Life, lead us to justice and peace!

Ms Sanna Ericksson of the Church of Sweden read a statement from the young Convocation participants. The Youth Statement thanked the churches and organizations for sending 12% of youth participants to the Convocation, encouraged young people "to continue with concrete actions for peace back home," and expressed their desire "to journey toward Busan together."

Professor Dr Fernando Enns, who served as the Moderator of the DOV Reference Group, recognized that the churches have come a long way in their ecumenical pilgrimage toward peace and justice. "Over the Decade, churches seeking to make peace in the community, with the earth, in the marketplace and with the peoples have gained greatly in understanding and learned much, Enns said. "And yet, we are not satisfied!"

In relation to the marketplace, "We are only starting to grasp the possibilities to care for one another," Dr Enns observed. In regard to the environment, "We are only beginning to see examples within some churches who accept the call to be responsible house-holders." As far as violence in the community is concerned, "We are only starting to create safe spaces for victims and perpetrators." And in relation to war and conflict, "We are only starting to focus on violence prevention and peace education, non-violent conflict resolution, and processes for the healing of wounded souls – in order to protect the most vulnerable."

"Therefore, Brothers and Sisters, our journey must continue. […] And we shall hold each other accountable," Dr Enns stated.

While inviting the General Secretary to make his closing remarks, Metropolitan Gennadiose recollected the difficulties during different stages of the organization and preparation of the IEPC. He added that, when the new general secretary assumed his responsibilities a little over a year ago, it was still unclear whether the IEPC would take place in the present way. He thanked the general secretary and the staff for the success of the IEPC.

"A dream has come true!" declared WCC General Secretary Rev. Dr Olav Fykse Tveit in his concluding remarks to the Convocation.

Noting that "This is a moment in the ecumenical movement when we see that our call to Just Peace has come to another level of consensus – in reflection, formulation and also commitment," he reaffirmed the WCC's commitment to bring the insights gained through IEPC to its upcoming WCC Assembly in Busan, Korea, and to make sure that they inspire the future work of the WCC.

He strongly thanked all those who had worked hard to make the IEPC a success, especially the staff in charge of organization and coordination.

Rev. Gary Harriott, General Secretary of the Jamaica Council of Churches, expressed his deep appreciation to all participants and the WCC for having held the IEPC in Jamaica. "This was the first time that such a major gathering of the World Council of Churches took place in the Caribbean, and we look forward to having you again."

Leaving Jamaica with Hope and Faith

With the end of the final plenary session came a palpable sense of relief. The long discussions, the patient waiting for a moment to speak on behalf of suffering people and the planet, the nervous frustration of the work for Just Peace were over.

"We did it! We did it!" one participant exclaimed.

> **"This is a moment in the ecumenical movement when we see that our call to Just Peace has come to another level of consensus – in reflection, formulation and also commitment."**

But "It's not over until we have prayed it," another person said, a little sadly – a short exchange that went to the heart of what distinguished the IEPC from any other gathering of NGOs involved in the work for peace.

It revealed the ever-present danger that we celebrate achievement too soon and fail to bring our work, the fruits of our labour, back to God in prayer and with humility. It showed how easily we are tempted to believe that our own endeavours have been enough, that spiritual life is an optional add-on.

The group responsible for preparing the spiritual life of the Convocation had prepared a deeply inspirational sending ceremony and prayer for the closing of this historic ecumenical event. The symbolic action and the sending prayer at the closing session helped people to leave the Convocation with hope and faith.

Hundreds of paper fish had been distributed as the participants entered the plenaries tent, and they had been invited to write their reflections and their own commitment on the fish. The stewards then moved through the tent with a net to "catch" the fish and there was a pause for reflections on the frustration and disappointment in work for peace as well as the comfort and joy of new possibilities and new encounters. John 21: 3-5 was read very slowly and prayerfully in four languages. As the worship ended, participants learned a new way of greeting one another with a sign of peace, the Ichthys sign, a fish drawn with a finger on the palm of one's neighbour's hand.

The rhythm of the Caribbean music was clearly heard once again, and participants sang the IEPC theme song. As they began slowly leaving the tent, many paused to say farewell to fellow participants, fully aware that together all had been part of an historic event pledged to build peace on earth.

II.
Message of the IEPC

The Message of the International Ecumenical Peace Convocation

I pray that, according to the riches of his glory, he may grant that you may be strengthened in your inner being with power through his Spirit, and that Christ may dwell in your hearts through faith, as you are being rooted and grounded in love. (Ephesians 3: 16-17)

We understand peace and peacemaking as an indispensable part of our common faith. Peace is inextricably related to the love, justice and freedom that God has granted to all human beings through Christ and the work of the Holy Spirit as a gift and vocation. It constitutes a pattern of life that reflects human participation in God's love for the world. The dynamic nature of peace as gift and vocation does not deny the existence of tensions, which form an intrinsic element of human relationships, but can alleviate their destructive force by bringing justice and reconciliation.

God blesses the peacemakers. Member churches of the World Council of Churches (WCC) and other Christians are united, as never before, in seeking the means to address violence and to reject war in favor of "Just Peace" – the establishment of peace with justice through a common response to God's calling. Just Peace invites us to join in a common journey and to commit ourselves to building a culture of peace.

We, nearly 1,000 participants from more than 100 nations, called together by the WCC, have shared the experience of the International Ecumenical Peace Convocation (IEPC), a gathering of Christian churches and inter-religious partners dedicated to the pursuit of Peace in the community, Peace with the Earth, Peace in the marketplace and Peace among the peoples. We met on the campus of the University of the West Indies (Mona) near Kingston, Jamaica from 17 through 25 May 2011. We are profoundly grateful to our hosts in Jamaica and throughout the Caribbean region who generously have provided a rich and spacious setting for fellowship and growth in God's grace. By the very fact that we met on the site of a former sugar plantation, we were reminded of the injustice and violence of slavery and colonialism and of the forms of slavery that still plague the world today. We have been informed by the severe challenges of violence in this context as well as the brave involvement of churches in order to meet those challenges.

We brought the concerns of our churches and regions to Jamaica; we spoke with one another here; now, we have a word to share with the churches and the world. We have encountered one another through Bible study, spiritually enriching common prayer, inspiring expressions of the arts, visits to local ministries and other service agencies, plenaries, seminars, workshops, cultural events, lecture sessions, wide-ranging deliberations and deeply moving conversations with persons who have experienced violence, injustice and warfare. We have celebrated the achievements of the ecumenical Decade to Overcome Violence (2001-2010). Our engagements have inspired us in showing that overcoming violence is possible. The Decade to Overcome Violence has generated many beautiful examples of Christians who have made a difference.

As we gathered in Jamaica, we were keenly aware of events in the world around us. Stories from our churches remind us of local, pastoral and social responsibilities for people who must deal daily with each of the issues we discussed. The aftermath of earthquake and tsunami in Japan raises urgent questions concerning nuclear energy and threats to nature and humanity. Governmental and financial institutions face the necessity of taking responsibility for their failed policies and the devastating impact on vulnerable people. We witness with concern and compassion the struggle for freedom, justice and human rights of the people in many Arab countries and other contexts where brave people struggle without global attention. Our love for the peoples of Israel and Palestine convinces us that the continued occupation damages both peoples. We renew our solidarity with the people of divided countries such as the Korean peninsula and Cyprus, and people yearning for peace and an end to suffering in nations like Colombia, Iraq, Afghanistan and the Great Lakes region of Africa.

We realize that Christians have often been complicit in systems of violence, injustice, militarism, racism, casteism, intolerance and discrimination. We ask God to forgive us our sins, and to transform us as agents of righteousness and advocates of Just Peace. We appeal to governments and other groups to stop using religion as a pretext for the justification of violence.

With partners of other faiths, we have recognized that peace is a core value in all religions, and the promise of peace extends to all people regardless of their traditions and commitments. Through intensified inter-religious dialogue we seek common ground with all world religions.

We are unified in our aspiration that war should become illegal. Struggling for peace on earth we are confronted with our different contexts and histories. We realize that different churches and religions bring diverse perspectives to the path toward peace. Some among us begin from the stand-point of personal conversion and morality, the acceptance of God's peace in one's heart as the basis for peacemaking in family, community, economy, as well as in all the Earth and the world of nations. Some stress the need to focus first on mutual support and correction within the body of Christ if peace is to be realized. Some encourage the churches' commitment to broad social movements and the public witness of the church. Each approach has merit; they are not mutually exclusive. In fact they belong inseparably together. Even in our diversity we can speak with one voice.

Peace in the Community

Churches learn the complexities of Just Peace as we hear of the intersection of multiple injustices and oppressions that are simultaneously at work in the lives of many. Members of one family or community may be oppressed and also the oppressors of others. Churches must help in identifying the everyday choices that can end abuse and promote human rights, gender jus-tice, climate justice, economic justice, unity and peace. The churches need to continue to confront racism and casteism as dehumanizing realities in today's world.

Likewise, violence against women and children must be named as sin. Conscious efforts are required for the full integration of differently abled people. Issues of sexuality divide the churches, and therefore we ask the WCC to create safe spaces to address dividing issues of human sexuality. At every level churches play a role in supporting and protecting the right of conscientious objection, and in assuring asylum for those who oppose and resist militarism and armed conflicts. The churches must raise their common voice to protect our Christian brothers and sisters as well as all humans who are subjected to discrimination and persecution on the grounds of religious intolerance. Peace education must move to the centre of every curriculum in schools, seminaries and universities. We acknowledge the peacemaking capacity of youth and call on the churches to develop and strengthen net-works of Just Peace ministries. The church is called to go public with its concerns, speaking the truth beyond the walls of its own sanctuary.

Peace with the Earth

The environmental crisis is profoundly an ethical and spiritual crisis of humanity. Recognizing the damage human activity has done to the Earth, we reaffirm our commitment to the integrity of creation and the daily life-style it demands. Our concern for the Earth and our concern for human-ity go hand in hand. Natural resources and common goods such as water must be shared in a just and sustainable manner. We join global civil society in urging governments to reconstruct radically all our economic activities toward the goal of an ecologically sustainable economy. The extensive use of fossil fuels and CO2 emissions must be reduced urgently to a level that keeps climate change limited. The ecological debt of the industrialized countries responsible for climate change must be considered when CO2 emission shares and plans for adaptation costs are negotiated. The nuclear catastrophe of Fukushima has proved once again that we must no longer rely on nuclear power as a source of energy. We reject strategies such as an increased production of agro fuel which hurt the poor by competing with food production

Peace in the Marketplace

The global economy often provides many examples of structural violence that victimizes not through the direct use of weapons or physical force but by passive acceptance of widespread poverty, trade disparities and inequality among classes and nations. In contrast to unfettered economic growth as envisioned by the neoliberal system, the Bible signals a vision of life in abundance for all. The churches must learn to advocate more effectively for full implementation of economic, social and cultural rights as the foundation for "economies of life."

It is a scandal that enormous amounts of money are spent on military budgets and toward providing weapons for allies and the arms trade while this money is urgently needed to eradicate poverty around the globe, and to fund an ecologically and socially responsible reorientation of the world economy. We urge the governments of this world to take immediate action to redirect their financial resources to programmes that foster life rather than death. We encourage the churches to adopt common strategies toward transforming economies. The churches must address more effectively irresponsible concentration of power and wealth as well as the disease of corruption. Steps toward just and sustainable economies include more effective rules for the financial market, the introduction of taxes on financial transactions and just trade relationships.

Peace among the Peoples

History, especially in the witness of the historic peace churches, reminds us of the fact that violence is contrary to the will of God and can never resolve conflicts. It is for this reason that we are moving beyond the doctrine of just war toward a commitment to Just Peace. It requires moving from exclusive concepts of national security to safety for all. This includes a day-to-day responsibility to prevent, that is, to avoid violence at its root. Many practical aspects of the concept of Just Peace require discussion, discernment and elaboration. We continue to struggle with how innocent people can be protected from injustice, war and violence. In this light, we struggle with the concept of the "responsibility to protect" and its possible misuse. We urgently request that the WCC and related bodies further clarify their positions regarding this policy.

We advocate total nuclear disarmament and control of the proliferation of small arms.

We as churches are in a position to teach nonviolence to the powerful, if only we dare. For we are followers of one who came as a helpless infant, died on the Cross, told us to lay aside our swords, taught us to love our enemies and was resurrected from the dead.

In our journey toward Just Peace, a new international agenda is of the utmost urgency because of the scope of dangers surrounding us. We call on the ecumenical movement as a whole, and particularly those planning the WCC Assembly of 2013 in Busan, Korea, with the theme "God of life, lead us to justice and peace," to make Just Peace, in all its dimensions, a key priority. Resources such as "An Ecumenical Call to Just Peace" (ECJP) and the Just Peace Companion can support this journey to Busan.

All thanks and praise to you, O Triune God: Glory to you, and peace to your people on earth. God of life, lead us to justice and peace. Amen.

III.
Opening Plenary Presentations

Voices from the Churches

Peace Is a Gift of God
Metropolitan Hilarion of Volokolamsk

Dear Brothers and Sisters,

We have assembled here in Jamaica not only to sum up the Decade to Overcome Violence declared by the World Council of Churches in 2001 but also to discern together the scale and forms taken by violence in today's world. The principle question we have to answer is what we as Christians can do together in the face of growing violence, aggression, exploitation and terror. Symbolically, the World Council has accepted the invitation of churches in Jamaica and chosen for this forum this very beautiful island, which at the same time is a place with one of the heaviest rates of violence in the world.

Violence pervades the life of humankind today. It would seem that peace-loving rhetoric has prevailed in international organizations and at an intergovernmental level, as political leaders and scientific and cultural figures talk incessantly about reconciliation, forgiveness, purification of memory and nonviolence. The United Nations keeps adopting ever-new resolutions condemning any forms of violence, and criminal legislation in many countries has introduced responsibility for crimes against humanity. International instruments clearly state that military interference constitutes ultima ratio, the last resort for curbing evil.

At the same time, TV screens send us a daily torrent of what could be called a systematic estheticisation of violence, cruelty, abuse and other manifestations of evil. Films with violent scenes appear to be very popular, especially among young people. A conclusion inevitably comes to mind: the commercial advantage of the distribution of such video products is so great that it makes it quite possible to close one's eyes to the glaring contradiction between official rhetoric and what we see on TV screens every day. Is the price the community pays for domestic violence, growing crime, terrorism and other dreadful things less than the profit made by producers and distributors of films focused on aggression? The modern pluralistic society seems unable to offer proper discernment of the disastrous consequences of this discrepancy between word and deed, since by definition it gives room to any evil justified by such notions as 'freedom of choice', 'freedom of speech', freedom of expression' and 'individual freedom'.

In our day, violence has acquired a structural and systemic character as it is no longer committed merely by individuals but by organized structures. This kind of violence should rather be called exploitation and injustice. Take for instance the methods and terms of trade and economic relations between rich states of the North and developing countries of the South, which more often than not are of an enslaving nature. As a result, poor countries become poorer while rich ones grow richer.

The list of diverse forms and manifestations of violence and injustice can be extended endlessly, but our task is to identify the cause of this evil and to overcome not the consequences but the causes. Regrettably, Christian churches speak out more often on specific problems arising for certain reasons without seeking to expose their cause. If Christians still can be 'a prophetic voice' in the world and not only the voice crying in the wilderness, we ought to fearlessly expose the injustice of modern society without fear of tarnishing our reputation in the eyes of the powers that be and the mass media under their control.

"The list of diverse forms and manifestations of violence and injustice can be extended endlessly, but our task is to identify the cause of this evil and to overcome not the consequences but the causes."

However paradoxical it may seem, the more we talk about justice in the world the less, alas, we see it in our life. We live in an atmosphere where double standards have prevailed, where cynicism predominates, concealed politically correctly under the mask of democracy and concern for human rights, which in fact tramples and distorts both.

There is at last a discussion in the world today not about an abstract infringement on the religious freedom of particular minorities but about the open persecution of Christians. It is no longer possible to hush up the fact that many persecutions have become well-planned indeed, not spontaneous persecution at all. Even the European Parliament, where certain members consistently sought to oust any mention of Christian values in European history, adopted for the first time in its history a truly revolutionary resolution on Christianophobia. In its wake, the Italian Parliament's House of Representatives adopted a similar resolution obliging authorities to oppose attempts to subject Christians to discrimination.

Today, reports are coming again and again about attacks against Christians in Egypt, Iraq, India, Pakistan and Indonesia and a number of other countries, predominantly Muslim. For instance, more than a half of the Christian population has already fled from Iraq because of the daily threats to their life.

In countries in which Christians are a minority, there is no effective system for their protection. For instance in Egypt, the police and military are reported to avoid interfering in mass assaults on the Copts while the Prosecutor's Office refuses to bring criminal proceedings against Muslim extremists, qualifying the continued bloodshed as 'interreligious clashes' for which, they say, both sides are to be blamed.

What are we doing as Christians today to protect our brothers and sisters in faith who are subjected daily to humiliation, threats and discrimination due to religious intolerance? Regrettably, more often than not, we do not go beyond statements, press releases, condolences and politically correct 'expressions of concern'. The hour has come to move to effective action. We urgently need to organize a system of protecting Christians against persecution. In the first place, it is necessary to set up information structures to monitor crimes committed because of religious hatred. The Christian community for all its disunity should unite and request the UN, governmental and international organizations to put an end to the persecution against Christians in today's world.

Christian churches and communities should put real content into their peace and human rights work, taking care in the first place of their brothers and sisters subjected to persecution in some parts of the world. St Paul calls us: As we have opportunity, let us do good to all people, especially to those who belong to the family of believers (Gal. 6:10); otherwise we will simply turn into one of hundreds of unobtrusive social institutions for promoting the building of peace.

"Peace is a gift of God sent from above to the people who have repented of their sins."

In Russia, there have been no religious wars or religious confrontations in our history. People in our country have been able to find a language of mutual understanding, friendship and good-neighbourliness despite their differences in faith, culture and ways of life. For developing inter-confessional cooperation, an Interreligious Council was established in 1998, in which leaders of traditional religions discuss arising complexities together and find ways to resolve them. A Council for Cooperation with Religious Organizations under the president of the Russian Federation has successfully worked for several years now. I will emphasize that the government has given great attention to the problems of peaceful co-existence of religions in multinational Russia. The way in which stable and benevolent relations were built and continue to be built between religions in Russia may serve as a lesson for using the same principles in the international arena as well.

Peace is a gift of God sent from above to the people who have repented of their sins. This world is lying in evil as it cannot build peace from itself, whatever peace concepts it may try to work out, for evil is an integral part of it. We remember the prophecy of St Paul: While people are saying, 'Peace and safety,' destruction will come on them suddenly (1 Thess. 5:3). God's peace is found elsewhere than in the artificial construction of peaceful co-existence or the legal regulation of social order mechanisms. We as Christians are called to point these ways out to the world, showing that it cannot be imposed either by progress or rationalism or various concepts of 'just peace'. Unity, about which so much was spoken in the history of the 20th century Christian churches, will be another example of meaningless and valueless rhetoric if we do not now unite our efforts to save 'ours in faith' who suffer from the ill will of those who seek to fill the earth with hate, enmity and bloodshed while calling to build a religious community on a global scale.

The alternative way is indicated in the Beatitudes. The Gospel teaches us that peace is to be built and strengthened without killing enemies but by killing hostility, as the Lord Himself did on the Cross (Eph. 2:16).

On behalf of the Russian Orthodox Church, I call upon both the powers that be and ordinary people of good will to show effective solidarity with persecuted Christians. The future of humankind should be built on peace and justice commanded by God, or there will be no humankind at all.

Peace Be with You!

Decade to Overcome Violence: An Overview

Rev. Dr Margot Kässmann

The greeting of Jesus as the risen Christ to his disciples has been a challenge and obligation to Christians and churches all over the world ever since he uttered these words.

Therefore, the issues of the "Decade to overcome violence" have been at the heart of the ecumenical movement since its early days. And I am convinced that the theological relevance of the topic and the ethical implications have to be part of the future work of the WCC.

When the churches of the world assembled in Amsterdam 1948, they declared that war is contrary to the will of God. After all the hatred and destruction of World War II, it had become obvious that churches as well as the nations and societies they lived in had gone astray from God's will for peace. That is especially true for the churches in Germany. But already in the midst of war, the ecumenical voice made itself heard. One example is Bishop George Bell who, in the British Parliament, spoke out against the bombardment of German cities. A courageous vote with regard to the enemy.

The issue of violence stayed on the agenda of the WCC. Is there any justification for violence – be it in war, in revolution for a just cause or in defence of human rights? At the Uppsala Assembly in 1968, Martin Luther King was invited as a speaker. He was assassinated, but his voice spoke to the Assembly anyway. And his voice is still to be heard; it is a very real message for today! In his speech, "The power of nonviolence" on June 4, 1957, he said: "We had to make it clear that nonviolent resistance is not a method of cowardice. It does resist. It is not a method of stagnant passivity and deadening complacency. The nonviolent resister is just as opposed to the evil that he is standing against as the violent resister, but he resists without violence. This method is nonaggressive physically but strongly aggressive spiritually."

As we come to the end of the Decade to Overcome Violence, I would like to highlight two sources especially. One is the conciliar process for justice, peace and the integrity of creation. When the churches came together for the sixth Assembly in Vancouver 1983, the churches of East Germany asked the WCC to call a Council for Peace like Dietrich Bonhoeffer had in 1934. In his central speech Alan Boesak from South Africa argued that churches cannot commit to peace while ignoring the reality of injustice in the world. Darlene Keju-Johnson in her speech related peace and justice to the reality of nuclear testing and waste in the Pacific. In the end, it became obvious: justice, peace and the integrity of creation must not be debated separately. We cannot talk about the one without having in mind the other. And this is not just an ethical issue. No, the "esse," the being of the church is in question with regard to those issues. A church that ignores war, injustice and destroying of creation is not church. It has become more than obvious that ecclesial and ethical issues are radically linked. Affirmation VI in the final document of the World Convocation for Justice, Peace and the Integrity of Creation in Seoul 1990 argued assertively for nonviolence. That statement had a major impact on the debate in Australia on the Gulf War, made a substantial contribution to the strong anti-war sentiment of the Canberra Assembly 1991 and finally led to the decisions in Johannesburg 1994.

> "A church that ignores war, injustice and destruction of creation is not church. It has become more than obvious that ecclesial and ethical issues are radically linked."

The other source is the Decade of Churches in Solidarity with Women. It was inaugurated during the WCC Central Committee meeting in Buenos Aires 1985. Bärbel Wartenberg had led the WCC delegation to the UN women's conference in Nairobi. Their report made very clear: the community of women and men in the church, as a former programme had been named, needed to be on the top of the agenda. The decade was launched in 1988 and had its final highlight in 1998 at the Assembly of the WCC in Harare. The last year of the decade was spent with team visits to the member churches. Official delegations of two women and two men each visited all member churches as "living letters" in order to find out what the reality of women in the life of churches was. The result was evident: violence against women is a vital issue in the majority of member churches. In the final report on those visits, we can find proof of the unwillingness of many churches to deal with the problem:

- "One church leader spoke of 'disciplining' his wife and being thanked by her later."
- "Several others queried the definition of 'violence', wanting to distinguish between violence that resulted in death, and 'just hitting.'"
- "The churches are responsible for the 'violence of silence.'"
- The report made evident that violence is not just a theme somehow "outside in the world." No, it is a topic within our churches, our relations as Christians. Thus, many women saw the Decade to Overcome Violence as a logical follow-up to the final report of the Decade of Churches in Solidarity with Women.

When the WCC Central Committee could meet for the first time in South Africa in 1994, Bishop Mogoba called for a Programme to Combat Violence as a follow-up of the Programme to Combat Racism. O yes, that seemed the right consequence. Member churches from all over the world reported on violence destroying the lives of people and entire communities. But, we asked then, is "combat" the right wording? The apostle Paul in his letter to the Romans writes: "Do not be overcome by evil, but overcome evil with good." (Rom. 12:21) But can violence be overcome? Has not violence been a fact of life ever since Cain and Abel? Here, a closer look at biblical and theological issues is needed.

In fact, there is ambiguity regarding the legitimization of violence within the Hebrew part of the Bible. Partly this is due to the differences in context and perceptions among the authors. Certainly the longing for a God who fights for the people and the understanding of crisis as a punishment from God are well known in almost all religions and all contexts, including Christianity. But alongside the clear references to a warrior God, a red thread of nonviolence runs through the Old Testament. This seems to be the much more exciting part because it is unusual and unfamiliar. Rather than being troubled or repelled time and again by the legitimization of violence within the Hebrew part of the Bible, we should point to texts like the story of Shiphrah and Puah, an account of courageous civil disobedience (Ex 1, 15-22). Or, take the well-known passage about the suffering servant (Isaiah 53) as an example. We can also think of prophecy like Isaiah, where swords become ploughshares (2,4). God gives Shalom. God liberates.

The message of the New Testament is very clear. In his Sermon on the Mount, Jesus opens a whole new set of categories. It is not the warriors, the heroes and freedom fighters, the strong and the brave who are blessed. No, it is the poor in spirit, those who mourn, the meek and those who hunger and thirst for righteousness, the merciful, the pure in heart the peace-makers and the persecuted ones. What a contradiction to the reality of this world! The church as a "sign of the kingdom" was present in the discussions at the fourth Assembly of the WCC in Uppsala 1968. This means that ecclesiological convictions and worldly matters are linked! The credibility of the church depends, among other issues, on the way it deals with violence!

After the Central Committee meeting in Johannesburg 1994, we asked ourselves in the governing bodies what might be a practical consequence. A reference group was created and met in Rio de Janeiro to discuss what should be the initial focus of the programme, given the complexity of the issue and the risk that taking on too many of its facets at once could make it difficult to find a profile. During the meeting, the participants were increasingly struck by the fact that large cities are a microcosm of the world as a whole. Thus, seven cities in very different regions in the world were chosen in order to show what violence means in the lives of people, to highlight churches' initiatives, and to connect them in order to learn from one another: Belfast, Boston, Colombo, Durban, Jerusalem, Kingston and Rio de Janeiro. I want to remember Salpy Eskidian at this point, who in person brought these cities and the Christian initiatives for peace and nonviolence together.

"The credibility of the church depends, among other issues, on the way it deals with violence!"

The Seven City Campaign was so convincing that after many difficulties, the assembly in Harare 1998 finally approved German Mennonite Fernando Enns' motion to prepare a Decade to Overcome Violence. The Decade was officially launched during the Central Committee meeting in Berlin 2001 – a very moving moment for me as a German. We lit candles near the Brandenburg gate where a wall had divided not only my country, but Europe as a whole for 28 years. One of the reasons the wall tumbled was that Christians in the German Democratic Republic had called for freedom, for justice, peace and integrity of creation. They brought the call "no violence" from the churches of Leipzig and Dresden and East Berlin to the streets of those cities and made a non-violent revolution possible.

But the past ten years have not turned the world into a peaceful place. Very far from it! Since September 11 2001, terrorism and the so-called "war against terrorism" have caused nameless suffering. Terrorists like Bin Laden have seen themselves as fulfilling God´s will in the name of Islam. Nations that declare themselves democracies have been led astray, using terms like "crusade" and "axis of evil" in order to legitimate military action and a seemingly legitimate demand to "kill or capture"! Trade of weapons is increasing fast and steadily. According to SIPRI (Stockholm International Peace Research Institute), the German part of the world market of weapons rose to eleven percent between 2005 and 2010 being surpassed only by Russia with 23, and the USA with 30 percent. Our economies profit from the violence and war that we lament. Churches cannot stay silent with regard to this dreadful evidence!

It is obvious today that religion plays a vital role with regard to peacemaking and overcoming violence. As the Roman-Catholic theologian Hans Küng says: There is no peace between nations without peace among religions. It is time that religion refuses to be misused by pouring oil on the fire of war and hatred. It is time to consequently deny that there is any theological legitimization for violence. There is no just war – that is what we have learned from history. There is only just peace. And that needs creativity, time, engagement and financing. In a convincing study, Markus Weingardt has studied 40 international conflicts to document how influential religiously motivated people can be in peace-making. They are able to build bridges between parties because they are trusted. They have symbols of peace like common prayer. They dare to talk to "the enemy."

We all know that those who believe in nonviolence are often seen as naïve, not understanding the reality of power and politics. Let us accept that! Jesus was naïve himself if we look at his life by the measures of success. In the eyes of the world, he failed, was convicted, suffered, died. But that dying man on the cross has been a challenge to the yearning for power and those who believe in victory ever since. The power of love is greater than the power of weapons and force. That is what we believe. What a message! We believe in God who is not almighty but comes as an infant, dies under torture and, thus non-violent and powerless, challenges violence and power. That is the point of reference for Christians. They have and the church has always gone astray in history when that was forgotten and violence and destructive power have been legitimated.

"The power of love is greater than the power of weapons and force... We believe in God who is not almighty but comes as an infant, dies under torture and, thus non-violent and powerless, challenges violence and power. That is the point of reference for Christians."

I am convinced that here in Kingston, we are not at the end of a journey. The end of the Decade to Overcome Violence should mark a new beginning in four foci for the churches of the world:

- We need clear theological convictions that violence is in no way to be legitimized by religion. There are two billion Christians in this world. If they radically stand up for nonviolence, dare to dream the dream of a world without violence, it would definitely make a difference. Peace be with you...

- It has to be our conviction that violence is not just one among other ethical questions to be debated. We talk about ecclesiological questions, about the being, the "esse" of the church. In a violent world after all failures in the past, the churches finally have to declare: There is no way to peace, peace is the way. Put the sword back into its place...

- All over the world, we find people who, out of their religious motivation, try to mediate conflicts. They need support, spiritually and financially. Reconciliation is not just part of the liturgy, but hard work in reality. Blessed are the peace-makers....

- Churches all over the world have to challenge the governments in their countries to stop producing, funding and purchasing weapons. It is a scandal that weapons production and trade is a source of economic wealth. Politics is not a separate reign that does not touch church interest. We are churches in the midst of this world and must act in it. They shall beat their swords into ploughshares...

Finally: In the end, we have to keep prayer and action in close contact. If we pray: "Blessed are the peace-makers" that means that we are blessed if we make peace. That can be a very radical message. The past has been full of challenges. The future will be, too. As Christians, churches and the ecumenical movement, challenge the forces of violence! We have a clear calling to overcome violence. Let us fulfill it!

Keynote Address

A New World Is Possible

Rev. Dr Paul Oestreicher

I dedicate this cry for an end to war to the memory of Elizabeth Salter, peace-maker, Quaker, lifelong servant of the ecumenical movement, staff member of the World Council of Churches and an initiator of the Decade to Overcome Violence and, therefore, of this Convocation.

Wherever you come from, whatever your church tradition, you may be Orthodox or Catholic, Protestant or Charismatic, Evangelical or Liberal, Conservative or Radical, all of us have come here because we wish to be friends of Jesus, rabbi, prophet and more than a prophet. To each one of us he says: You are my friends if you do what I command you ... This I command you, to love one another as I have loved you. Is anyone, anywhere, excluded from that love? Here is the answer that Jesus gave to his friends: "It is said 'you shall love your neighbour and hate your enemy'; but I say to you, love your enemies and pray for those who persecute you."

That is how the man in whom we see the face of God spoke, lived and died. As his enemies were killing him, he prayed for them to be forgiven. Jesus was not only speaking to each of us individually; he was addressing the people of God as a holy community. The prophets of Israel spoke to their nation. Often the nation did not want to hear.

Gathered together in Kingston from all corners of the earth, Jesus speaks to us now, to us, a small cross section of his sanctified people. Do we want to hear him? Our record suggests that we do not. Most of our theologians, pastors and assemblies, Orthodox, Catholic, and Protestant, have bowed down ever since the time of the Emperor Constantine in the third century, bowed down deeply to empire and nation rather than to the single new humanity into which we are born. We have made a pact with Caesar, with power, the very pact that the early Christians called idolatry. Because the newly converted ruler declared it to be our duty, we have squared it with our conscience to kill the emperor's enemies, and to do this with Jesus on our lips.

Under the sign of the Cross, Christian nations have conquered and massacred the children of Islam. In 1914, my German father went to war with the words God with Us engraved on his belt buckle. The British soldiers whom he was trained to kill had no doubt that the same God was on their side. When in 1945, a bomber set out, loaded with the world's first nuclear weapon, a single weapon which was about to kill one hundred thousand women and children and men in the city of Hiroshima, the aircraft's crew were sent on their way with Christian prayers. The war memorials in the cathedrals and cities of Christendom attest to the fact that we, like our brothers and sisters in Islam, regard those who have died in battle for the nation as having secured their place in heaven, and that now includes those in the coffins arriving from Afghanistan and draped in the 'sacred' Stars and Stripes.

Unless we change, unless the Church moves to the margins and becomes the alternative society that unconditionally says no to war, no to the collective murder that every embattled nation or tribe, every warring alliance, every violent liberation movement, every fundamentalist cause, and now the War on Terror declares to be just, until we throw this justification of war, this 'just war' theology into the dustbin of history, unless we do that, we will have thrown away the one unique ethical contribution that the teaching of Jesus could make both to the survival of humanity and to the triumph of compassion.

I commend to you religious thinker Karen Armstrong's highly significant *Charter of Compassion*. A Hindu religious follower like Mahatma Gandhi thought that Christianity would be a good idea – if only Christians practiced it. If we were to show compassion for those whom we have good reason to fear, the new world that Jesus called the Kingdom would come a little closer. That is within our power. Albert Schweitzer in his philosophy of civilization simply called it reverence for life.

This Convocation will not yet be the Universal Christian Peace Council of which Dietrich Bonhoeffer dreamed, long before Hitler's obedient servants hanged him. But we could help to pave the way to such a Council, a Council speaking with the authority of the whole Church, if, here and now in Kingston, we were ready to say: it is impossible both to love our enemies and to kill them, it is impossible both to reverence life and to be in league with the military-industrial complex, the killing-machine that rapaciously consumes levels of wealth that are beyond our mathematical imagination.

War and the arms trade that feeds it cannot make life for the people on our small planet more just or more secure. It is not simply that crimes are committed by all sides in every war. War itself is the crime. Its preparation alone globally consumes more than a hundred times the resources that could provide clean water to every child on this planet. Even before the latest perversions of science and technology are put to their lethal use, thousands of children die unnecessarily for lack of clean water.

Jesus was not an idealistic dreamer. He was and remains the ultimate realist. The survival of our planet demands nothing less than the abolition of war. Albert Einstein, the great physicist and humanist, already knew that early in the last century. He repeated it often with a clarity and credibility that few Christian pacifists have matched.

"War itself is the crime. Its preparation alone globally consumes more than a hundred times the resources that could provide clean water to every child on this planet. Even before the latest perversions of science and technology are put to their lethal use, thousands of children die unnecessarily for lack of clean water."

The abolition of war is possible. It is as possible as was the abolition of slavery, the slavery that still haunts the history of this nation of Jamaica. Wilberforce and his evangelical friends, who campaigned to end it, were thought to be unrealistic dreamers. Slavery surely was part of our DNA, necessary to every society's economic survival. The churches were up to their necks in maintaining slavery, the bishops of the Church of England unanimously upheld it. In the same way, many Christians are wedded to a society that cannot let go of the cult of the good soldier or even the holy warrior. Wilberforce and his determined friends triumphed against all odds. Slavery was made illegal. Its defenders withered away. That needs to become the fate of war. If the churches of the world fail to embark on such a campaign, we will have nothing of unique significance to say on the subject of world peace.

What are our chances of winning this battle? Some will say: slavery, exploitation, and trafficking in human beings still go on. Yes, but it is universally acknowledged as both morally wrong, and illegal. Passing legislation to abolish war will not immediately eliminate armed violence. What it will do is to make absolutely clear that to resolve conflicts by military means is illegal, with its perpetrators brought before an International Court of Justice.

Will we then remain in bondage to the principalities and powers, or will we wrestle with them and thereby enter into the glorious liberty of the children of God?

This struggle, if we embrace it, will be at least as tough as that of Wilberforce. Devotion to and respect for every nation's military tradition is as undiminished in church as in state. The Roman dictum: *si vis pacem, para bellum*, if you want peace, prepare for war, holds sway. It is a powerful lie. Yet those who believe it are neither stupid nor evil. History, however, shows that if we prepare for war, war is eventually what we get. Jesus put it quite simply: Those who live by the sword will die by the sword.

Unless we learn to resolve our conflicts – and conflicts there will always be – unless we learn to resolve them without militarized violence, our children's children may no longer have a future. Love of those who threaten us, care for the welfare of those whom we fear, is not only a sign of spiritual maturity, but also of worldly wisdom. It is enlightened self-interest. Military strategists glimpsed that when, in the Cold War, they spoke of common security. If my potential enemy has no reason to fear me, I am safer too.

So, it is time for the still small voices of the historic peace churches, hitherto respected but ignored, to be taken seriously. That is the main reason why, as an Anglican priest, I have also chosen to be a Quaker, a member of the Religious Society of Friends. Quaker history, often a story of suffering, witnesses to the biblical insight that love casts out fear.

"Love of those who threaten us, care for the welfare of those whom we fear, is not only a sign of spiritual maturity, but also of worldly wisdom. It is enlightened self-interest."

So, dear friends of Jesus, can we agree in Kingston to work for the day when the majority of our fellow human beings begin to see collective violence, to see war, in the same way as they see individual murder?

At the moment war, once it starts, is held by most of our neighbours to be honourable, probably necessary, and sometimes noble. Language disguises the bloody, cruel reality. Heroes, it is said, lay down their lives for the nation. In reality, they are trained, if possible, to stay alive and to kill the citizens of other nations. Armies, we are told, are there to protect our women and children. In real life, women and children are war's first – and currently the numerically greatest number of – victims.

When – as in England a few weeks ago – a crown prince marries in a Christian cathedral, he is expected to wear full military regalia. Such symbols are powerful. That is the extent of our problem. Even when the Pope comes on a state visit, he is received, like every head of state, by soldiers carrying fixed bayonets that are designed to kill, rather than by children bearing flowers. His Holiness accepts the military rituals, as do practically all our churches. Do we even register the absurdity?

We are comfortable with military chaplains embedded with the men and women who are trained to kill. If they were a questioning, prophetic presence, they would undermine the cohesion and the morale on which every army depends. They are welcomed because they raise troops' morale.

The taxes I pay, though once I tried unsuccessfully not to, help to finance Britain's Trident submarines. The sailors who man them have no right to disobey the order, if it were ever given, as it could be by a British prime minister, to commit genocide. They are conditioned to do the unthinkable in my name.

You will before not long be left in doubt that this Convocation is about the world's need for a just peace. That is, I guess, what has brought us here. However, to speak of a more just peace would be nearer the truth. The struggle for greater justice will remain a task for every generation, for as long as human society exists. Our faith, our common humanity, our love for one another commit us to this struggle. But we should never give way to the mistaken assumption, as some Christians sadly do, that 'until there is perfect justice, there cannot be peace'. Rather, peace, the rejection of collective violence, is a precondition for the world of tomorrow that will always need to be made more just. Killing each other can only undermine that task. To oppose evil with violence is to drive out the Devil with Beelzebub. It will not work.

I am under no illusion. The price to be paid for nonviolent resistance to evil is as high as any soldier is expected to pay. Nonviolent resistance to evil will never be a quick fix. It will call for long suffering and patience. It will be a living expression now of the new world that is not yet.

"Peace, the rejection of collective violence, is a precondition for the world of tomorrow that will always need to be made more just. Killing each other can only undermine that task. To oppose evil with violence is to drive out the Devil with Beelzebub. It will not work."

The Ploughshares Movement is one example of nonviolent direct action against the symbols of modern warfare. Like the Berrigan brothers at the time of the Vietnam War, such peaceful resisters are prepared to break laws that protect the arsenals of violence. Juries may acquit them or may send them to prison. The fate of Jesus was worse, was fatal. When he angrily overturned the tables of the corrupt financial dealers in the Temple forecourt, challenging greed in league with priestly power, much like the bonus culture of today's corrupt banking system, whose life did Jesus put at risk in that one-man demonstration? Only his own. How absurd then, that many Christians use this example of righteous anger to justify the violence of war, when in fact it demonstrates the very opposite.

What I have put before you in rather stark simplicity is nevertheless deeply complex. Having spent my life studying politics, I do not believe that there is any room for pacifist self-righteousness. I have not come to Kingston to demonize those who choose the military option. They are part of us, the many, and we the few. We must find ways of co-opting them into the peaceful struggle. The critics of principled nonviolence are neither knaves nor fools. We must answer them wisely and patiently. They will rightly ask pacifists like me many serious questions: how, for example, is law and order to be maintained globally without heavily armed nations? On this point, there is already good news. In the light of the last century's history of unparalleled violence, international law is paving the way for genuine alternatives.

In theory, war is already largely outlawed. There are courts to try not only crimes committed in war, but the crime of war itself. But how are the laws of peace to be enforced? It is in their policing that there is still little experience. Yet there is some. When soldiers under United Nations command are trained, as police in our streets are trained, not to kill enemies, but to prevent or to end violent conflicts, we are already on the way to the new world. The great majority of the armed forces of New Zealand, my second home, are already engaged in the Pacific as peace-keepers, and are proud to be. Violence itself is their enemy. There is good news too in the experience that a critical mass of peaceful, unarmed people, often young people, from Leipzig to Cairo and beyond, can bring down tyrannies. That 'love is stronger than hate' is, as Desmond Tutu often reminds us, a political as well as a spiritual truth.

When the still-young discipline of Peace Studies is given the same resources in the world's universities as those that are given to Security Studies and the development of weapons systems, we will have made real progress. When women, raped and victimized in every war, are given an equal say in how we order our lives, we will have advanced even further. And with the military now recruiting women, will they be able to transform its rigidly patriarchal traditions?

Hardest of all, peace will demand the dethroning of the military-industrial complex. Dwight D. Eisenhower, America's top World War II general and then its president, warned the American people shortly before the end of his administration of its insidious power, a late but not too late insight. Such a peace demands a seismic global rethink. Its organization will be as demanding as the organization of war. Every discipline will be involved: law, politics, international relations and economics, sociology, gender studies, personal and social psychology, and: last but, for us, not least, theology, the way we interpret the will of God.

There will always remain a dialectical tension between the struggle for justice, and the need to keep the struggle peaceful. We now know too that this new world will also depend on our will and capacity to cherish and preserve the natural environment of which we are part. War desecrates and pillages nature and squanders its precious resources.

Yes to life means no to war. Humble men who can boast of no Nobel Peace Prize have paved the way. In the midst of patriotic fervor, they have simply said no. Let me tell you of two brave, wise farmers.

During the Second World War, Franz Jägerstätter defied Hitler's command to take up arms. 'Jesus forbids me to'. His 'no' led straight to prison. A devout Catholic, his bishop came to visit him. 'Franz, if you persist in your refusal, you will be executed. Surely you cannot do that to your wife and children?' His reply: 'Bishop, do you want me to kill Russian husbands and fathers?' Franz was executed in 1944. His wife Franziska stood by him to the end. Franz was virtually disowned by his church. Two generations later, a German Pope beatified him.

"There will always remain a dialectical tension between the struggle for justice, and the need to keep the struggle peaceful. We now know too that this new world will also depend on our will and capacity to cherish and preserve the natural environment of which we are part. War desecrates and pillages nature and squanders its precious resources."

Archibald Baxter was a New Zealand farm labourer at the time of the First World War. He belonged to no church, but had diligently read the New Testament. In 1917, he refused to serve. They dragged him to the trenches in France, tortured and almost killed him, did all they could to break his will. They failed. He had no formal education, but his memoir has become a classic of peace literature. Defending his refusal to kill, Baxter replied to his critics: 'The only lasting victory that we can win over our enemies, is to make them our friends'.

KYRIE ELEISON   CHRISTE ELEISON   KYRIE ELEISON

IV.
Thematic Plenaries Presentations

Peace in the Community

Affirming the Dignity and Rights of All and Nurturing Values of Mutuality

Martin Luther King III

Thank all of you for your warm welcome. I want to also thank the leadership of the World Council of Churches for inviting me to join you today and giving me the opportunity to be a part of this International Ecumenical Peace Convocation.

Let me also thank the people of Jamaica for their gracious hospitality and goodwill that has been extended to me on this visit to your beautiful country, just as you welcomed my mother, Coretta Scott King and my father, Martin Luther King, Jr. when they visited Jamaica in June, 1965.

Reverend Thompson, fellow program participants, members of the World Council of Churches, it is a great pleasure and an honour to be with you today and to share my thoughts with you on this occasion.

I have been asked to address this plenary session on the topics of "affirming the dignity and rights of all and nurturing values of mutuality and interdependence." These topics resonate with great familiarity with me, since my parents taught them to my siblings and me as core values on a daily basis. The importance of affirming the dignity and rights of all people was emblazoned in my consciousness as a central principle of all my dealings with everyone, even as a child.

As civil rights leaders, my parents were acutely aware of the need to respect the dignity and rights of all people, most especially one's adversaries. For them, it was the great cause of their times, particularly with respect to African Americans, who had been denied their rights and their human dignity as standard practice in the segregation era. Passing these values on to their children was really second nature to my parents.

My mother was an activist in the struggle for dignity and human rights even before my father became a leader. She was involved in human rights campaigns as a college student, well before she met him. My mother was raised in the African Methodist Episcopal Church, which has a very strong 'social gospel' tradition. She also had the unique experience of attending the Lincoln School as a young girl, where a largely Quaker faculty taught social change values. She followed her older sister to Antioch College where social justice values were taught to all students.

After they married and moved to Montgomery, he became a community and national leader who was dedicated to achieving respect for the dignity and rights of African Americans through the application of nonviolent resistance.

This was the unique aspect of my father's leadership in the struggle for human dignity and civil rights; leveraging the power of nonviolence in a very deliberate way to challenge racial segregation. I emphasize the word 'deliberate' here because, when the civil rights movement began in 1955, the people of Montgomery did not respond non-violently without preparation. Instead there was a very well-organized effort to teach the African American citizens of Montgomery the basic principles and methods of nonviolence. My father had intensely studied the life, work and teachings of Mohandas K. Gandhi and he made a decision the adapt some of Gandhi's methods to our struggle for dignity and civil rights in Montgomery.

My father did not start the Montgomery bus boycott. That was sparked when Mrs Rosa Parks refused to give up her seat on a city bus to a white man, as was the custom in those days. And then a group of community leaders decided that a bus boycott was in order.

Nor did my father campaign or ask to become the leader of the protest. Instead he was chosen to be the leader, partly because he was new in town, had no enemies and was well-liked, and partly because he was recognized as a good speaker.

And yet, it is interesting that they chose the one man in town who had read a dozen or more books about Gandhi's nonviolent campaigns. By the time my father was first asked to serve as spokesman for the Montgomery improvement association, he was already very well read about the power of nonviolence as a method for challenging social oppression. He had already thought seriously about how organized nonviolence might be used to secure dignity and rights for African Americans. And so, he was well-prepared for that leadership role. With hindsight, it is not hard to imagine the hand of God in his anointing as spokesman for the Montgomery bus boycott.

But it was not only his intellectual development that led Martin Luther King, Jr. to become a champion of human dignity and civil rights. He had the powerful example of his father, my grandfather, Reverend Martin Luther King, Sr., a man who embodied and radiated dignity in his bearing and in all of his dealings with people. His mother, my grandmother, Alberta Williams King was the same way. Just in the way they carried themselves and conducted themselves, they insisted on having their dignity respected and in respecting the dignity of all people.

My grandfather was also a civil rights leader in Atlanta. In 1935, he led a voting rights march to Atlanta's city hall and later he led another march for equal pay for African American teachers. He would never back down from racial injustice, and this lesson was not lost on his sons.

Another source for the strong emphasis on human rights and dignity in the life and leadership of Martin Luther King, Jr. comes from his Christian training. As the son and grandson of Christian preachers, my father was very well-educated about the teachings of Jesus, which are very much about nonviolence. Jesus taught the values of unconditional love and forgiveness, treating the poor and oppressed with kindness and generosity and about the power of unearned suffering as a redemptive force for good. These are all cornerstone principles of nonviolence that are found in the Sermon on the Mount and other events in the life of Jesus of Nazareth.

I am not saying that the Christian faith has a monopoly on the spiritual principles that undergird nonviolence. I believe you can find mandates for nonviolence in the holy scriptures of many religions.

But Martin Luther King, Jr.'s leadership as a nonviolent revolutionary was very much in the spirit and tradition of Jesus Christ. And yet as one who received his Ph.D. in systematic theology, he was well-acquainted with the spiritual teachings of all faiths. Concerning the nonviolent philosophy that empowered the American civil rights movement, he said "Christ furnished the spirit and motivation while Gandhi furnished the method."

And so, my concern for human rights and human dignity has deep roots, going back generations and as an integral part of my faith. The struggle for human rights for all people of every race, religion and nation is one to which I pledge my wholehearted support for as long as God gives me breath. And I see this ongoing struggle as a great ecumenical challenge meriting the support of people of all faiths.

Today, as we strive to affirm the dignity and rights of all people, many tenacious forms of discrimination continue to undermine human rights. There is still racial discrimination. There is discrimination based on religion, nationality, age, gender and sexual orientation.

I believe economic rights – the right to food, shelter and employment – are human rights that should be available to all people, everywhere. In my opinion, freedom from poverty, want and deprivation is a fundamental human right. Every nation should actively work to eradicate the forms of discrimination that keep people living in poverty.

The most common method of enforcement of discrimination being used around the world is violence. Most regimes that oppress people use forms of violence to control their populations. And when liberation groups retaliate against violence with more violence, what you get is civil war.

But there is an alternative. One of *the* most important lessons we learned in the civil rights movement in the United States, as did Gandhi in India, is the tremendous power of the philosophy and strategy of nonviolence. When oppressed people get organized and practice disciplined nonviolence, they can produce far-reaching social change.

"Today, as we strive to affirm the dignity and rights of all people, many tenacious forms of discrimination continue to undermine human rights. There is still racial discrimination."

Now, as for the other part of my topic, "nurturing values of mutuality and interdependence," this is another way of affirming the importance of cooperation and connectedness, which are very much needed in our world. We talk a lot in our societies about the virtues of competition and individualism. But in many countries, especially my country, we have glorified competition to the point where it is counter-productive. Certainly competition has a place in economics and sports. But we urgently need more cooperation, more recognition of our mutuality and interdependence to help us understand why it is wrong to tolerate extremes of wealth and poverty.

I believe that doing a better job of nurturing the values of mutuality and interdependence among the young people of our nations will also help us to prevent war and create peace. The poet Longfellow once said that "if only we could read the secret history of our enemies, we should find in each man's life sorrow and suffering enough to disarm all hostility."

Conflict is an inevitable part of life. There will always be conflict. But we must impress upon each new generation that there are more productive ways to deal with conflict than violence toward our adversaries. This is what we are doing at the King Center, an organization founded by my mother after my father was assassinated in 1968, and which I now serve as president and chief executive officer. We are determined to have an impact on fulfilling my father's dream by educating and training people in the philosophy and methods of nonviolence that empowered the leadership of Martin Luther King, Jr. In this endeavour, we welcome your support.

By taking the time to educate ourselves about the sorrow and suffering and hardship being experienced by our adversaries, and encouraging them to do the same toward us, we are sowing the seeds of greater understanding needed to create the beloved community envisioned by Josiah Royce and Martin Luther King, Jr.

In March of 1968, just three weeks and one day before he was assassinated, my father delivered a sermon at the national cathedral in Washington, D.C. On that day he delivered a clarion call for recognition of the mutuality and interdependence of all humanity. He said, "Through our scientific and technological genius, we have made of this world a neighbourhood and yet we have not had the ethical commitment to make of it a brotherhood. But somehow, and in some way, we have got to do this. We must all learn to live together as brothers or we will all perish together as fools. We are tied together in the single garment of destiny, caught in an inescapable network of mutuality. And whatever affects one directly affects all indirectly. For some strange reason I can never be what I ought to be until you are what you ought to be. And you can never be what you ought to be until I am what I ought to be. This is the way God's universe is made; this is the way it is structured."

I should note that, in his election victory speech in Chicago, President Obama quoted my father's line about "mutuality" and "the single garment of destiny."

My father saw mutuality and interdependence as a cosmic truth and an inescapable part of the human condition. But instead of celebrating this beautiful mutuality, we spend so much time, money and effort engaged in my-way-or-the-highway conflicts. Too often the spirit of reconciliation is replaced by cutthroat competition, in which contesting parties see the destruction of their adversaries as the only solution to their problems. Of course, it never works, because violence always begets more violence and, as my father often said, an eye for an eye leaves everybody blind.

And today it is kind of ironic that we have even more manifestations of the "scientific and technological genius" my father referenced in that quote. Indeed, we have amazing tools for affirming our mutuality and interdependence in the internet, cell phones, skype and so many other communications devices being invented every day. And yet in some ways, we seem to be using these wonderful inventions to distance ourselves from each other. I am sure many of you have had the experience of going out to a romantic dinner, only to see young couples who should be looking in each other's eyes, instead reading their email and texting on cell phones.

My point is that, too often, we are not using these new communications tools to advance our spiritual and emotional connectedness, nor to affirm our mutuality and interdependence. We need to make more of an effort to use technology to promote greater understanding, empathy and compassion between people, not as a device to "cocoon" ourselves in isolated worlds. I know we can and must do better if we make a conscious effort to do so.

One of the things we must do in every nation is to recommit ourselves to a shared global vision.

On December 10, 1964, my father, Martin Luther King, Jr. was presented the Nobel Prize for Peace in recognition of his leadership of the civil rights movement in the United States. My father always considered the African American freedom struggle to be a part of the world-wide freedom movement. And he often said that he was deeply concerned about ending poverty and war everywhere.

When he accepted the Nobel Peace Prize, this is what Martin Luther King, Jr. said:

> I have the audacity to believe that peoples everywhere can have three meals a day for their bodies, education and culture for their minds, and dignity, equality and freedom for their spirits. I believe that what self-centered men have torn down, men other-centered can build up. I still believe that one day mankind will bow before the altars of God and be crowned triumphant over war and bloodshed, and nonviolent redemptive goodwill will proclaim the rule of the land.

My father had a dream, not just for the United Sates, but for making the entire world a better place. He talked about creating a "beloved community" in which people of every race, religion and nation could live together in peace and harmony and work together for the common progress of humankind.

In the beloved community of his global dream, poverty, hunger and homelessness will not be tolerated because international standards of human decency will not allow it. Racism and all forms of discrimination, bigotry and prejudice will be replaced by an all-inclusive spirit of sisterhood and brotherhood. In the beloved community, international disputes will be resolved by nonviolent conflict-resolution and reconciliation of adversaries. Love and trust will triumph over fear and hatred. Peace with justice will prevail over war and military conflict.

The beauty of nonviolence is that it provides lasting change, because there is no aftermath of bitterness and hatred to feed an endless cycle of revenge and retaliation. We found that nonviolence confers on its practitioners a unique credibility that can win the hearts and minds of not only the public, but even enemies, in a way that violence can never match.

The nonviolent philosophy and method that liberated India from colonial domination and African Americans in the United States, has been adapted and used with success in many nations, including Poland, the Philippines, the Bahamas, South Africa, and now Egypt and Tunisia. All over the world people are beginning to tap into the power of nonviolence to expand and protect human rights.

"The beauty of nonviolence is that it provides lasting change, because there is no aftermath of bitterness and hatred to feed an endless cycle of revenge and retaliation."

And as nonviolent movements begin to connect across national boundaries around the world and share information via the internet, we will open up new possibilities for global campaigns to advance human rights and social justice in all nations.

As my father once said, "the struggle for freedom is one long front crossing oceans and mountains…the brotherhood of man is not confined within a narrow, limited circle of select people. It is felt everywhere in the world… out of this struggle will come the glorious reality of the family of man."

Meeting this challenge will require commitment and much hard work from all of us. But with prayer, faith and cooperation, there is every reason to believe that we will succeed, and our efforts will herald a new era of great progress in securing civil and human rights for all.

With this shared commitment, let us affirm the bonds of mutuality and interdependence that unite freedom and justice-loving people everywhere. Let us embrace the future with a radiant spirit of hope and optimism, sisters and brothers of all races, religions and nations, united and determined to build the beloved community for all humanity.

With this vision, we can put an end to humanity's nightmare of poverty, racism and militarism, and go forward into a more hopeful future, united and determined to create a more just, compassionate and peaceful world.

Thank you and God bless you.

The Dalit Struggle for Dignity

Asha Kowtal

I am here representing the people of my community – the erstwhile '*untouchable*' people, about 250 million in South Asia and elsewhere in the world. Let me give you some glimpses of the life world of my people.

In a recent incident near Mumbai, a Dalit woman, Rani, saw a mob of people surround her husband, tie him down on the ground and mercilessly attack him. She ran to his rescue, but the three women among the mob attacked her. Then each of the six men there, one after another, raped her, as the dominant caste women encouraged them. As soon as the couple regained consciousness, they left the farm, went to the police station to register a complaint, but the police did not accept it. They returned home to file a complaint in their own village. But when the people saw both of them, they kidnapped the husband. A few days later he was found murdered. There the story ends, but what remains is an echoing silence of violence.

Alongside Rani's story, I also wish to amplify the cries of Kamala and hundreds of other women raped every day because they are dependent on the powerful. Today I cry for Yellamma and hundreds of young girls sexually abused by the dominant caste men because of religious legitimization. I want to give expression to the inaudible voices of Savitaamma and thousands of people from my community who clean human excreta with bare hands.

I stand before you on behalf of Arun and hundreds of other young students who end their lives and drop out unable to bear discrimination and humiliation even in premier educational institutions in India. I echo the pleas for justice of eight members of one family who were burnt alive in Kambalpalli recently because they refused to let their land be taken away by dominant caste people. I place before you the plight and humiliation of thousands of elected representatives who are constantly harassed, challenged and killed because of their aspirations for political power. I highlight the misery and sufferings of thousands of people who are denied food and water when they resist oppression and discrimination.

I mourn with men of the Bhootmange family in Khairlanji near Mumbai, whose women were dragged out from their homes, raped publicly and murdered because they dared to file a criminal complaint against the dominant castes. I also want to protest on behalf of the little children who are prohibited from sitting in the front rows of the classrooms and are forced to clean the toilets in their schools. I groan with the menfolk of my community who stand helpless when their wives and sisters are paraded naked in the village streets.

I present to you Satish and many others in urban India who are not allowed to live in a neighbourhood of segregated housing – similar to ghettoization. I stand with people and communities who are discriminated against and refused relief materials after tsunamis and similar natural disasters.

Dear friends, I have come here to expose the cruelty of the CASTE system, which legitimizes and perpetuates violence and discrimination against millions of Dalits and the majority of Indians. Now what exactly is this Caste system? Caste is a system of hierarchical social organization in which the locations of people are determined by birth. This system is peculiar to the Indian sub-continent, resulting in discrimination and exclusion of millions of people, and is considered as the largest systemic violation of human rights anywhere in the world.

Having been deeply affected by stigma and shame, the Dalits are segregated in both rural and urban areas, denied opportunities and access to resources and deprived of participation in public life. As such, they are the poorest of the poor, the most uneducated, the most unemployed and the most vulnerable. These, my friends, are the features of the culture that is violent in itself. This culture has infected the ethos of Indian society to such an extent that the State, Judiciary, media and even academia have turned casteist. Because of the manifold violations of their dignity as human beings, they become vulnerable to various other forms of violence. I want to highlight the predicament of Dalit women as victims of two cultures of violence – caste and patriarchy.

What we see here are two types of violence. One is 'discrimination'. Discrimination disempowers, deprives, denies, dehumanizes and diminishes the capacities of life. The other is the 'backlash violence' that is unleashed against Dalits when they assert their rights and demand justice. Landlords and the police use various methods to crush resistance. My dear brothers and sisters, today I want us to think about how to teach nonviolence to the powerful instead of the disempowered. In other words, how can we aspire for peace without confronting the violence which is deeply embedded in our cultures and communities?

India boasts of itself as a booming economy and is recognised as a global economic power. It is also hoping to become a member of the 'Security Council' in the UN. India is also applauded for its rich ancient tradition of wisdom and cultures. But as a person pushed to the margins of society, I am unable to see myself as a part of that India when most of my people continue to live in extreme poverty, earning a mere Rs. 20 to Rs. 50 per day (less than a Dollar). I can go on giving you a lot of statistical information, but I want us to think of Dalits as human beings, as people aspiring for dignity and life. And in their aspiration, there are possibilities for peace with justice. There are possibilities for social transformation. There are possibilities for our own liberation and transformation. As I speak about the Dalits, I also think of many others who are likewise discriminated and denied life, justice and peace. I think of the people who are struggling against racism, the Indigenous people, the minorities and all others who have been made vulnerable to violence by religious and cultural legitimizations.

Today, I call upon you to join these struggles of the despised and the discriminated. It is a struggle for dignity; a struggle for respect and through it let us strive for a world of peace with justice.

Violence of Patriarchy and Sexism:
A Focus on Women in Conflict Zones – Palestine

Muna Mushahwar

I am a mover for gender justice within the WCC and I come to you from a land that has long known turmoil, injustice and suffering. A place that has known martyrs for freedom, both men and women. Its children as well as the elderly remember and are intimately acquainted with being at the receiving end of displacement, discrimination and denial of the most basic human rights which the rest of the world takes for granted.

I stand before you today in beautiful Jamaica, while last week my people were once again brutalized by occupation as we commemorate 63 years of the Palestinian displacement and occupation by Israel.

The process of creation of a "refugee people" that was started 63 years ago continues to the present day. The catastrophe, *Al Nakbah*, that began with the displacement of seven hundred thousand Palestinians other than those who were killed, persists today with over 6 million displaced Palestinian refugees around the world and the continuing quest for freedom and dignity.

I ask you to stand with me in a moment of silence and solidarity for the suffering and loss of innocent lives. I ask you to reflect on the mothers that have lost their children this week and have to yet again pick up the pieces of a life that will never be the same again. Thank you.

You must all be wondering how this relates to violence of patriarchy and sexism. The answer to that is the fact that in conflict zones, when the survival of the people is on the line, women's suffering gets marginalized, pushed to the background while the more important issues are dealt with.

In the middle of political crisis, women find themselves in the very difficult position of, on the one hand, fighting and fending off the aggression of an occupation that threatens their lives and those of their loved ones. And on the other hand, the oppression of not being able to speak of their social and domestic problems. Even though that they can express refusal of the aggression of occupation, we find that often they are unable to do that when it comes to aggression from within their own social surroundings for fear of being labelled as unpatriotic if they were to criticize male national authority. Palestinian women have found themselves in the dichotomy of being pushed forward toward independence from patriarchal constraints and self-sufficiency by political events that have shaped our history, but at the same time weighed down by social and cultural constraints that maintain a patriarchal hold on them.

Having been at the frontline of the conflict since its beginning, some chose to participate in the armed struggle and became freedom fighters, well acknowledged and respected in Palestinian history for their sacrifices. Others found themselves in a position where there were forced to choose between having their children shot or being removed from their home, as happened with my mother's own family who came from Haifa in the North. Of course, as there was no real choice in the matter, mothers had to gather whatever they could from what was their normal life and try to create a new one for their family and children to ensure survival. Often they became the sole provider for the family. They could not have the luxury of feeling grief. Throughout the struggle they have been in a position of constant combat in a non-violent resistance both on the materialistic level as well as the psychological. The terrain for combat being no longer limited to the field but extending into their militarized home, under threat of demolition or attack. Even childbirth has become an act of non-violent resistance, with pregnant Palestinian women being prevented from reaching a hospital, forced to give birth at checkpoints and losing their newborn child as a consequence.

Occupation not only maintains the legacy of no luxury afforded to Palestinian women, but in more recent times has been reinforcing the patriarchal attitude toward them in society. While our young women are encouraged to pursue higher education within Palestine, the fact that a concrete wall of 8 meters constructed by Israel divides up the Palestinian territory hinders movement and therefore, these young women have to travel longer detour roads, being subjected to the possibility of harassment by opportunistic perpetrators. Social and economic burdens prohibit these young women from pursuing their education

In recent years, severe psychological symptoms such as depression, anxiety, post-traumatic stress disorder are reported to have severely increased in Palestinian society under the current circumstances, especially among women, numbers rising to 62% of married women reporting psychological abuse and 23% reporting physical abuse.

"Honour crimes" committed against women on the grounds of "tarnishing family name and honour" or "collaboration with the occupation" are still taking place, and perpetrators are still protected by law. 32 women were killed between the years 2004-2006; 12 of these murders occurred in Gaza. In 2009 13 women were killed.

Palestinian women held in detention by the Israeli government face different forms of violence, according to a UNIFEM report published in December 2010. Torture, harassment, verbal and physical abuse, medical negligence, poor living conditions with lack of fresh air and crowded holding cells – practices that clearly go against international law and the UN regulations for the treatment of prisoners.

Through all these issues, occupation has become a tool that affords promoters and defenders of patriarchy in Palestinian society the opportunity to keep the status quo with regard to women's conditions and issue. Excuses of "more pressing political issues," "nationalism" "protection of honour" are used conveniently to avoid dealing with what they perceive as a Pandora's Box: the moment it's open, there is no knowing where it might lead.

Despite that, positive signs of change within the Palestinian society have started budding through Palestinian women's organizations that have been raising awareness about these issues and advocating equality and partnership. The Palestinian National Authority has recently adopted a national strategy promoting gender equality and equity as a result of collaboration between the Ministry of Women's Affairs, the United Nations Entity for Gender Equality and the Empowerment of Women as well as several non-governmental organizations working in the Palestinian territories.

But while Palestinian women in the Palestinian National Authority areas have some flicker of hope in that respect, Palestinian women living in Jerusalem such as myself find that we have yet another ghost to be haunted by; a constant threat of losing the "right" to live in our City. If I am absent from the city for any prolonged period of time, be it for education or work, or if I for example, were to marry a Palestinian from the West Bank or Gaza or a foreigner, that person would not be allowed to live with me in Jerusalem. I would therefore be forced to live where he does. But by doing that, Israel strips me of my "residency right" in Jerusalem and I become yet another refugee. I lose the right to raise my children in the city that I was born and raised in and would only have memories to tell them about as my parents do, telling my brothers and I that "this used to be our house that we were forced to flee from," or "this used to be grandfather's workshop." I would not be allowed to visit my mother's grave, which as it is, I have to give a weekly explanation to some Israeli soldier of why I need to get through the road block they placed a few meters outside the cemetery.

So, as a Palestinian Jerusalemite woman, I am restricted in my choice of a life-partner, education and work, and have constantly to prove to the state of Israel that the centre of my life continues to be in Jerusalem.

I would like to emphasize that the issues raised do not depend on religion. It is often mistakenly assumed that Christian women fare better than their Muslim counterparts. The fact is that while there might be a slight difference to the advantage of Christian women, the issues remain the same. In fact, in our churches, women still face inequality when it comes to issues such as succession orders and ordination, to name just a couple.

In asking ourselves "What is the role of the church in all of this?" I see two clear answers.

As a woman, I believe that we cannot have justice in the community without having it within our safe haven of the church.

As a Palestinian Christian woman, I believe that the church has a huge role and must take responsibility in stopping the mis-interpretation of Scripture that allows the injustice committed against the Palestinian people and justifies it. It needs to make clear the distinction between the biblical "Israel" and "chosen people" and the current political entity of the state of Israel.

In 2009, Palestinian Christians took a stand with a unified voice in issuing the "Moment of Truth" document, also known as The Kairos Palestine Document. This was a message of Love, Hope and Faith to bring peace as well as justice according to the teachings of Our Lord to our beloved land. And we ask Christians all over the world to read it, reflect upon it and support it.

Israeli Army Chief of Staff Moshe Yaalon said in August 2002: "The Palestinians must be made to understand in the deepest recesses of their consciousness that they are a defeated people."

I stand in front of you today, despite all the grief and injustice that my people have known at the hands of Israel, and I ask you: Do you see a daughter of a defeated people?

Just and Inclusive Communities for Peace:
A Process of Building Networks of Interdependencies

Tânia Mara Vieira Sampaio

I am immensely grateful for the happiness I feel at this moment of sharing. It is a great honour and responsibility to talk to you about what I have learned from the essence and wisdom of many women, men, children, young people and old people and, especially, the poor people of Brazil and Latin America. I bring in my body the marks of what I've learned from the community's search for a more just and inclusive society and for peace.

I keep remembering the smile and intense gaze of a man whose name I do not know, who stopped me a few days ago and spoke the following words: "My dear lady, you look very sad, very sad indeed. Don't be so sad. Life is beautiful." I had been walking down the road without realising that what I was feeling inside, my sadness and a feeling of the most profound powerlessness, was reflected on my face. It was very difficult to bear the killing of a community leader. The smile of the unknown man invited me to meet him. Suddenly, that poor downtrodden man, who spends his days looking after the cars parked on the roads in order to earn a bit of money for his work (one of the many self-employed people in Brazil in recent years), that man with his gaze and concern for Others who he did not know, was able to revive in me feelings of happiness and hope. Here was a person who thought about Others and was able to care for me in such a loving way that I keep remembering his face.

The respect for life shown by that unknown man prompts me to begin this moment with an act of profound respect for Life: the Life of all living beings of the ecosystem, lives that are the most diverse and indispensable threads in the great Web of Life. I don't mean life in an abstract and universal way, but rather the tangible life that brightens our bodies in multiple related processes.

I want to start a dialogue. In order to do this, although it might sound paradoxical, I believe that moments of silence are timely. In a mixture of absence and presence, I invite you who are present to seek in your memories those who are absent here but present in the daily life of your communities. I invite everyone of you to feel the movement of your body in silence, without rushing to reply, without feeling any pain because you do not know the truth, without ... an infinity of certainties.

I invite you to seek in the power of the air, water, fire and earth an opportunity to dialogue about just and inclusive communities and the celebration of Peace. Let us feel the air as we breathe in and out, allowing life to circulate around our bodies. I mean bodies in a holistic way and not as a body-spirit dichotomy. Let us breathe in and breathe out several times as we search for the *Ruah,* the *Pneuma* of the Mystery that makes us living beings. While we breathe, let us remember the lives of the women, men, children, young people and old people who are part of our lives. [...] Let us feel silence and memory.

In the powerful image of fire, I invite your memory to make present the tangible lives of the combative people we know in our communities. [...] Let us feel silence and memory.

In the vital strength of water, today threatened with scarcity, let us remember the lives of the women, men, children, young people and old people whose strength is stolen every day in our communities. [...] Let us feel silence and memory.

From the vigour of the earth, whether the most arid or fertile, let us make present the lives of those who cultivate the seeds despite all the hardships they face. Lives that sow, lives that announce it is possible to harvest a new fruit. Peace is born and will continue to be born as a result of people planting justice in all the different communities around the world. [...] While we feel silence, let us remember the names of the people we invoke in this vital Eucharist. In whatever tone you want to (high or low), pronounce a name followed by another name so that we know to whom our lives are related. [...] Let us quieten the sound of our voices again and feel silence and memory.

The movement of listening and silence is *kairós*. It is a timely moment to appreciate that we are "learners," beings who are undergoing a constant process of education, in a process of opening ourselves that replaces ready-made and universal discourses.

Human languages are precarious. Sometimes they are too fragile to capture all the experience of faith that we feel. The truths that nurture us therefore can only approach the Transcendent, they cannot reduce it to our formulations. To insist on owning the absolute truth about God, on the basis of a tradition of faith, would be to make God subservient to our possibilities and would contribute little to a process of dialogue.

My mind goes back to José and Ana who immediately understood that, although they attended different churches, they should fight together in their neighbourhood. Both of them felt the power of God within them. As time went by, the community rooms of the residents' association were the scene of many meetings, moments of celebration to which each brought their symbols of faith, their songs, their discourse about God. Their communion was not bound by institutional liturgies. The movement of life, with its demands, set the tone of the ecumenical and inter-religious liturgy celebrated there.

In the daily lives of these two people and many others, I learned that our own experience of God can be seen as *a possibility of approaching the Mystery,* but not the only one!

I think that for us to begin any dialogue, it is essential to recognize that differences exist between interlocutors and it is also essential to listen to the other person. In this context, I want to share how communities in the poorest neighbourhoods have worked with the churches and their educational institutions and universities, something I have been involved in for the last 30 years. This triple alliance has allowed us to make profound connections.

It is important to explain that access to formal education in Brazil and Latin America is restricted to only a small part of the population. Although access to university in Brazil has improved in the last decade and the percentage of people with access has risen from 5% to 14% of the population, this only goes to show that education is still a privilege of the few. In the knowledge-based society in which we live in these times of globalization, poor communities need to appropriate knowledge quantitatively and qualitatively much more quickly than they do at the moment.

I was listening to Neuma, a young black woman aged 19, presenting her work at university. She explained how she had experienced something that would change the way she held her body for the rest of her life. It was a very strong feeling and it made us all feel very emotional. She said that ever since she was a child, she learned that when black people passed close to police officers, they should keep quiet, hunch their body and lower their head. They couldn't look them in the face, they couldn't look them in the eye. They were always to blame. Their crime (even though they had done nothing wrong) was the colour of their skin. And so she learned to always hunch her body. However, one day at university, as she was walking along, she encountered some police officers, also studying at the university, who were standing in her way. She would have to walk among them to continue on her path. She had a few seconds to reflect and decide what to do, but these were seconds that carried the experience of years of community organization, three years at university, and strong links with black people who she looked up to (some of her teachers, who already had doctorates). She decided she had the power to stand up straight, raise her eyes and walk right between those police officers in a way that she, and many other black people had never been allowed to do because of the strongly racist mentality of society in our country. Standing up straight, looking at people in the eyes, this was Neuma giving us a wonderful lesson.

Such empowering processes as these have helped to show that new knowledge and new categories of analysing reality were necessary to promote emancipation, empowerment, participation and decision-making by individual people and communities.

Among the paths leading to this construction of knowledge, overcoming obstacles and confronting forms of structural violence, were contributions from the theory of complexity and the theory of gender. There are other theories, but I have chosen these two because of their significance for the community experience in which I live.

The first contribution, the theory of complexity, sees the ecosystem as interdependent and complex and human beings as different rather than superior, and introduces a new insight that proposes building networks to promote relations of connectivity between different living beings. A second contribution, the theory of gender, with its emphasis on asymmetric social relations, not only between men and women, but also between ethnic groups, social classes, generations and beliefs, shows that there is no single universal human being and affirms the heterogeneity or plural nature of social groups. The main analytical focus of both theories is power relations. To reflect on the hierarchy of power in social relations is necessary in order to rescue the body as a unique place for the experience of being in the world, because it is these social relations, manifested in the exercise of power, that either oppresses people or makes them free. Making it urgent to establish another concept of power designed to promote networks that promote ideas of connectivity and interdependence.

People could be perceived as beings with desires and passions as well as needs, with all the implications that this signifies. This key to the interpretation of power allows people to confront and combat the sacrificial logic of the market, which prejudices the lives of people and promotes a sacrifice that masks and covers its perversity because it signifies the real death of people. A violent death, planned for the quarter of the world's population who do not have dignified working conditions, health, housing, education, leisure, pleasure...

This perverse religious logic of the market has been subjected to a structural critique. We must unmask and denounce the idols created by human hands, as is the case of the market, a sacred cannibalism that feeds on the deaths and the decrees of death of its victims. We cannot combat a sacrificial logic by naïvely denying the existence of the market, but we can repudiate how it is worshipped and we can redesign technological and scientific development. We can intervene in its dynamics, using its own instruments, to build a world that includes everyone, on the basis of power relations exercised through networks of interdependence.

To be open to others is a learning process that we need to see as an urgent educational task, because we face social relations of power that traverse our body. Human beings do not naturally respect and understand Others. They can and need to be educated to do this.

From this community comes to us the great ethical challenge: affirm the life of Others in a world that has room for all. The ethics in this educational process need to encourage humans to want to find in Others their fundamental reference for building the identity and principle of justice. The ethics of solidarity and of gratuity consist of a constant movement that accepts the differences in Others. This involves discomfort and dismantling. Or more radically, an existential availability for Others who present an inflexibly different face that, however, requires a detached attitude. As happened to us in our relations with Leandro in the daily life of the university.

A 17-year-old with Down's Syndrome, Leandro began to attend the Body-Expression Project a year and a half ago. The project is attended by 220 children with various disabilities. He was curious about dance and wanted to learn and perform. In recent months, his happiness has been circulating around the university, as he made new friends and told them he was the dancing teacher of a project that looks after poor children outside of school hours. A few weeks ago, we were present at a lovely rehearsal performance by his pupils, who are preparing for a dance festival at the university.

The I and the Other are infinitely responsible. As I learned with the Toba Indigenous people of the Argentinean Chaco, for whom the first person is not I but YOU, and the second person is HE and the third person is I. The Tobas see the world in a different way and have different power relations. When conjugating verbs, the first person is the Other (contrary to our Western logic). They therefore believe that poor people, as such, in themselves, do not exist! If someone in their society is poor, I am responsible for creating this situation and I am therefore responsible for doing something to change it. I can only live with dignity if the Other lives with dignity.

The Other is only complete when, as a consequence, they fracture ourselves, not leaving us unharmed. The ethical value of differences is the invitation to consolidate fair and inclusive communities in a daily process of "learning." The taste and wisdom of that unknown man, of Neuma, José, Ana, Leandro and the Indigenous people therefore invite us to be silent and enfold ourselves in the vital energies of air, fire, water and earth.

[Translated from Brazilian]

Achieving Peace: To Learn from Various Religious Traditions

Deborah Weissman

I am honoured to have been invited to speak at this important conference. In March of 1990, I participated in the WCC convocation in Seoul on Justice, Peace and the Integrity of Creation. The Palestinians and Israelis who were there worked together and issued a joint covenant. If only it had been adopted by our respective governments, we could have saved thousands of human lives on both sides in the ensuing years.

I come from a very troubled part of the world, where I have lived for the past almost 39 years. "Overcoming violence" is a crucial challenge for all of us but particularly for my region, the volatile Middle East. The common wisdom is that religion is a problematic factor that fans the flames of hatred and violence. But for many of us, religion can also be a positive factor, promoting peaceful dialogue. For about seven years, I was privileged to be part of the WCC's interfaith initiative called "Thinking Together." Within that group, we explored a number of questions, including the question of religion and violence. We realized that our religious cultures may indeed contain potentially problematic texts and traditions, but they also contain tools for alternate interpretations of those texts, as well as spiritual and cultural resources for developing a more positive approach to the Other.

Throughout the world today, religions are involved in violent conflicts. The image of religion in the world today — and, I'm sorry to say, especially in the Middle East — is an image of extremism, xenophobia and violence. Now, I won't argue that this image has no truth to it. In the name of religion, atrocities have been committed. What is it about religion and religions that accounts for this unholy alliance between faith and extreme violence? Well, many people of faith seem to have absolute faith that allows no questioning of authority and makes no room for other truths. When we interpret present-day reality through ancient scriptures, we may lose touch with those around us and their human needs. And when we expect reward for our actions in the world-to-come, it may impel us to be violent to others in the world-that-is.

But, I don't really believe that is the case. I think it's more a question of the extremist, violent forms of our religions being given a great deal more exposure than the rest of us. After all, a bombing, an attack on worshippers, the language of incitement — these are more newsworthy than peaceful dialogue and coexistence. Harmony among groups doesn't sell newspapers.

I would maintain that our efforts to achieve peace could stand to learn a great deal from the various religious traditions. I'd like to suggest at least five areas in which this could take place:

1. Religions provide people with a particular sense of identity, rootedness, community and ultimate meaning. Particularism implies assumption of historical responsibility for an identifiable community. At the same time, an exclusively universalistic approach sometimes engenders a shirking of responsibility. For example, as a child of the 1960's, I recall members of my cohort who spoke in the name of universal love; they simply hated their parents, siblings, neighbours and so on. There is ultimately something not only immature but in a certain way immoral about that position. A morally responsible human being has to act within a particular context in which he or she assumes responsibility for particular people. It is rootedness in the historical experience of a particular group that can nurture moral behaviour.

As an example of this, I would like to relate the story of the French town of Le Chambon-sur-Lignon, mentioned in your booklet on a Just Peace. During the Second World War, five thousand Christians there saved approximately the same number of Jews. Pierre Sauvage, an American Jewish filmmaker hidden in the town as an infant, went back in the early 1980's to research the motivation for this impressive rescue operation. In his documentary, "Weapons of the Spirit," he reached the conclusion that several factors were responsible; but, ultimately, the main reason for their resistance, he maintained, was the collective historical memory they shared of having themselves, as Huguenots, been persecuted as a religious minority in the 17th century. This, to be sure, was an echo of the biblical injunction, "And you must understand the soul of a stranger, for you were strangers in the land of Egypt."

2. Religions give us traditional cultures, which are the repository of the accumulated human wisdom of generations of people who may have faced dilemmas similar to our own. Wipe out "tribal" identities and you wipe out the cultural anchoring of moral imperatives. Without the stories different peoples have of their own suffering, what identification will they develop with the suffering of others? Without a sense of tribal honour, what motivation will they develop for decent behaviour? Indeed, as philosopher Michael

Walzer has suggested, "…the members of all the different societies, because they are human, can acknowledge each other's different ways, respond to each other's cries for help, learn from each other and march (sometimes) in each other's parades."

3. It is precisely our monotheistic faiths that have given us the notion of a merciful and compassionate God Who expects us to emulate Him in our human behaviour, *imitatio dei*. We generally have, as well, stories of saintly individuals and groups from whom we can learn.

4. At least two of our religious cultures are based on complex legal systems. I'm referring to *Sharia* within Islam and *Halacha* within Judaism. These systems take lofty ideals of peace and social justice and translate them into everyday, incremental actions. We, too, must learn to translate our dreams for peace into concrete steps we can take in our day-to-day lives.

5. Perhaps the most basic thing we can learn from religion is the notion of hope. When we believe in some transcendent power that promotes the Good, we have a way of coping with the despair that almost inevitably arises from our apparent lack of success. One of my friends in Jerusalem is Bishop Mounib Younan, the Palestinian Lutheran Bishop of Jerusalem, who was recently elected President of the LWF. When I despair — and that is much of the time — Mounib reminds me, "As long as you believe in a Living God, you must have hope." Or, as a great 20th century rabbi wrote, "…one should not despair, thinking that one cannot make peace, but rather one should pursue peace today and also tomorrow and on the day afterwards, until one reaches it. " (*Chafetz Chayim, Shmirat Halashon, Sha'ar Haz'chirah*, Chapter 17)

I would echo those who have suggested that the true clash in today's world is not "between civilizations" (as argued by Samuel Huntington) but within each civilization or religion — a clash between the forces of fundamentalism or extremism and those of moderation, tolerance, or what I might call "religious humanism." Particularism ought not to obscure the universal nature of God and God's creatures. Particularism is not synonymous with chauvinism. Also, sometimes it is precisely when people feel that their own identity is under attack that they respond violently. Again, I will bring a quotation from Walzer: "When my parochialism is threatened, then I am wholly, radically parochial…and nothing else.… Under conditions of security, I will acquire a more complex identity than the idea of tribalism suggests." Our goal, then, should not be the eradication of group identities but their empowerment through ensuring the safety and security of the different groups. And I disagree with something in your booklet: Zionism as such is not the enemy. There are certain interpretations of Zionism that are problematic, just as there are certain interpretations of Palestinian nationalism or indeed even of Islam that are problematic. But Martin Buber was a Zionist, and I am a Zionist who believes that the best fulfilment of Zionism will come when there is a Palestinian state living in peace alongside the State of Israel.

May I add one more point? In our part of the world, we have two deeply traumatized peoples who both see themselves as the victims. Both sides sometimes forget that victims can also be victimizers. Victimhood gives one a sense of self-righteousness and promotes national unity. But it also obscures our responsibility for unjust behaviour.

I will conclude with a quotation from this week's Torah portion, the one that will be read by Jews all over the world this coming Sabbath. We will read the portion called *B'chukotai,* containing the last two chapters of Leviticus. Lev 26: 6, "And I will give you peace in the land, and you shall lie down, and none shall make you afraid..." May this be God's will. Amen.

Peace with the Earth

Dona Nobis Pacem: Peace with the Earth

Elías Crisóstomo Abramides

"The earth, having no tongue cries out sighing:
Why are you people polluting me with many evil things?"
Troparion – 9th ode

"The heart that has learnt to love has pity for all creation"
Writings of St. Siluan the Athonite

First Hour. After his consecration in October 1991, His All Holiness Bartholomew, Archbishop of Constantinople-New Rome and Ecumenical Patriarch, became the 270th successor of the Apostle St. Andrew.

A central activity of Patriarch Bartholomew is his well worldwide-known efforts to increase environmental awareness around the world, caring for the good creation of God in order to preserve life on planet Earth, our home, in an environment in peace with its Creator. His constant achievements and positive impacts have earned him the honorific title of "Green Patriarch," building the so-much-needed "Peace with Creation."

Second Hour. Established in 1989 by late Ecumenical Patriarch Dimitrios, 1 September is known as the Day for the Protection of the Natural Environment, "when prayers and supplications should be offered for all Creation and for the reparation of the impairment caused to the natural environment." It gave birth to the "Time for Creation" in the church calendar starting on 1 September and ending on 4 October of every year.

Every September 1, the Ecumenical Patriarch issues an encyclical letter on the environment. I shall quote some of his key concepts expressed along these many years.

"Humanity, both individually and collectively… has succumbed to a theory of development that values production over human dignity and wealth over human integrity… This is why nature 'groans and travails' in all its parts" (Rom. 8:22) .

The Ecumenical Patriarch signalled our present attitude of constant abuse: "The beauty of creation and our tragic abuse of it."

He insisted that "few positive steps have been made on the arduous path toward true and stable reconciliation of humankind with our surrounding physical world… The so imperatively needed reconciliation, whenever and wherever it is accomplished, represents a 'par excellence' spiritual event."

In November 1997, Ecumenical Patriarch Bartholomew clearly affirmed that:

> to commit a crime against the natural world is a sin. For humans to cause species to become extinct and to destroy the biological diversity of God's creation; for humans to degrade the integrity of the Earth by causing changes in its climate, by stripping the Earth of its natural forests, or destroying its wetlands; for humans to injure other humans with disease; for humans to contaminate the Earth's waters, its land, its air, and its life with poisonous substances: these are sins.

In relation to water he affirmed:

> Just as water is the essence of all life, water is also the primary element in the life of a Christian, where the sacrament of Baptism marks the sacred source of spiritual life… It can never be regarded or treated as private property or become the means and end of individual interest. Indifference toward the vitality of water constitutes both a blasphemy against God the Creator and a crime against humanity.

With reference to climate change he declared:

> Climate change constitutes a matter of social and economic justice. For those who will most directly and severely be affected by climate change will be the poorer and most vulnerable nations… as well as the younger and future generations… There is a close link between the economy of the poor and the warming of our planet…. The web of life is a sacred gift of God – so precious and ever so delicate.

Finally, last year, on 1 September 2010, he stated that: "We hold, therefore, that there is a dire need in our day for a combination of societal sanctions and political initiatives, such that there is a powerful change in direction, to a path of viable and sustainable environmental development."

Third Hour. In the five summer seminars that were held annually from 1994 to 1998 at the Theological School in the Island of Halki (Heybeliada), the close connection between environmental issues and education, ethics, communication, justice, and poverty was learned.

In the eight International symposia conducted biannually from 1995 to date by the Ecumenical Patriarchate, we have explored the impact of our wasteful lifestyle on the waters of the Aegean Sea, the Black Sea, the Danube River, the Adriatic Sea, the Baltic Sea, the Amazon River, the Arctic Sea and the Mississippi River.

Together with theologians, scientists, politicians and journalists, the Ecumenical Patriarch recognized in a tangible manner the responsibility that we all bear in the crisis that will inevitably take humanity to a situation where Peace with the Earth could be unattainable, thus provoking a disgraceful attack on Peace with the Earth, as we have already been witnessing present times.

Fourth Hour. Another World is possible – Glory to God and peace on earth! Yes, indeed, another world is possible and it is not a world of the future. It is the world of the South, perhaps with less material riches, less sophisticated, simpler, but full of spirituality, emotions, good feelings, faith, family ties, solidarity, love and beauty.

Our natural environment is beautiful. It still keeps a lot of the peace and the perfect balance the original good creation of God had. However it faces challenges and aggressions which are received daily.

Greed and pride and an exacerbated consumerism imposed by the established economic order has discarded the role of human beings as priests of creation, turning them into its exploiters and abusers, treating all its constituents including human beings as commodities.

It is imperative to achieve a change of paradigm which will bring peace, dignity, justice and love to the lives of all human beings.

There should be a profound and sincere repentance – a "metanoia" – of an order not previously understood by many, followed by a true transformation – a "metamorphosis" – of our hearts and minds to give expression to that repentance in our everyday life. Only then might we be able to restore the perfect peace and natural balance and equilibrium of the original creation.

However to be in Peace with the Earth, there must be Peace in the Earth. With justice and love, peace is attained and God is praised. "The heart that has learnt to love has pity for all creation" we read from the writings of St.

Siluan the Athonite. Peace, Justice and Love are concepts and feelings that go together.

We are sharing the enriching perceptions of our diversity, a symbol of Christian hope for the future, and a testimony of our ceaseless will to preserve the peace, the perfection, the balance and the beauty of the good Creation of God – and most important, the will to preserve Life, the most precious gift that was given to us by God.

Dona nobis pacem - Give us peace, we pray. May God grant us the wisdom to act on time!

Recapturing the Lost Embrace

K. M. George

In the story of creation in the book of Genesis, Adam woke up from a deep sleep to find a charming figure standing beside him. She smiled at him. He loved her at first sight and said to her tenderly, "Bone of my bones and flesh of my flesh" (Gen 2: 21-23). He called her *Hawwah* (Gen 3:20).

Adam is taken out of the dust of the earth, so his name means *earthly*. He is subject to death.

Hawwah means life, mother of all life.

What is earth without life? An arid, inhospitable place, the ultimate void of death.

What is life without earth? Rootless, unable to survive, doomed to wither away.

Adam and Eve, Earth and Life, embraced each other – a life-giving embrace in love and peace. Shalom.

The Holy Scripture begins the story of all creation with this primal embrace between earth and life.

We are gathered here in Jamaica because we, children of Adam and Eve, are deeply distressed that a fatal divorce is now taking place between earth and life, our first parents. We are threatened in our very existence. The crisis of our times is precisely that the earth is being emptied of all life and life is being uprooted from its ground.

Three weeks ago, we celebrated the Resurrection of our Lord Jesus Christ (a rare common Easter date for all Christians). We proclaimed with joy that Christ is risen from the dead and has beaten death by death, granting life to all those who are in the tombs – enslaved to the chain of death-dealing forces, injustice and corruption, violence and war…

Let me tell you a personal story, I celebrated the Easter liturgy at the Indian Orthodox Cathedral in New Delhi. In the evening of Easter Sunday, the joyful hymns of Resurrection still ringing in our ears, a friend of mine and I took the night train to Benaras, India's most ancient and venerable city for Hindu pilgrimage on the banks of the holy river Ganges (Ganga). There were the usual sights of men and women ritually bathing in the holy river, yogis chanting mantras looking at the rising sun or sitting in silent meditation, disciples falling down to earth before their gurus, funeral pyres burning the dead and sending up smoke to the sky mixed with the camphor-smelling air…

The ancient river, matrix of a great civilization, was flowing quietly carrying all the filth of a polluted and crowded city and the sins of innumerable repentant pilgrims. I was reminded that Josephus, the Jewish historian in the first century CE, had identified the river Ganges with the river Pishon, one of the four rivers that parted from the great river that flowed out of the Garden of Eden, as narrated in the Bible (Gen 2: 10-14). I was also painfully aware that this holy river considered in Indian mythology to have originated in heaven, flows down from the snow-clad Himalayas where snow caps are gradually disappearing and age-old glaciers are melting because of global warming.

Watching the gentle ripples of the mother Ganges, the life-giving force of water that nourished a great civilization, one is at the same time anguished at the possibility of it drying up because of human greed and inordinate consumption. Yet in Benaras, one cannot but notice the profound spiritual quest of humanity paying homage to the five elements of nature that sustain life – earth, water, air, fire and the sky (space).

From Benaras, we went to Saranath where the Buddha, the Enlightened One, preached his first sermon some 2,500 years ago. It was the message of *karuna* or compassion, not only to human beings but to all sentient beings – a message that began to change the face of Asia 25 centuries ago.

However, it is distressing to note that the Buddha's message of compassion to all living beings including plants and animals, and his revolutionary movement against the caste system, his rejection of the Brahmin God and Scriptures – all stood in stark contrast with the violence in our cities against women and children, against Dalits and the poor, the simmering conflicts within and between our nations and the greedy, exploitative march of some of our booming economies on the wings of neo-liberal globalization.

Yet Buddha, as depicted in his various images, remains calm and composed, radiating a peace that is contagious. Near the Buddha *stupa*, the peace monument, we met an American, a top executive from a well-known business firm. He said he wanted to drive out the dominant male values of competition, aggressivity and profit from the corporate culture, and bring in feminine values of intuition, compassion and care.

From Sarnath, I went alone to Calcutta, leaving my companion to his work, taking the night train to the Northeast coast of India along the

Gangetic plane. In Calcutta, I was staying close to the "Mother House," where Mother Teresa is buried. After my work with Serampore University research department, every evening I joined the Sisters of Charity for the evening meditation and prayer. There I saw Christians, Hindus, Muslims, and people of all colours praying at the tomb of the Mother, that small, fragile woman who showed the compassion of Jesus to the poorest of the poor, the destitute, the orphan and the leper. She always spoke about the love of Jesus. Millions are inspired by her example.

A little bit like the two disciples on the road to Emmaus, we had to struggle in our ignorance and insensitivity with the meaning of the series of experiences – all in the Easter week. Relying on the Risen Christ, our invisible co-traveler, for interpretation and insight, I found a few convictions grow stronger in my mind:

A first conviction is that there is a deep connection between the three levels of experience that we successively encountered:

- The reverence shown to the five elements of earth and water, air, fire and sky. No life would emerge or be sustained without them.
- The compassion shown to all sentient beings including the millions of micro-organisms, known and unknown, that invisibly sustain our life.
- The tender love and compassion shown to human beings, made in God's image, especially the least and the lost of our own brothers and sisters.

We need to affirm in joy and gratitude all these different levels as one single reality. Peace and justice are not simply human issues to be debated and worked out in isolation, but integrally related to the respect and compassion to the myriads of created existence that God saw good. All carry the stamp of God's Will and Love. All life is hatched in the uterine warmth of the Holy Spirit, the Life-Giving Breath of God.

A second conviction is about enlarging the biblical image of the Body of Christ to the whole creation. Ancient sages in many civilizations had taught about the organic oneness of the body of the universe. Christ the Word incarnate of the Creator God has assumed a material body, the very stuff of our human body and of the universe. Christ thus has given us a new perspective on the organic and holistic nature of the body of creation that surrounds us. Our sacramental vocation as God's image is to continually transfigure this world into the luminous, peace-giving, healing and reconciling Body of Christ in justice, love and respect. The great Cappadocian Fathers called the human body and soul "fellow servants yoked together" in the quest for *theosis* or divinization. The whole creation has a profound share in our body and the divine right to be tenderly cared for in view of its participation in God's glory. Justice is essentially loving care to a member of our own body.

A third conviction is that our present paradigm of progress and development is to be radically questioned by our churches, if not condemned outright. What do we mean by achieving a "higher standard of life, increasing production, maintaining a modern lifestyle" and so on? Crawling daily through the choking traffic in our poor cities, breathing in carbon smoke and filthy dust raised by the ever-surging number of motor vehicles, we are bound to ask, "Is this progress and development? Is this the greatest human achievement? Is this civilization?"

At the Miami airport, you see written repeatedly in bold letters in the Sky Train between terminals "Eat, drink, fly, shop. Eat, drink, fly, shop." Of course you are forbidden to ask, "Eat what, when and where? Why shop and at what cost? Fly where? For what?" Questions are taboo in the "global criminal economy," as phrased by Manuel Castells.

At Benaras Hindu University, I talked to a professor in Gandhian studies about the relevance of Mahatma Gandhi. He said respectfully, "Gandhiji may be relevant for the post-capitalist West, but not for pre-industrial India." I didn't ask him about E. F. Schumacher of *Small is Beautiful* fame, or Arne Naess the Norwegian deep ecologist or Martin Luther King Jr. or Nelson Mandela – all those who followed Gandhi.

Mahatma Gandhi was teaching Indians to be locally self-sufficient in food and clothing and live in such a way that you do not drain the resources of the Mother Earth. He said that there is enough in our world for everybody's *need* but not for everybody's *greed*. Our total inability today to see the difference between need and greed is at the root of all violence. In fact, every form of greed is violence against others, against nature. This critical distinction is to be maintained in every sphere of life – from the simple act of eating our bread to the ambitious projects in biotechnology and information technology as well as in space and nuclear technologies. To know the limit and discern the alternative is wisdom. Only then is a different world – a just and peaceful world – possible.

Finally, in the context of acrimonious debates about anthropocentrism and androcentrism in theology or about the strong and weak anthropic principles in cosmology, we may recall what St Isaac of Nineveh (a seventh-century ascetic bishop in the Persian church, the man who shed tears of compassion, even for the devil) said of human body smell. He says that Adam the first human being had a very pleasant body smell that attracted all birds and animals to him. They approached him without any fear or intimidation. But when he sinned, his body smell became repulsive and threatening. All creatures were scared and they fled from him because his smell smacked of violence. (This is our condition today. We have the killer's foul odour which we try to cover up with perfumes and deodorants.) St Isaac suggests that our calling today is to regain the lost fragrance of humanity through the path of holiness, self-discipline and compassionate love.

This is the "aroma of Christ" about which the Apostle Paul tells the Corinthians. We are the aroma of Christ, the aroma that leads from life to life (2 Cor 2:14-16). This is restoring peace with the earth, recapturing the lost embrace between Adam and Eve. *Shalom.*

A Maya Perspective on Peace with the Earth

Ernestina López Bac

We receive strength from today's wisdom.

The spirituality, theology and worldview of the Indigenous peoples of Mesoamerica (Central America and Mexico) who are descendents of the great Maya civilization have their oral source in the experience and testimony of their wise elders. There is also their Sacred Calendar, which for each day gives guidance and direction for living in relationships of balance, harmony and communion, both with human beings and with Nature.

Today, Waijxaqui Kawoq, or "Storm Force 8" represents self-generated energy. It expresses the force that makes things happen more quickly. It is the energy that drives forward more quickly our responses to what is happening, making them more rapid and clarifying the end result. It is somewhat revolutionary in that it makes happen what must happen.

This energy is especially useful in our human lives, above all when there is stagnation, or obstacles in the way, or procrastination.

The activity of this energy is to be seen when changes take place, life springs up, action is taken and enlightenment occurs. It gives people the strength, the energy which is essential for avoiding domination by problems, routine, imbalance, stagnation or fear of risk-taking.

With this energy and wisdom, let us make our own the words of María Chávez Quispe, a sister, companion and friend of those present here. She tells us:

> "This city in Jamaica is a city where the original populations were exterminated by the conquistadores. We must remember the presence of those absent ones, who are challenging this International Ecumenical Convocation for Peace to make its contribution to eradicating the past violence in this place.
>
> "We greet all the ancestors of these Caribbean lands and ask permission from them to tread this ground from which their blood cries out. We also ask permission from the heart of each one of those here present, from

the heart of God, Mother and Father, from the heart of this land and space which is welcoming us, and from all those persons who are the heart, root and seed of this Caribbean land. And we ask that the blood of our sisters and brothers who were exterminated here may be the energy and strength that will sustain from its deepest roots this project of 'peace with the earth.'"

The Values of Mayan Philosophy (*Ru k'ux'Maya'na'oj*)

I shall now briefly share with you some of the basic values that have sustained the life, worldview, philosophy, spirituality and theology of the Indigenous peoples of Mesoamerica (Mexico and Central America), and more specifically Guatemala, until the present day.

The experience and concept of VALUES in this presentation can be translated as "the heart and energy of thought and wisdom of the Indigenous or original peoples of Abya Yala."

The heart and energy of thought and wisdom. That is the name given to "all the values underlying a person's identity in their life in society and in their relation with Nature." They sustain family and communal life, inspire creativity and attitudes which build and decide – in other words, they are a manifestation of spirituality.

It also means a person's attributes and ability to be and remain in relationship with all human beings, with Nature, with ancestors and the departed. Such attributes and abilities are sustained by these VALUES.

The heart of wisdom gives strength and clarity to the thinking which is the basis of people's social and communal life. It creates consistency in thinking and knowledge. The heart of wisdom is to be found and shown in tales, narratives, myths, rituals, examples, stories, fables, teaching, activities, attributes, events, ceremonial speeches and other social phenomena.

Values are naturally passed on from generation to generation in social relationships, in family life and activities, in spirituality and through the educational practices of the community.

Values are learned and exchanged between communities. They are carefully maintained and observed, because it is considered that they have a direct relationship with people's freedom and dignity.

Values provide the foundation for living in peace with justice, for sustaining creative productive work, for developing art, science and thought. In other words, in the setting of these people's culture, values maintain the dignity and freedom of the Maya people and of all the Indigenous peoples in this multicultural society which is building an intercultural culture.

Living with one's heart and the strength of the thinking and wisdom of these peoples is responsibly and consistently to accept to the uttermost Jesus' commandment so to act that there is abundant life (John 10:10), particularly today when life is being trampled underfoot more than ever.

I shall now give some details of these basic values in relation to Nature and the human person.

The Value of the Great Meaning and Presence of God in Everything

The sacred value of Nature. All that exists in Nature has its raison d'être, its role and its protector. The whole of creation is sacred. Hence the expressions, "Our mother earth, our father sun, our grandmother moon," which appear in ceremonial prayers.

It is manifested in the recognition of the *nawal*, or protector, of the mountains and valleys, the rivers and the lakes, the seas and the winds. It also finds expression in the concepts "Heart of the earth, Heart of the lake, Heart of the sea."

There is an obligation to care for and protect the earth and Nature. It also guides us to acknowledge that Nature holds us in life and that family and community are constructs within it. We are thus intimately united with Nature. People are educated from childhood about this value.

In this value, Maya spirituality shows one of its basic principles: the inter-relatedness of Nature, human beings, and the Heart of the Heavens.

There is a conversation with the earth. The earth is constantly giving us messages, advice and warnings on how we should conduct ourselves toward the beings living on it.

The *Popol Wuj* (the Maya Quiché sacred book) tells how, when the creation of the earth was ended, guardians and protectors of Nature were created and balances set up:

"So the earth was created when it was formed from the Heart of the Heavens and the Heart of the Earth. Those were the names given to those who first made it fertile, when the heavens were suspended above and the earth was submerged beneath the water. So the work was brought to perfection, after it had been executed after thought and meditation on how it could be brought to a happy ending. Then were made the small wild animals, the guardians of all the forests, the spirits of the mountains, the deer, birds, lions, tigers, serpents, snakes, rocks and the guardians of the reed beds."

The Heavens and the universe are sacred in character

This value finds expression in our acknowledgment of the existence of the Heart of the Heavens, GOD, who is the centre and energy of the universe. These peoples call him *Juraqan*.

By observing and noting the phenomena of the universe, we order our lives and find direction. From the universe we draw strength for living. We, together with Nature, are part of it.

In order to be able to practice and live out this value and that of the sacred character of Nature in Maya culture, the present-day lunar sacred calendar of 260 days was created and perfected. It is the product of a spiritual and mathematical combination of twenty categories and thirteen degrees of value.

The universe gives us an indication of its immensity and orderliness, and so animals and human beings hold conversations with it and learn from it.

This intimate relationship between human beings and the universe is shown above all in oral tradition and some narratives in the sacred scriptures. For example, when the two heroes *Junajpú* and *Ixbalamke* died, we read:

"Thus they departed, having conquered all those of Xibalbá. They then ascended in the midst of light and were immediately taken up into heaven. One belonged to the sun and the other to the moon. Then the vault of heaven and the face of the earth became bathed in light. And they dwell in heaven (*Popol Wuj*, ch. 14, pt 2).

Values Concerning People's Lives

The value of one's star, one's mission. This is a basic value of the Maya peoples. It is based on the acknowledgment that we each have our own star to accompany and guide our personal vocation in life.

It is the strength and protection that bears along all human beings from their conception and is continually evident throughout their lives.

It is a value that contributes to the recognition of the dignity of man and woman, of the boy and the old man, of the girl and the old woman, of the young woman and the young man.

It is a basic value in the life of the Maya peoples. It is based on the recognition of one's own "star, light, gift," which accompanies and guides each person's mission and vocation in life.

This value has a direct relationship with the growth and development of the person. Children and young people are brought up and guided according to the day on which they were born (in the lunar calendar) and their star or mission. Their upbringing is complemented with education in values, together with their learning methods of production and affirmation of their cultural identity.

The potential and possibilities of each human being are seen as of value at their birth and throughout their lives, so that they can contribute new ways of meeting needs, new ways of resolving conflicts, new techniques and knowledge for the life of human beings and of Nature to their community.

In that way, the energy of the light, the star of each person is seen as being of value together with the education given by their family. They will thus be able to develop and serve their people and be capable of strengthening their relationship with the Heart of the Heavens and keep alive the memory of their ancestors.

The concept of "Light-star-gift-mission" is not exclusive to Maya culture, but is also for valuable all human beings, irrespective of the culture they practice or live by.

We all have our "Light-our star" and thus we all have our own protection in order to live out the mission which is ours, to protect the life of every individual, of Mother Earth and the whole universe.

It does belong to Maya thinking but it will also help people in other cultures to find direction for their lives.

The value of meaning and state of peace, a sense of responsibility. This is the name given to "the spiritual force that produces harmony, balance, calmness and peace." It is a predisposition of every person and is developed and shaped with the help of family so that one can take on responsibilities.

It is the strength that is called on, asked for or instilled in solidarity with others, so that people have the energy that helps toward physical and psychological recovery. Also, when a person is at the point of death, it is invoked by those around the sick person to provide a sense of strength and calmness for a peaceful death. It is a mature and responsible attitude, and it is the social quality that families look for in young people as they enter into marriage.

It is a mature approach and attitude that enables people to engage in dialogue and reach agreement. People are educated in this and in all values from their earliest age in order to strengthen their capacity to take decisions with the aim of achieving their goals and responsibly to take on their commitments.

Families in which this value is not lived out are broken families.

The value of protecting everything because everything has life. This is the value that guides and makes understandable the moral and social standards and the spirituality of the Maya peoples. It is applicable at all levels, from the supreme value of human existence in the various settings in which it has developed to the existence of the elements of Nature; from the value of human activity and work to the balance of things, the cycle of natural phenomena, animal and plant life; from the guardian spirit of the individual to the guardian spirit of the earth, the sea, the rivers, the lakes, the mountains, etc.

The educational process in Maya families develops and applies the value of protecting all that has life, because it is the basis for shaping people's lives and living and experiencing spirituality.

It is the strength that holds together in solidarity the relations between individuals and the community and relations between peoples.

Teaching about this value given by the elders to families in their community can be grouped under the following heads:

1. You should protect and care for your life and your person.
2. We human beings should protect one another and be considerate toward one another.
3. You should protect and consider your neighbour.
4. We should protect and care for all that exists on the face of the earth.
5. You should care for and maintain your work tools.
6. You should protect the things that are of use to you and to your community.

This value finds its deepest expression when a person is capable of standing in for another when they see that that person is experiencing pain and anguish. It is being merciful and compassionate both with human beings and with Nature and the whole universe. It is a sense of mutual consideration and respect, strengthened with protectiveness and loving care.

It is a permanent condition of human life. It is passed on to sons and daughters and transcends the community. It is a foundation for peace.

The value of taking and giving advice. This is the great value that keeps society firmly and dynamically organized so that it can direct its life and find solutions to conflicts.

It is of supreme importance both in the educational system of Indigenous peoples and communities, and also in the educational system of the country. The value of "taking or receiving advice" is one of the pillars in the process of democratization in a multi-cultural multi-racial nation.

The Indigenous communities that have been able to maintain this social organization have been able to do so because of the continued existence of their values, because of the sharing with people giving wise advice and because of the practice of "celebrating advice-giving" with and for the community.

The value of gratitude and thanksgiving. From these basic values there arise many others:

- Achievement of goals, fulfilling of tasks and commitments
- The value of work in our lives, the significance of work
- The value of protecting everything because it has life. Having and feeling compassion

- Respect for the words of our fathers and mothers, and of our grandfathers and grandmothers
- Honesty in all our speaking. The truthful word. Always telling the truth.
- Helping one another, cooperating with neighbours and the community
- Beauty and cleanliness in our lives. Clean transparent work well done. The service we give.
- Helping to maintain the vitality of the spirit in the body. We should endeavour to maintain the vitality of the spirit in people's bodies and in all that lives and exists on the face of the earth.

Finally, underlying the experiences I have shared is anthropologist Isabel Sucuqui Mejía's text on *The scientific bases of May spirituality*. (Isabel Sucuquí Mejía holds a master's degree in social anthropology and is an Indigenous woman from the Maya Quiché culture of Guatemala. She is a living witness to the great academic abilities of the Indigenous individuals and peoples of Guatemala, Mexico, Central America, Latin America and the Caribbean and to the great human and spiritual values that they experience and contribute to humankind.)

Save the Earth and Peace with the Earth
Adrian Shaw

Scotland, like most European countries has a carbon-based economy dependent on oil, gas and coal for transportation, heating and electricity supplies. Scotland's total emissions of carbon dioxide are over 40 million tons. This is a similar figure to Bangladesh, but Scotland has a population of just 5 million while Bangladesh has a population of 150 million.

The impact of global greenhouse emissions was presented to the conference by the Rev Tafue Lusama of Tuvalu, who highlighted the potentially catastrophic impact of climate change on Pacific islands. Countries in North America and the European Union, along with China, produce over half of the world's emissions of carbon dioxide, its biggest volume of greenhouse gas and the principal cause of climate change. Churches in the north have to respond to the call for help from churches in the Pacific and elsewhere to cut the emissions of greenhouse gases, but what practical steps can they take?

The Church of Scotland has sought to respond to this challenge:

"The Church of Scotland is concerned that climate change poses a serious and immediate threat to people everywhere, particularly to the poor of the earth; and that climate change represents a failure in our stewardship of God's creation. We accept the need to reduce the emissions of greenhouse gases urgently to avoid dangerous and irreversible climate change; and to promote a more equitable and sustainable use of energy." (General Assembly 2009)

To help congregations, the church has urged local churches and congregations to take three steps. Churches should

- Be aware of their impact
- Take action to reduce their carbon footprint
- Get involved in community activities

These three points are discussed in more detail below.

Be Aware

Climate change represents a failure in our duty to care for creation. Its likely impact across the world in this century means we cannot ignore it and it will not go away. Congregations should learn about climate change, its causes and its consequences. How much energy do members of a church congregation contribute to the problem in their church buildings, in their homes and in their travel? The Church of Scotland suggests that members of congregations start with church buildings. From energy bills, congregations can work out how much energy is used in their church buildings in a year and then do a simple sum to work out the carbon footprint. There are a variety of carbon footprint calculators online to help you do this.

What was the carbon footprint of travel to the IEPC?

Approximately 1000 delegates travelled to the IEPC in Kingston, Jamaica from around the world. The return air flight from Scotland was responsible for emissions of 1.6 tonnes of carbon dioxide. If we assume that on average each delegate who flew to the IEPC was responsible for one tonne of carbon dioxide, then the total for the convocation would be 1000 tonnes. This is about the same as the amount of carbon dioxide produced by twenty large churches in Scotland each year.

Take Action

The 2009 Church of Scotland General Assembly challenged all congregations to make a 5% reduction year on year in their carbon footprint. This has stimulated a wide response of reactions from positive to unenthusiastic. Some congregations have made a commitment and have taken effective action, but many others have struggled to do this. There are a variety of reasons why members of churches feel unable to act, but at the root of the problem is the challenge of relating care for creation to practical action. For this to happen requires a new way of thinking, and a collective commitment.

Get Involved

The Church of Scotland, along with other denominations, is encouraging congregations to become eco-congregations. The ecumenical eco-congregation movement started in Britain and Ireland just over a decade ago. In Scotland, it has become the largest community environment movement in the country with over 270 registered congregations and is now growing internationally. Eco-congregations must demonstrate that they are taking steps to care for creation

- In their worship;
- In managing their church and other church property, including its energy use;
- By getting involved in community action, either locally, nationally or globally.

Being an eco-congregation thus challenges congregations to explore in worship and in action what it means to care for creation. The programme also makes awards to encourage and reward achievements. To get an award, a church must demonstrate action in all three areas and show that they know and are trying to reduce their carbon footprint. Congregations have become involved in a variety of national or international actions. For example, congregations organized a service before The Wave, a large climate change march held in Glasgow before the Copenhagen climate change conference, encouraged church members and church leaders to attend and were then invited to lead the march by other participating groups.

Going International

This approach has been proved to work in Britain and Ireland and is now developing in other countries including Canada, Hungary and South Africa. It is becoming an international movement. Can your church get involved too?

Eco-Congregations in Action: An Example. The islands of Westray and Papa Westray are to the north of Scotland in the Orkney archipelago. The minister, the Rev Iain Macdonald, and members of the congregation have worked with other members of the community to promote renewable energy to reduce their dependence on fossil fuels and to take advantage of the wild and windy weather that is often a feature of the islands. For example, the church on Westray is now heated by a ground source heat pump and a small wind turbine. Recently, the community has established a community business to install a large wind turbine on Westray that can meet much of the island's electricity demand. This demonstrates how a congregation can be at the heart of community responses to climate change.

Peace in the Marketplace

A Talk Show on Peace in the Marketplace
Omega Bula

This plenary session was a talk show which tried to raise issues of economic injustice as a source of violence and propose solutions for discussion. The intension was to highlight the connections between economic injustice and violence within a context of struggles against gender and racial injustice and the process of economic globalization that continue to marginalize the poor.

What in your view is economic-related violence?
How can this be avoided?

Economic-related violence is when a woman is forced to work in the most vulnerable sectors of the market economy in order to sustain her family. She dreams of a "different world," a world without poverty. She lives in a country God has blessed with abundance in arable land, fresh water, mineral resources, resilient men, women and young people who work hard each day for sustainable livelihoods. But they have been impoverished – made poor by unjust local and global systems – systems that are economic, political, cultural, and social. Women struggle the most within these systems, and this is why they dream of a different world every day.

Poverty for women in these countries means that they have hardly any money for basics you may take for granted elsewhere – such as health care, food, shelter, clean water, sanitation, their children's education and access to many other life-giving necessities. It means one meal a day for many families, poorer nutrition, reduced capacity for work, less democratic participation, vulnerability to many things that come with structural/physical and emotional violence as they seek livelihoods in the most dangerous occupations.

Just to give you one example, women are most at risk to having the HIV virus and the dreaded AIDS. They are more vulnerable biologically, socially, culturally and economically. The absence of economic independence has led to the loss of rights to safe sexuality, power of decision-making, and unequal gender relations in many aspects of life. This is not about women becoming prostitutes, no, it is about how men gain control over women's lives [bodies] in a context of poverty, making women highly vulnerable to infection.

The major issues have to do with a lack of control over own sexuality and sexual relationships; poor reproductive and sexual health; neglect of women's health needs such as nutrition and basic health care; harmful cultural practices and teachings; stigma and discrimination which lead to women being abandoned, blamed, violated and ostracized from family and community. Women carry the psychosocial and physical burden of care and support for the sick in the family. The HIV pandemic has revealed the worst of broken relationships and the worst you can experience in gender injustice.

Do Market Values Support or Promote Violence?

Values of the neoliberal economic model or free-market economies that thrive on greed and profit are based on the "domination ethic" as opposed to the "cooperation ethic." Systems based on domination are by nature violent. They need winners and losers in order to survive. They cannot sow peace and security because they survive on structural violence in the economy and the Earth. As explained by Marcus Borg, the difference between these two ethical approaches to managing God's household are these:

The domination ethic
- the "domination ethic" survives on exploiting and distorting God's gift of life because of its unrelenting human greed;
- domination is made manifest in the wasting of the planet's resources that brings suffering, despair, and violence; that plagues all peoples, communities, and creatures throughout God's world;
- this complex human-made web of domination has been named empire; the many forms of empire are the primary obstacles to God's purposes of justice, equality, and reconciliation between peoples, nations and within creation;

- those who suffer the most from this system of domination anywhere in the world are impoverished women and men, young people and children; they are migrants denied rights and dignity; they are people of colour who experience racism; they are the surplus people in an economy that can choose when and how to exploit their labour;
- they are marginalized, vulnerable and powerless because they face the barriers of race, gender and class.
- they experience on a daily basis economic structural violence, emotional violence, physical violence, mental violence, sexual violence and spiritual violence. These are the ones who end up living on the streets, run-down neighbourhoods; they are undernourished, landless, unemployed, uneducated, and exploited. They live face to face with death. They are the targets of the charity industry that comes from the crumbs of the tables of the rich.

The cooperation ethic
- The "cooperation ethic" survives on the realization of the common good; whether it is in the context of family, group, community, the world at large.
- An approach that rejects control and domination in all its forms – including patriarchy – and opts for communal interdependence in the economy and the earth.
- Relies on God's covenant of grace which continues to provide abundant life in all of creation; and that the weaving of right relations sustains life and the wholeness of one Earth community in all its diversity.
- Seeks to create sustainable alternatives for the common good; such as life-giving economies. Ecumenically, we have benefited from understanding development as building sustainable communities. An approach and process that integrates poverty, wealth and ecological justice analysis; an approach which includes the struggle for rights and dignity.
- Our task as church-based development agencies is to increase the participation and capacity for action of those who have been made poor, marginalized or powerles, to work at building right relations
- The cooperation ethic seeks the restoration of relationships of respect, nonviolence, peace among all people and within God's beloved one Earth community in all its diversity.
- We are challenged to choose life, and resist empire. There are no losers or winners when we choose life. Everyone, including the Earth, wins.

Peace, Economic Injustice and the Orthodox Church

Emmanuel Clapsis

The peace-making vocation of the church is a dynamic process of a never-ending personal and communal transformation that reflects the human and fallible struggle to participate in God's Trinitarian life. St Nicholas Cabasilas epigrammatically summarizes the Orthodox view on peace-making: "Christians, as disciples of Christ, who made all things for peace, are to be 'craftsmen of peace.' They are called a peaceable race since 'nothing is more characteristic of a Christian than to be a worker for peace.'" In being "craftsmen of peace," the Orthodox churches unite themselves in prayer, vision, and action with all those Christians who pray that God's Kingdom will come on earth as it is in heaven. The aspiration to live in peace and justice unites Christians with people of living faiths and ideologies in a shared vision, hope, and actions for less violence, injustice, and oppression. An effective intervention in situations of conflict, injustice and oppression requires the churches not to ignore what is possible to learn from advances in political sciences and economics as well as from successful economic and political policies and practices that aim to transform conflicts into life opportunities.

In addressing the root causes of injustice and violence in the marketplace, the Orthodox churches recognize the autonomy of the inherent rationality of the market and leave the development of economic theories and policies to those who understand better its dynamics. The churches, however, critique economic theories and practices based on their performance and their effects upon the people. Their criticism should contribute toward a revisionary logic of the market that favors economic practices that generate greater opportunities for a more equitable and just distribution of power and resources.

Today, one-and-a-half billion people live in areas affected by instability, conflict or large-scale, organized criminal violence. The causes of conflict arise from economic, political and security dynamics. Political exclusion and inequality affecting regional, religious or ethnic groups are associated with higher risks of civil war, while inequality between richer and poorer households is closely associated with higher risks of violence. The disparity between the rich and poor between and within nations is increasing. Unemployment is on the rise, pushing more and more people into poverty, malnutrition, poor health, depression, violence, insecurity, fear, and desperation. There are nearly one billion undernourished people on our planet and this number is increasing by 68 people every minute; that is more than one every second. The human cost of violence cannot be ignored by anyone who considers all human beings to be icons of God.

The economic and monetary crisis that leads to an increased disparity between rich and poor is understood mostly by the Orthodox Churches to be primarily a "spiritual" and/or cultural crisis. It is attributed to unrestrained individualism that leads to an excessive desire for wealth and to consumerism. Individualism and consumerism have disconnected people from loving God and their neighbour, thus preventing them from reflecting in their lives God's love for all creation.

St John Chrysostom, a notable preacher of the undivided church, stated that not to be an advocate of the poor would be "the worst inhumanity."[1]

Being the advocate of the poor led him to refute point by point all the arguments by which the affluent justified the marginalization of the poor and their indifference toward them. Christ in a privileged manner is identified with the poor. The poor are not the spectacle of human misery and suffering that evokes compassion or disgust, but they are the icons of Christ, the presence of Christ in the broken world. This is their dignity! If you refuse to give bread to the poor, you ignore Christ who desires to be fed: "You eat in excess; Christ eats not even what he needs... At the moment, you have taken possession of the resources that belong to Christ and you consume them aimlessly."[2] The poor for St John Chrysostom are the liturgical images of the most holy elements in all of Christian worship: the altar and the body of Christ.[3]

The Orthodox Churches advocate a culture of compassion in which people share their material resources with those in need. Charity and compassion are not virtues to be practiced just by those who have the material resources and means. They are virtues that promote the communal love that Christians should have for all human beings. Every human being, regardless of whether he or she is rich or poor, must be charitable and compassionate to those lacking the basic material resources for sustenance.[4] St Basil exhorts the poor to share even the minimal goods that they may have.[5] Almsgiving leads people to God and grants to all the necessary resources for sustenance and development of their human potential. However, a voluntary sharing of resources in the present world is not enough. Building a culture of peace demands global and local institutional changes as well as new economic practices that address, in a more fundamental way, the root causes of poverty. It calls for a fusion of the Christian culture of compassion with the knowledge that we have acquired through experience and the advances of social science about the structural sources of poverty and its multifaceted

---

1. John Chrysostom, *Homily 10 on Almsgiving*, 10. 1 in *The Fathers of the Church*, vol. 96 (Washington, D.C.: Catholic University of America Press, 1998), p. 131

2. PG 58.493

3. *Epistulam II ad Corinthios, Homilia* 20.3

4. Ibid. 10. 13:

5. *Tempore Famis et Citatis*, PG 31.320-321.

aspects that urgently need to be addressed through reflective concerted actions.

In an increasingly fragmented world, the Orthodox churches acknowledge and defend the dignity of every human being and cultivate human solidarity. In addressing violence in the marketplace, even if people accept in their hearts the virtues of justice and peace, the market operates with its own autonomous logic and economic practices. It is guided by the belief that there can be a "total free market" in which unregulated competing economic relationships of individuals in pursuit of their economic gains can lead to optimum good. It advocates that free markets without government "interference" would be the most efficient and socially optimal allocation of resources. Many economists and institutions of global development agencies embrace economic globalization as indisputable reality and suggest that there is no alternative to this. They assume that Neoliberalism contributes to the prosperity and the equitable development of all nations. Unfortunately, though, its economic practices have not been designed to meet the immediate needs of the world's poor people. Global inequalities between nations and within nations are widening. Joseph Stiglitz, former World Bank Chief Economist (1997-2000) and Nobel Laureate in Economics, notes that economic globalization in its current form risks exacerbating poverty and increasing violence if not checked, because it is impossible to separate economic issues from social and political issues.

The Orthodox churches are not in a position to suggest concrete alternatives to economic globalization. Neither do they intend to endorse or reject complex economic policies and practices that regulate the global economy. Yet, based on the eschatological orientation of the Christian gospel, Orthodoxy believes that all political and economic theories and practices are subject to criticism and modification aimed at overcoming those aspects of them that generate violence and injustice. The logic of the market must not only seek the maximization of profits favouring and serving only those who have economic capital and power. Economic practices must ensure just and sustainable development for all people. We cannot talk about a free economy without entering into particular judgments about what kinds of exchange are conducive to the flourishing of life and what kinds are not. The churches are led by their faith to take an active role in fostering economic practices that reflect God's peace and justice. These economic practices integrate in their logic those elements of social life that promote a culture of compassion that unites all human beings in peace and justice. Indispensable aspects of this culture are: respect for the dignity and the rights of all human beings; equitable socio-economic relationships; broad participation in economic and political decision-making; and just sharing of resources and power.

Once, we put human faces to all those millions of people who suffer the consequences of an inequitable distribution of power and resources, it becomes evident that it is an indispensable aspect of the church's mission to the world to be involved through prayers and thoughtful actions in noble efforts to eradicate poverty and injustice.

Peace in the Marketplace: Misplaced Concreteness of the Market

Roderick R. Hewitt

Everyone's after the dishonest dollar,
Little people and big people alike
Prophets and priests and everyone in between
Twist the words and doctor the truth.
My people are broken-shattered!
And they put on Band-Aids
Saying, "It's not so bad. You'll be just fine" (Peace! Peace!)
But things are not "just fine." (There is no peace!)
(Jer. 6:13, *The Message*)

The Mona campus of the University of the West Indies (UWI) in Kingston, Jamaica, was chosen as the site for hosting the historic global ecumenical gathering of the WCC Peace Convocation. The venue may have been chosen because of its functional assets that met the needs of the convocation. However, it is paradoxical that the site also represented a powerful memorial symbol when the global market system during the era of colonial rule thrived through the economic violence of the sugarcane plantation. Prior to the founding of the UWI, the area was famous for its sugar estate on the Liguanea plains. Remnants of the aqueduct that brought water from the Hope river to the cane fields are still visible. This site that is now used as an educational institution for the empowering of people was once dedicated to the systematic disempowering of enslaved Africans through economic violence. The system of enslavement that was used against African-Jamaicans had its basis in three major sets of factors: (1) its profitability, (2) its practicality, and (3) its justifiability in European racist thought.[6] This system of total control was built on brutality that was characterized by domination, exploitation and oppression. It was the response of African-Jamaicans to this evil system that shaped the quality of their resistance to enslavement.

---

6. Maulana Karenga, 1993, *Introduction to Black Studies,* University of Sankore Press, Los Angeles, p.122.

It is my objective to explore the sub-theme of "Peace in the Market-place" and to share some perspectives as a member of the WCC-AGAPE group. I do so as one whose worldview has been shaped by the realities of the Jamaican and Caribbean contexts. However, the polyphonic sounds of this region have been further enriched by wider ecumenical learning through living, studying and working in other contexts of Europe and Africa. I will approach the subject with a deep sense of humility, considering that I am, along with the vast majority of the peoples of Jamaica, heirs of the ances-tors that survived the onslaught of the global market[7] that profited from the commoditization of enslaved Africans. This marketplace resulted in the holocaust of millions of Africans who were forcibly taken across the Atlantic to the Americas between the 15th and 19th centuries as human cargo and traded in the marketplace.[8] There is a direct relationship between market forces and issues of exclusion and alienation on the basis of race, class, creed, colour, gender, ethnicity and culture. Therefore, I will not approach the sub-ject as a neutral critic but as an active participant and a wounded healer. The methodological tools of reflection will draw upon the works of the prophetic voices of social justice: Jimmy Cliff who uses the medium of reggae music to facilitate change in the social and economic order.

Welcome to Jam Rock

The choice of Jamaica for the holding of this global peace conference is a stark recognition and reminder that this small country with only 2.7 mil-lion people has one of the highest homicide rates in the world. In spite of its enchanting and rich culture mixed with the most picturesque environ-ment and hospitable people, the recurring question is: Why Jamaica is so violent? Violent crime did not emerge overnight or during the past decade. The history of Jamaica can be read from the perspective of different epochs of violence since the arrival of the Spaniards in 1492. The socio-economic fabric of the country was built on structural violence of the-then global marketplace. The demand for commodities such as tobacco, sugar, bananas led to Africans being traded not because they were black but for economic reasons. Africa provided the European colonial empire a large, cheap and replaceable labour force that was in close reach of the Americas. The geno-cide of the Indigenous Tainos people by the Spaniards in the first century of colonialism was followed by another two centuries of enslavement of Afri-cans and later Indians from India through the indenture system.[9]

---

7. When used with capital letters Market refers to the global organizing principle of the economy and trade within and between nations. When market is used with the small "m," I am referring to the local contextual expression and implementation of the global Market.

8. Eric Williams, 2003, *From Columbus to Castro: The History of the Caribbean*, Andre Deusch, London, pp.136-155,

9. Ibid. Eric Williams, 2003, pp. 46-57,136-155, 347-360.

This brief introduction suggests that the problem of violence in this land cannot be simply solved through the good intentions of an inefficient criminal justice system. The tentacles of violence are deeply embedded in the historical error perpetrated by the systemic oppressive and inhumane socioeconomic system.[10] A visit to the local prisons or "correctional centres" as the government loves to call them, will expose the sickening presence of vulnerable young black men wasting away in the prime of their lives. They are products of an inhumane marketplace structured to throw away black people, especially young black men, who are deemed to be of low economic value to the state and its allies in the marketplace. You can hardly find persons of other ethnic background or those belonging to the middle or upper socio-economic class languishing within the penal institutions. The implications are that even the justice system is corruptly controlled by the market forces, because justice is least accessible to those suffering from inequality, poverty, unemployment and marginalization.

Unmasking the Violence of Peace

What then do we mean when we say peace in the marketplace? The understanding of *peace* doesn't always mean exactly the same thing every time the word is used because the word has an important range of meanings. However, for this paper, I want to draw on the Jamaican use of the term. The persistent experience of de-humanizing social, political, religious and economic structures over many centuries has influenced the people to link the experience of peace with respect in all areas of life. To be respectful to "the other" means the practicing of just relationships. When this fails to happen, the person speaks of being "dissed," which is the opposite of "respect." At work is a scheme that is aimed at destroying their experience of wellbeing that must be resisted at all cost. There is no room for compromise when your humanity is threatened. Resistance on all fronts is an imperative.

Pangernungba, an Indian SCM programme staffperson and human rights and peace activist invites us to engage in hermeneutics of suspicion over the use of the concept peace.[11] He argues that it is a political word being used to unleash violence and that our responsibility is to unmask its deception:

"We live in a world where order and stability 'rest on' or are 'born of' violence. Peace has become an animated 'political word'; it is used as the most

10. George Beckford, 1992, *Persistent Poverty (Underdevelopment in Plantation Economies of the Third World*, Oxford University Press, pp.30-52

11. Pangernungba, 2003, *Unmasking the Violence of Peace*, Student World, Ecumenical Review, World Student Christian Federation, Vol.LX111, 2003/1, Serial Number 247, Budapest, Hungary

effective weapon of power and domination where violence can flourish only under the 'name' and 'shadow' of peace... the most bloody and unjustifiable violence continues to be unleashed in the name of peace. Irrespective of how, where and when and in what name it is done; its sole purpose is to rip the earth, cultivate vicious cycle of violence and perpetrate unending poverty, marginalization and impoverishment of the world's majority population. Beyond this politics of peace, we witness a large section of humanity whose experience of peace is synonymous to violence, death and destruction. Commitment to the task of unmasking the 'painted face' of peace has become imperative."[12]

His critique mirrors those of the prophet Jeremiah, whose reflection on his 8th century BCE nation led him to conclude that there is such a reality as "false peace" especially within the context of economic justice of the marketplace.[13] Pangernungba further argues how contemporary capitalism's ideology of peace is advanced as a countervailing equalizer to harmonize the violence caused by the instruments of domination (globalization).[14] One must be extremely careful how the word peace is used; in the neoliberal economic order, peace has been co-opted by tyrants to carry out violence and achieve their political aim of total domination. Also the powerful global political and economic institutions use the concept of peace to strengthen their control of capitalism through the global economy and market.

In this scenario, a postcolonial critique is required to deconstruct this false ideology of peace that is perpetrated by an unjust neoliberal economic order that is doing so much violence in the marketplace. Jimmy Cliff, the premier Jamaican song writer and singer, penned these words about peace within the local context:

"How is there going to be peace when there is no justice? Oh no! Oh No! How is there going to be peace when there is no justice? Someone is taking more than their share, of the bounties of this land and that not fair. Some people got more than they need while there's so many hungry mouths in the world to feed."[15]

He has identified the root cause of the problem as structural greed, in which the world's economic and political order (dis-order) is unjustly organized to benefit the few privileged ones who already have more than their fair share of the earth's resources. The peace that is sought is just-peace, or peace with justice. Cliff's analysis is in harmony with the biblical words of the Psalmist that "justice (righteousness) and peace shall kiss ((embrace)

---

12. Ibid.
13. Jeremiah 6:1-13
14. Ibid. Pangernungba, 2003, *Unmasking the Violence of Peace*,
15. Jimmy Cliff, 1991, Breakout, ARC CD, Holland

each other (85:10), and the prophet Isaiah asserts that "The fruits of righteousness shall be peace" (32:17).

WCC programme executive for Economic Justice Rogate Mashana offers an alternative vision of the market that is seen as a gift from God based on a just sharing of resources and on just exchange of goods. The "free market" model has resulted in a world economic crisis that the ecumenical community must address in order to limit the inevitable fallout of ecological crisis and climate change. [16] Market forces will naturally emerge for the trading of goods. However, the market is a double-edged sword. Its advocates claim that it is the best tool to protect and build a strong nation, but it is also claimed by others to be a weapon of mass destruction that is designed to enrich the few at the expense of destroying many lives.[17] In the Jamaican context, injustice is the driver of violence, and this paper argues that it is consummated, incubated, and given growth hormones for its development in an unjust marketplace that impacts far more negatively on the wellbeing of the poor.

This paper invites us to explore the notion of "Peace in the Marketplace." But the invitation is rooted in contradiction. Peace and the market seem to be, on one hand, partners in providing stability for investors so they can maximise their profits and, on the other hand, they relate as enemies in a historic embedded conflict because their objectives are diametrically opposed to each other. The polyphonic voices of the Caribbean regional context, shaped by its diverse life situations, suggest that any exploration of "Peace in the Marketplace" must embrace a methodology of approach that recognizes that there are different ways to interpret the issue and to act upon it. Walter Rodney, the Guyanese political scientist, argued that the market is an instrument that transfers value from the South to the North to develop the North and underdevelop the South.[18] Using the language of "free trade" to deceive southern countries with promises of economic development, the un-free relationship has ensured the opposite because what the northern wealthy countries want is access to exploit the resources of these southern nations. Daley and Cobb, Jr. make reference to the warning of Alfred North Whitehead about "the fallacy of misplaced concreteness."[19] They argued that because of the high degree of abstraction present in the discipline of

---

16. Rogate R. Mshana, *Addressing The Global and Economic Crisis: Alternatives and Challenges for the Ecumenical Movement* in Patriricia Sheeratttan-Bisnauth, ed. 2009, *Power To Resist and Courage to Hope: Caribbean Churches Living out the Accra Confession*, World Alliance of Reformed Churches and Caribbean and North America Area Council, Geneva

17. Jimmy Cliff, 1991, Breakout, ARC CD, Holland

18. Walter Rodney, 1983 *How Europe Under develop Africa*, Bogle-L' Ouverture Publications, London

19. Herman E. Daley & John B. Cobb, Jr. 1989, *For The Common Good(Redirecting the Economy Toward Community, the Environment, and a Sustainable Future)*,Beacon Press, Boston, p.25

economics, it is particularly liable to this fallacy of misplaced concreteness. I wish to acknowledge that this fallacy is also present within the discipline of theology of which I am a practitioner. The perspectives that follow are therefore tentative and random thoughts about an aspect of life that is in need of urgent transformation.

Dale and Cobb also argued for the misplaced concreteness of the market, claiming that:

> "Its strengths are to be found in its capacity to use independent, decentralized decisions to give rise not to chaos... Individual consumers know their preferences better than anyone else and act directly to satisfy them in the marketplace. Individual producers know their own capacities and options better than anyone else and they too act on this information in the market."[20]

In western economies, the market is given divine and infallible status. It is fused into the democratic model of governance and made sacred as the most efficient institution for the production and allocation of resources. There is an insatiable competitive drive for profit that ensures that there are winners (those who can best know and use market information) and losers (those who failed to know and use market information). The 2008/09 "market failure" has served to expose the inherent weakness of this global institution because of its capacity to erode its own standards and requirements by destroying competition and increasing monopoly power. This economic Beast thrives on unrestrained self-interest, even at the expense of the common good of the community.

About two kilometres from the site where the Convocation has gathered is another important meeting place called Papine market. This market is the place where farmers from the rural hilly communities bring the produce to sell from their vulnerable subsistence way of life. This is also the marketplace where the urban enterprising poor who have bought ground provisions from rural sellers at another market in downtown Kingston that is paradoxically called Coronation market add on their marked-up price and resell them for a profit; the Papine market caters for University students and up-town middleclass purchasers. The infamous Coronation market operates, in a limited way, under the authority and security of the municipality. However, there is an alternate system of governance sponsored and administered by the rough justice of "Area Leaders" that are popularly called "Dons." The rural sellers must pay extortion protection money in order to sell "in peace." This kind of peace can be very costly. The experiences of these rural sellers would

---

20. Ibid, pp.44-45

surely question the appropriateness of the title "peace in the marketplace." Their stories speak of the unpredictable nature of the market that unleashes violence on those trying to make an honest living. There are many marketplaces in this nation that mirror the wider regional and global marketplace. They have one thing in common, and that is: they are built on unjust competition that gives immediate and permanent advantage to those who have the largest amount of capital. In this market ideology, everything and everyone is commoditized as a product for sale at a right price.

Our Hands Are Not Clean

The Jamaican experience confirms that the church is part of the marketplace that unleashes violence that denies people fullness of life. The church is not a neutral voice in this most important issue because its hands are not clean. Christians and the church as a global religious institution are part of the market system and therefore part of the problem. This has been the case from the time Columbus arrived in the region with the church being an integral part of the colonial political and economic project. Both needed each other to survive. The arrival of Protestant evangelical missionaries was also part of the British colonial project, and the contemporary arrival of American missionaries propagating their prosperity gospel constitutes an extension of a wider market-driven strategy and agenda. Its goal is to facilitate the redefinition of Christianity away from its traditional solidarity with an ethical social market economy that ensures social and ecological sustainability of competition to an unbridled monetarist-driven understanding of the market where only the strong survive. The church must speak on economic issues not as a political party but out of a clear understanding of its commitment to the Gospel's call for justice in all areas of human life. No amount of easy talk will solve the problem, because many vested interests are benefiting from an unjust marketplace. In 2008, Jamaica experienced a double whammy fallout from the global financial crash that was made worse with a crash in the local alternate "get rich quick"/ponzi investment schemes built on sheer greed. It revealed how compromised sections of the church were, especially those TV "mega-church" leaders who majored in preaching a designer prosperity priority gospel that gave support to a corrupt financial system built on greed and deception. Instead of preaching fidelity to good stewardship of money that eschews greed, some of these populist pastors, in their addiction to the love of money and avarice, led many of their flock astray. Jeremiah's assessment is correct: "Everyone is after the dishonest dollar, little people and big people alike. Prophets and priests and everyone in between twist the word and doctor the truth" (6:13).

Greed as the Motive for a Successful Marketplace

The economic success of the market is measured according to how high the returns that investors received are, not necessarily how much is invested for sustainable development of the people and country. Indeed, Jesus was right when he entered the temple and confronted the merchants of corrupt financial practices who were blessed by the religious establishment. This was a well-planned protest that constituted much more than a purely religious act. He openly exposed the unethical and corrupting practices that were present in unaccountable religious institutions. The poignant words of Jesus identified that the religious market can become a corrupting place that blesses and protects "a den of robbers" (Luke 19:46). Jesus had earlier warned in Luke 12:13-21: "Beware of Greed. Watch out! Be on your guard against all kinds of greed! A man's life does not consist in abundance of possessions!" This resulted in his teaching about the snare of greed. Greed has costly consequences for the wholesome development of human communities! The 2008/09 global financial crisis demonstrated how the under-regulated markets can go rogue because their interest lies not in the common good of the community but in manipulating money and commodities in favour of the short-term interests of the wealthiest and most powerful. The singular goal of the global markets is to serve the private goals of maximising profit for the powerful few rather than seeking to meet the basic human needs and right of peoples and their communities.

Toward a Christian Political Ethics

On cannot do justice to this subject without drawing on the prophetic works of a great Latin American theologian and ecumenist, José Bonino, who in 1983 wrote the seminal text: "Toward a Christian Political Ethics" for the 1985 WCC Vancouver Assembly. He passionately argued then for the need of Christian political ethics that will give shape to the vision of a just, participatory and sustainable society.[21] The key tenets of this ethics asserts that this world of economic integration is one where power is concentrated in the hands of a few. He warned the church nearly thirty years ago not to champion a blind acceptance of political and economic power with a theology of order/peace because the church must become a revolutionary agent for change on behalf of the poor.[22] Bonino is right when he states that the modern world has to pay a frightful price for the recovery of ethics.[23] To a great extent, the moral failure of the marketplace was also a failure of the church's political ethics in the public sphere.

21. Jose Miguez Bonino, 1983, "*Toward a Christian Political Ethics,*" Fortress Press, Philadelphia, p.9
22. Ibid, pp.21,24
23. Ibid, p.20

The Market Does Not Accumulate Moral Capital

The most powerful life-denying virus unleashed by the market is the corrupting individualistic self-interest that destroys trust and the moral strength of community-building of the values of honesty and integrity. The market intrinsically depletes moral capital (Fred Hirsch: 1976). It is for this reason that the ecumenical community must not retreat in addressing this important matter of the market because its impact on the social and biophysical can be life-threatening. People suffer as a result of economic systems that unleash structural violence that lead to death and disfigurement and diminish human well-being and potential. The unjust marketplace constitutes the maintenance of indirect violence. When there is peace in the marketplace, then the values of nonviolence, economic welfare, social welfare and ecological balance are affirmed. So, if we are to speak of peace in the market-place, it constitutes putting up resistance against enslaving forces of power relationships that perpetrate structural violence against all oppressed groups.

Exposing the Masks of the Marketplace

Commenting on the crisis in Zimbabwe, Prof Tinyiko Maluleke asserts that those who engage in crime and violence that may result in murder often need allies and accomplices behind them. They hide behind masks so that they are not identified by victims. These masks may be physical, metaphorical, cultural and ideological. If this perspective were to be applied to the marketplace, what are the masks that camouflage the reality of violence and death? Firstly there is the mask of democracy.[24] Democracy that is meant to foster a good constitution and laws that facilitate good governance, political stability, economic and social, development and protecting the common good is often hijacked by powerful economic forces that bribe politicians who are susceptible because they lack strong political ethics. Good governance is therefore a prerequisite for peace, respect for human rights and social progress and just economic growth.

Next, money has become the currency for morality in the marketplace. It behaves like an addict that uses money as substance abuse. This addiction to the drug of the uncontrolled market has lead to the death of many. The operators of the market are smartly dressed and sit before impersonal computers and every weekday on the stoke of a bell that declares the opening of the market, the touch of a finger results in the movement of billions of dollars that may result in the life or death of millions of people around the world while the anonymity of the market ensures that no one is held accountable.

---

24. Unpublished paper presented at CWM/South African Council of Churches sponsored conference on Zimbabwe in July 2007: "Overcome Fear with Faith."

Subverting the Culture of Violence

In a global context where 1.4 billion humans live in extreme poverty and the wealth of the world's three richest individuals is more than the gross domestic product of the world's 48 poorest countries, a radical alternative must be implemented to address the ever-widening economic disparity.[25] The extremes of over-consumption and deprivation are therefore regarded as forms of violence that threaten the common good of societies because there are perpetrated by political priorities that give attention to the maintenance of high military expenditure at the expense of those that give people fullness of life such as decent living, good health and educational facilities. There is growing recognition that there is a clear need for change in the way that the global market is governed, but the most difficult challenge is finding the political will to make the change. Conversion of the market economy to meeting the needs of all and not the few will not be achieved by voluntary measures because the market system is never satisfied with what it has earned as profit. The goal is always more. It serves itself at the expense of others, profit before people, especially the most vulnerable who are preyed upon and forced into debt.

Economic Justice in the Marketplace as a Missional Priority

Therefore, if genuine change is to come to the marketplace, then it will require an ecumenical partnership of all people of goodwill who can rise above the short-term self-interest and focus on the common good. Such a broad-based ecumenical partnership is necessary to lobby governments, the business and financial sectors to embrace laws that promote effective, good and ethical governance that promotes and ensures peace and unity among the people. The church's commitment to the ministry and mission of Jesus necessitates that it takes sides with justice and refuses to remain silent in the face of the gross dishonesty in the marketplace and the seeking of profit regardless of human cost.[26] Hendricks argues that justice was formative and foundational to the ethics and morality, the world-view and social consciousness upon which Jesus carried out his ministry[27]. The missional priority of the churches must be centred on liberating diakonia that consistently puts before the national, regional and international policy-makers the plight of the poor. This ecumenical global partnership should establish standards of the global marketplace that are based on economic justice that consistently gives priority to a sustainable model of international trade. The prayer that Jesus taught his disciples to pray reminds us that his mission to giving people fullness of life involves forgiveness of debt. This constitutes an

---

25. Just Peace Companion, 2011, World Council of Churches, Geneva, p. 11
26. Obery Hendricks, Jr, 2006, *The Politics of Jesus*, Doubleday, NY, p. 29
27. Ibid.

indispensible corrective measure to overcome the exploitative ways of commerce that is practiced by the forces of political and economic empire.[28] If the church and the wider ecumenical community fail to act decisively, then they risk being charged by the message of the prophet Jeremiah: "They dress the wounds of my people as though it were not serious, 'Peace, peace' they say, when there is no peace... they have no shame at all!" (6:14-15)

I will use again the question that Jimmy Cliff posed to have the last word on the sub-theme: "Peace in the Marketplace": How can there be peace when there is no justice?

Peace among the Peoples

Hiroshima and Peace among the Peoples

Setsuko Thurlow

I am pleased to have this opportunity to share with you small parts of my experience upon the bombing of Hiroshima.

I was a 13-year old school girl on 6 August 1945 at 8.15 am. I suddenly saw the brilliant bluish-white flash outside the window. I remember the sensation of floating in the air. When I regained consciousness in the total darkness and silence, I found myself in the debris of the collapsed building.

I began to hear my classmates' faint voices: Mother, help me; God, help me. Then suddenly a hand started shaking my left shoulder and a man's voice said: "Don't give up, keep moving, and keep pushing. I am trying to see you. We see the light coming through the opening, crawl toward it and get out of here as quickly as possible."

By the time I came out, the debris was on fire. That meant that most of my classmates were burnt to death alive.

There were bleeding, ghostly figures. They were naked and battered, burnt, blackened and swollen, parts of their bodies were missing, flesh and skin dangling from their bones, some with their eyeballs hanging in their hands. We girls joined the ghostly procession, carefully stepping over the dead and dying. There was deathly silence, only broken by the moans of the injured and their pleas for water: "Water, water, please give me water," but we had no containers to carry water in.

We went to a nearby stream to wash off the blood and dirt from our bodies, then we tore off our blouses, soaked them with water and hurried back to hold them to the mouths of the dying who desperately sucked in the moisture. We kept busy with the task all the day; we did not see any doctors or nurses.

---

28. Ibid.

Out of a population of about 360,000, most of them were non-combatant women, children and elderly who became victims of the indiscriminate massacre of the atomic bombing.

By the end of 1945, approx. 140,000 had perished and, as of the present day, about or at least 260,000 have perished because of the effects of the blast heat and radiation, and the effects are still felt today, 66 years later.

In spite of the characteristic effects of the atomic bombing, the unimaginable defeat of Japan, and the humiliation of occupation by foreign troops, we survivors were able to begin to see the meaning of our survival in terms of historical perspective and global context, and transcend our personal tragedies. We became convinced that no human being should ever have to repeat our experience of inhumanity, illegality, immorality and cruelty of atomic warfare.

We identified our mission as warning the world of the danger of nuclear weapons. Convinced that humanity and nuclear weapons cannot co-exist, and that for the total abolition of nuclear weapons is the only path to security and the preservation of humankind and civilization for future generations, we have been speaking out around the world for the past several decades on this subject.

To you the participants of this programme, I wish you productive and successful deliberations.

Comments on Peace between the Peoples

Patricia Lewis

I wish to thank God and the World Council of Churches for this opportunity. 160 million dead from conflicts in the 20th century is a conservative estimate, and of direct deaths only. 160 million deaths. Why?

[Lewis pointed to the fundamental 'inequality' between creation and destruction. To create something – from nurturing a human life to building a community – takes a long time. To destroy it takes seconds.] So much love and effort to create beauty; so little time to destroy it.

[Lewis observed that the "How" is widely known – whether by oppression, dehumanization, using weapons, chemical weapons, firebombing, cluster-bombing, nuclear bombing, the list is endless.]

But why? Is it the inability to address conflict early? Is it the inability to share the earth's resources equitably? Is it our ability to see the other as separate, not like us? Is it our fundamental human nature to be aggressive? Or is it the speed at which we, children of God, can destroy without even thinking through the consequences? Are we not wise enough as a species?

But we are wise – sometimes – and we see that God-given wisdom over and over again. Think of all the people who have stood up, without violence, to end oppression. We have seen many cases of promoting peaceful change today and throughout history, and yet somehow we don't trust in those experiences. We are always thinking the worst.

Let's take nuclear disarmament. Change when it comes will come quickly because people in the military will recognize, as they almost already do, that nuclear weapons have no military use at all, and that their magical symbolism rests on the willingness to use them. That is the essence of nuclear deterrence. It no longer exists, if it ever did. They also realize that you cannot make small mistakes with nuclear weapons. There is no calling them back, so they are extraordinarily dangerous.

We can say the same thing to war. Why can't we look to abolish war? It may seem crazily idealistic to many of us, but why is it that we only see the hurdles and not the possibilities? Where is our faith? We already have conflict prevention and peace-building in the UN and that is having considerable effects. But we, particularly in the West, need to take the planks out of our own eyes, and apply conflict prevention strategies to all or our countries. We need to work together in our own countries to address these underlying issues, support people who are oppressed and find ways to make change within each situation without violence. We do know how to do this and to believe that change can come peacefully. We need to understand that we can prevent man-made deaths in the 21st century, but we do have to work for it together.

What do weapons of mass destruction do to our souls? This is a very big subject for me. I am thinking here not of the people who are targeted but the people who are using them in the name of their own security. By that I mean everyone in the countries that possess nuclear weapons – that includes China, France, Israel, India, Pakistan, Russia, the United Kingdom, the United States. It also includes all who are under the so-called "nuclear umbrella" – for example, Canada, Norway, Germany, Netherlands, Poland, Hungary, Greece, Turkey. We are all relying on these weapons in the name of our security, and that means that we are all prepared to exterminate whole cities, to exterminate whole civilizations in the name of our security. So my question is: what has that done to our souls and is this part of the fundamental malaise that we see throughout the world today? Is this ability to think about killing so many other people in the name of our security underlying a large part of the evil that we see? Are we part and parcel of this?

My challenge to this room is "What are we doing?" For those of us who live in these countries or who come under the nuclear umbrella – for example, in Australia, Japan, South Korea, Taiwan, Philippines, you are all under that nuclear umbrella – what are we doing to prevent this enormous evil that we are perpetuating in the name of our own security?

V.
Bible Studies

Peace Will Come through God's Action

Prepared by Fulata Mbano Moyo, Anastasia Dragan, Jooseop Keum, Theodore Gill, Gervasis Karumathy, and Tamara Grdzelidze

Introductory Remarks
on Contextual Bible Study

Contextual Bible Study methodology is a brainchild of Liberation Theology. It suggests an interactive study of a biblical text. Contextual Theology cannot be *taught* because it is the voices of participants that matter. It allows the context of a reader and a biblical text to be in dialogue; the aim of this dialogue is to raise awareness leading to transformation.

There are five key "Cs" that summarize this methodology:

1. Community. It is important to receive an invitation from a community. Questions raised in the course of interpretation are answered by participants themselves. Sometimes it makes sense to record a process of interpreting according to Contextual Theology because some of the participants may be illiterate; it is empowering for them to know that what they said was noted. This kind of reading is not an interpretation by an individual but an engagement of all voices with the text. The process of such an exercise is more important than its product.

2. Context. Social location of a *reader* matter. Two realities, of interpreters as well as persons mentioned in text and the original audience, are to be taken seriously into account.

3. Criticality. Hermeneutical tools of exegesis and interpretation are used by the facilitator who forms questions to cater for critical reflection. If a text, like Tamar's Rape, deals with sexual violence, special interpretive tools must be used.

4. Consciousness. Raising awareness about an issue at the heart of the community. The tendency is to read the Bible with hermeneutics of trust, and to find solutions through such interpretation. One of the aims of the

Contextual Bible Study is to see the Bible as a tool of liberation, yet also of oppression. For example, the Bible was used to justify apartheid and racism; it is still used to justify a brand of Zionist ideology supporting Israel's occupation of Palestine.

5. *Change.* Interpretation and understanding lead to transformation (positive change). How to design a Contextual Bible Study? It has two types of questions: *exegetical* (literary or critical-consciousness questions that draw on tools from academic biblical studies); and *interpretive* (community-consciousness questions that draw on feelings, experiences and resources from the community). To formulate questions, the study facilitator uses hermeneutical tools of exegesis (uncovering the meaning of the biblical text within its historical and social context) and interpretation (reading the biblical text from the context of the participants/interpreters).

Peace in the Community

The Rape of Tamar (2 Samuel 13:1-22)

"Some time passed. David's son Absalom had a beautiful sister whose name was Tamar; and David's son Amnon fell in love with her. Amnon was so tormented that he made himself ill because of his sister Tamar, for she was a virgin and it seemed impossible to Amnon to do anything to her. But Amnon had a friend whose name was Jonadab, the son of David's brother Shimeah; and Jonadab was a very crafty man. He said to him, 'O son of the king, why are you so haggard morning after morning? Will you not tell me?' Amnon said to him, 'I love Tamar, my brother Absalom's sister. Jonadab said to him, 'Lie down on your bed, and pretend to be ill; and when your father comes to see you, say to him "Let my sister Tamar come and give me something to eat, and prepare the food in my sight, so that I may see it and eat it from her hand."' So Amnon lay down, and pretended to be ill; and when the king came to see him, Amnon said to the king, 'Please let my sister Tamar come and make a couple of cakes in my sight, so that I may eat from her hand.'

"Then David sent home to Tamar, saying, 'Go to your brother Amon's house, and prepare food for him.' So Tamar went to her brother Amnon's house, where he was lying down. She took dough, kneaded it, made cakes in his sight, and baked the cakes. Then she took the pan and set them out before him, but he refused to eat. Amnon said, 'Send out everyone from me.' So everyone went out from him. Then Amnon said to Tamar, 'Bring the food into the chamber, so that I may eat it from your hand.' So Tamar took the cakes she had made and brought them into the chamber to Amnon her brother. But when she brought them near him to eat, he took hold of her, and said to her, 'Come lie with me, my sister.' She answered

him, 'No, my brother, do not force me; for such a thing is not done in Israel; do not do anything so vile! As for me, where could I carry my shame? And as for you, you would be as one of the scoundrels in Israel. Now therefore, I beg you, speak to the king; for he will not withhold me from you.' But he would not listen to her; and being stronger than she, he forced her and lay with her.

"Then Amnon was seized by a very great loathing for her; indeed, his loathing was even greater than the lust he had felt for her. Amnon said to her, 'Get out!' But she said to him, 'No, my brother; for this wrong in sending me away is greater than the other that you did to me.' But he would not listen to her. He called the young man who served him and said, 'Put this woman out of my presence, and bolt the door after her.' (Now she was wearing a long robe with sleeves; for this is how the virgin daughters of the king were clothed in earlier times.) So his servant put her out, and bolted the door after her. But Tamar put ashes on her head, and tore the long robe that she was wearing; she put her hand on her head, and went away, crying aloud as she went.

"Her brother Absalom said to her, 'Has Amnon your brother been with you? Be quiet for now, my sister; he is your brother; do not take this to heart.' So Tamar remained, a desolate woman, in her brother Absalom's house. When King David heard of all these things, he became very angry, but he would not punish his son Amnon, because he loved him, for he was his firstborn. But Absalom spoke to Amnon neither good nor bad; for Absalom hated Amnon, because he had raped his sister Tamar."

Questions and Observations

In the context of the International Ecumenical Peace Convocation, the purpose of this text is to provide a focus for the theme of "Peace in Community." It must be recognized from the start, however, that rape is a highly-charged subject. Asking participants to draw from their own, and their community's experience requires a pastoral approach and a willingness to be flexible in response to what may be shared in discussion.

How might we address the Rape of Tamar according to the methodology of contextual Bible study? Rape is often referred to as a text of terror, and this text does not normally appear in the liturgical calendars of most churches. In theological gender studies, it is used to break the conspiracy or chain of silence that often exists around issues of sexual abuse in a community. Study of this seldom-used text is employed as a means of transformation. It is a tool that helps open up the process to discuss issues which are important in church and society.

Exegetical questions:
What is this story about?
Who are the main characters of this story?
What do we know about each main character?
How much do we know about David's family?
What do we know about the people who told the story?"

One study group reacted to these questions in the following way: We will learn more about the place of women, and about rebellion, in David's time if we read 2 Samuel 20.

- It is important to understand the background to this story of the Rape of Tamar, and events before and after it.
- The story foreshadows the sorts of tensions that will trouble the house of David for some time.
- Amnon was the firstborn: if something happened to him, Absalom would benefit.
- David is the prototype of humanity and highly appreciated in various theological traditions. He expresses only anger and does not act upon his son's misbehaviour.
- Tamar was not treated as a person, as a Thou. It is a story of men; women do not count.
- The text was edited before or after the Babylonian captivity – what meaning did the people of that time find in it?
- The Bible is bold in telling "secret stories," even to the discredit of the royal family.
- How much did Tamar know about this law? Was it most concerned with unity, rights or the institution of marriage in Israel?
- Did it help the household of David to keep silence over this incident (or other similar incidents)?
- Does it make sense to maintain "peace" by not revealing our own or our leaders' faults/transgressions?

Interpretive questions:

- Have we violated people like Tamar in our own contexts?
- By "violation," do we mean only sexual violence, or any kind of violence against women?
- Is the marginalization of women "violence"?

See Judges 19 on voices of women; amazingly, in 2 Samuel 13 Tamar receives no female support whatsoever.

- How do our own theologies address the problem of sexual violence against women?
- What would you do to maintain integrity in your community after such an incident?
- How does an abused woman reflect what God is?
- What kind of resources do we have to address the problem of sexual or other kind of violence? What is "just peace" in terms of *our* communities?

Peace with the Earth

The Peaceable Kingdom (Isaiah 11:6-9)

"The wolf shall lie down with the lamb, the leopard shall lie down with the kid, the calf and the lion and the fatling together, and a little child shall lead them. The cow and the bear shall graze, their young shall lie down together; and the lion shall eat straw like the ox. The nursing child shall play over the hole of the asp, and the weaned child shall put its hand on the adder's den. They will not hurt or destroy on all my holy mountain; for earth will be full of the knowledge of the Lord as the waters cover the sea."

Peace with the Earth

The theme of a day is to bring to light violence against the earth, overexploitation and destruction of the creation by humanity. The present dominant civilization treats the whole creation in a violent way, as clearly expressed in climate change and water crises. The Bible teaches us that there is a possibility of change, of *metanoia*: change of paradigms, mindsets, lifestyles and instruments of international law. These changes may result in "the peaceable kingdom" – a traditional description of Isaiah 11: 6-9.

Under the present challenges, churches are expected to contribute by their action to highlight the importance of life-giving agriculture, efforts made for mitigating of and adapting to climate change, advocacy work with others for fair, ambitious and binding international agreements.

Invited Speakers?

Three suggested speakers on this theme who may invite people to participate in a study group could be someone from the Pacific region, speaking on the resettlement of populations because of the rise of sea level; someone from Latin America, bringing Indigenous perspectives on relating to the earth; someone from an eco-congregation or green church speaking about ecological concerns addressed at the congregational level.

The way Isaiah 11: 6-9 is interpreted has a lot to do with what we will do with God's gifts and callings in our lives. Either we will think the gospel is not being effective and legitimize our interpretation with a futuristic interpretation, or we will insist on crying out for God to work in our lives and overcome our weak faith so that we may find ways to help those around us. The verses, portraying a transformed creation, seem to demand a setting of either the millennium or of the new heavens and earth. Since we do not see a transformed creation where wolves can dwell with lambs or leopards with baby goats or calves with a young lion, it is too easy for us to consign this passage into a file for some future application. If we succumb to this temptation, we are unaffected by God's Word.

Harmony Restored: The Peaceable Kingdom

"Species lie down together:
Can nurture overcome nature?
Can Spirit overcome genetic wiring?
How are we to be 'civilized'?"

By favouring the figurative interpretation, some have seen this passage as a description of the work of the Spirit in the church starting with Christ's coming.

In this view, the verses refer to the New Testament age and beyond: we see the results of the Spirit's work in the New Testament, though we realize it will be fully realized only in the age to come. We perceive this in two areas:

1. Christ's wonderful transformation of the people around him through his Spirit-anointed ministry. We first see that Christ simply transformed everything around him. God's Spirit was released through his life into the lives of others. As much as the other disciples opened themselves to this Spirit, the effect of Christ's rule changed their lives. We see a reverse of the curse that was put on man in the garden of Eden where Adam and Eve ran from God. Now God's life is re-established in Christ. We note that during his temptation in the wilderness, the wild animals did not bother him:

And he was in the wilderness forty days being tempted by Satan; and he was with the wild beasts, and the angels were ministering to him. (Mark 1:13).

2. *The kingdom of God (heaven) where God's presence is seen in and through the church.* Although some dispute the dating of the phrase "kingdom of God" in the time of the historical Jesus, they are overrun by a number of clear scriptural references. The phrase is used more than 150 times in the New Testament.

What is your own vision of "the peaceable kingdom" here on Earth?

Peace in the Marketplace

Give Us Our Daily Bread (Matthew 20:1-16)

"For the kingdom of heaven is like a landowner who went out early in the morning to hire men to work in his vineyard. He agreed to pay them a denarius for the day and sent them into his vineyard. About the third hour he went out and saw others standing in the marketplace doing nothing. He told them, 'You also go and work in my vineyard, and I will pay you whatever is right.' So they went.

"He went out again about the sixth hour and the ninth hour and did the same thing. About the eleventh hour, he went out and found still others standing around. He asked them, 'Why have you been standing here all day long doing nothing?'

"'Because no one has hired us,' they answered: "He said to them, 'You also go and work in my vineyard.' When evening came, the owner of the vineyard said to his foreman, 'Call the workers and pay them their wages, beginning with the last ones hired and going on to the first.'

"The workers who were hired about the eleventh hour came and each received a denarius. So, when those came who were hired first, they expected to receive more. But each one of them also received a denarius. When they received it, they began to grumble against the landowner. 'These men who were hired last worked only one hour,' they said, 'and you have made them equal to us who have borne the burden of the work and the heat of the day.'

"But he answered one of them, 'Friend, I am not being unfair to you. Didn't you agree to work for a denarius? Take your pay and go. I want to give the man who was hired last the same as I gave you. Don't I have the right to do what I want with my own money? Or are you envious because I am generous?'

"So the last will be first, and the first will be last." (NIV)

A Second Story - Give Us Our Daily Bread

At 5:00 am, still dark, a group of migrant workers started to gather in Ansan station square. No later than 5:30 am, about 100 laborers were gathered. At 6:00 am, a mini-van arrived and a man selected ten people and disappeared with them. Ten minutes later, another van came and took five more and left. No more vans came, but people did not move away until around 9:00 am.

Then, most of the people who had hoped for their "daily bread" went back home. Five or six persons opened their suitcases and started to sell small items of souvenirs from their home countries. Three or four persons started begging. About ten people were "standing around" the square. Some were dazed by the sun. Some were sighing.

In Korea, there are about one million migrant workers. Most of them work for so-called "3D" jobs which means "dirty, difficult (physically) and dangerous." Many of them work as unskilled laborers in the construction industry. However, due to the impact of the global economic crisis in 2009 and the collapse of the housing market, many of them have no daily job. For them, "Give us our daily bread" is not only a petition in the Lord's Prayer or a line from the liturgy, but a matter of life and death!

Introductory Questions

1. What is the parable of the labourers in the vineyard about?
2. How many times did the landowner hire labourers?
3. Why were those labourers standing around at the eleventh hour at the marketplace? Who did go back home and who did not, and why?
4. How much is the average wage per day for a normal unskilled labourer in *your* own context (this is the equivalent to a denarius in Jesus' time)? What is the minimum wage per day in your country?
5. Please fill in the following template:

	Time of Hiring	Time of Finishing Work	Hours of Working	Expected Payment due to Working Hours	Actual Payment by Landowner
1	Early Morning (6:00)	18:00	12 hours	1 denarius (10 asses)	1 denarius (10 asses)
2	Third Hour (9:00)	18:00			
3	Sixth Hour (12:00)	18:00			
4	Ninth Hour (15:00)	18:00			
5	Eleventh Hour (17:00)	18:00			

Why did the men who were hired first complain at the end of the day? Would you accept this payment if you were among the people who worked for twelve hours? Which is more difficult: working in the vineyard, or waiting for employment in the daily labour market?

Denarius

In the *Roman currency* system, the denarius (plural: *denarii*) was a small *silver coin* first minted in 211 BC. It was the most common coin produced for circulation but was slowly *debased* until its replacement by the *antoninianus*. The word "denarius" is derived from the *Latin dēnī* "ten times," as its original value was 10 *asses*. Its purchasing power at the time of Jesus, in terms of buying bread, has been estimated at about US$20. Historians say that the daily wage for an unskilled labourer or a common soldier in the Roman empire was 1 denarius, without tax. (By comparison, a labourer earning the *minimum wage in the United States* in 2005 made US$58 for an 8-hour day, before taxes.)

Parables

How do we understand the parables of Jesus? We often use parables when we try to explain something in a simple and easy way in moral and religious teachings. In the synoptic gospels, parables are the key methodology of Jesus' teaching. Approximately one third of his teachings use parables, particularly when he met crowds who were mostly illiterate. Jesus' parables are simple stories which are easy to remember. However, although his parables were simple and easy to understand, the meaning of the parables is deep and highlights the core values of the kingdom of God. Therefore, each parable demands a very careful reading and interpretation.

The Parable of the Vineyard

The aim of Jesus' parable of the labourers in the vineyard is to teach about the kingdom of God (verse 1). The context of the parable is massive unemployment. Many labourers were standing around in the marketplace without work (vv.3, 6). When the owner of the vineyard asked them: "Why have you been standing here all day long doing nothing?" (v.6), they replied, "Because no one has hired us" (v.7). Some of the rich people and policy-makers say that the poor are poor because they are lazy. However, here we meet the crowd of labourers who have no job opportunity although they want to work!

Then the next question is regarding a fair wage. Even in the case of the labourers who can work 365 days in a year, one denarius per day was not enough to reach the minimum wage of today. It was less than half of it, and the labourers would have to work almost 24 hours per day to earn the minimum wage. Moreover, for those people who have daily jobs only six months in a year, is one denarius a sufficient wage for labourers?

It seems the first were enjoying their everlasting privileges. The last had no basic means, such as education, to climb the socio-economic ladders. In this context, Jesus taught this parable on what it means to have a just economy in the kingdom of God.

First, the just economy in God's kingdom involves equal opportunity. In the parable, the owner hired the workers five times. In Hebrew prophecy, the vineyard normally means the people of God and the "owner" is God (cf. Isaiah 5:7). The economy of God's kingdom provides equal work opportunities for everybody so that they can sustain their life and realize their God-given gifts.

Second, there was an equal distribution based on needs. Whether they worked for twelve hours or just one hour, all received equally a denarius which can support them to buy daily bread for their family. Of course, it was not fair! There were no criteria for this payment. It was based neither on quantity nor quality of labour. However, if we consider that a denarius was a minimum wage for survival, it is understandable.

Third, "Lead us not into temptation"! For those people who worked for twelve hours, it was an unreasonable calculation.(12) It was a totally unacceptable, unfair payment. In the midst of the recent global financial crisis, there was the scandal of millions of dollars in bonuses being paid to the financial workers in Wall Street or London City. The CEO of the UBS bank justified this greed as being inevitable in order to employ top-quality financial managers. Those people who created the crisis were putting on different masks, presenting themselves now as problem-solvers. Therefore, in the laws of the economy that we know today, the first will always be the first and the last will be forever last.

We are living in a competitive society where everything is measured by numbers. Even human beings are listed as those who are the first and who are the last, who is the biggest and who is the least. Possessing more than others and accumulating massive wealth is becoming the only measure of security in the God-less market. The temptations of excessive wealth and greed lurk in every corner of the marketplace. In the logic of the market, there is no space for God's grace in relieving human suffering. The market leads us into the temptation of worshipping Mammon.

Concluding questions

1. Is there peace in the current global and local marketplaces? If not, why is there no peace? If yes, is it pax Romana or pax Christi?
2. Is there justice in the marketplace? If yes, is justice enough to bring peace to the market?
3. Is Jesus really talking about peace in the marketplace? What then does the last verse of the parable mean?

Economy of God's Kingdom

Read together Isaiah 55:1. "Come, all you who are thirsty, come to the waters; and you who have no money, come, buy and eat! Come, buy wine and milk without money and without cost." The market is the place where access is denied to those who have no money. Everything is priced in the market, even human beings. In this context, however, let us remind ourselves that a totally different market does exist in the kingdom of God where, although we have no money, we still may have life in fullness. If in Isaiah 55 we find the vision of a life-giving economy, the text of Mathew 20 is a case-study in how to actualize it: The economy of the first who take care of the last as the first – is possible! An economy of the first and the last sitting and feasting together in the house of the Father – is possible! (Luke 15:11-32)

Peace among the Peoples

Christ Is Our Peace (Ephesians 2:11-22)

So then, remember that at one time you Gentiles by birth,
called "the uncircumcision" by those who are called "the circumcision" –
a physical circumcision made in the flesh by human hands –
remember that you were at one time without Christ,
being aliens from the commonwealth of Israel, and strangers to the covenant of promise,
having no hope and without God in the world.

But now in Christ Jesus
you who once were far off have been brought near by the blood of Christ.

For he is our peace; in his flesh he has made both groups into one
and has broken down the dividing wall, that is, the hostility between us.

He has abolished the law with its commandments and ordinances,
that he might create in himself one new humanity in place of the two,
thus making peace,
and might reconcile both groups to God in one body through the cross,
thus putting to death that hostility through it.

So he came and proclaimed
peace to you who were far off and peace to those who are near;
for through him both of us have access in one Spirit to the Father.

So then you are no longer strangers and aliens,
but you are citizens with the saints and also members of the household of God,
built upon the foundation of the apostles and prophets,
with Christ Jesus himself as the cornerstone.

In him the whole structure is joined together and grows into a holy temple in the Lord;
into whom you also are built together spiritually into a dwelling place for God.

The Kingdom of God and Christian Community

The second chapter of Ephesians says of Jesus Christ, *He is our peace* (Eph. 2:14).

The author of this document is writing to a Christian congregation made up of both Jews and non-Jews, or "Gentiles." He recognizes that they are often described as distinct factions within the church, "the circumcision" and "the uncircumcision." The Greek word for "Gentiles" is *ethné*, the root for the English words "ethnic" and "ethnicity"; some versions of the Bible translate the term as "the nations" or "the peoples" and, like the Hebrew word *goyim*, it signifies all nations *other than* Israel. In this sense, "the Gentiles" were set apart by Jewish authors as "the others" or "the Other," as people distinctly different from members of their own community.

The author writes as a Jew by birth. He adopts assumptions that distance him from those who come from Gentile backgrounds. In this section of the letter he addresses "*you*" Gentiles (2:11) "who once were far off" (2:13; cf. Col. 1:21) as opposed to the chosen people of Israel – apparently, the author's own biological relatives – "who were near" to God (2:17) even in the past. These historic compatriots within the commonwealth and covenant of God are contrasted with the Gentiles who were "aliens" and "strangers." It is clear from such words and phrases that members of the earliest church at times viewed their own membership as internally divided.

There are a number of New Testament passages that testify to divisions and jealousies separating Christians. Even within the earliest Jewish-Christian congregation in Jerusalem, there were disagreements among the Aramaic-speaking and Greek-speaking believers (Acts 6:1). In Paul's letters, tense relations between Jewish Christians and Gentile Christians is found as a recurring theme (for example, Gal. 2:11-14; Rom. 3:1-2, 21-30; and 1Cor. 1:22-24 where the terms "Jews" and "*Greeks*" are used). The gospels feature accounts in which Jesus is linked with non-Jews; among these Gentiles are the wise men from the East (Matt. 2:1-2), the Syro-Phoenician woman (Mark 7:24-30//Matt. 15:21-28), the "good Samaritan" (Luke 10:29-37), the Samaritan woman at the well (John 4:1-42) and at least two Roman centurions (Matt. 8:5-13; Mark 15:39 and parallels). One of the purposes of these passages is to demonstrate that Christ's good news is not restricted to the lost sheep of the house of Israel but extends to all.

A point made repeatedly by New Testament authors is that divisions among Jewish and Gentile believers are incompatible with the kingdom of God that Jesus announced. The letter traditionally addressed to the church at Ephesus puts this message in terms of bringing down a barricade: Where once there was a "dividing wall" between one group and another, a barrier composed of "the hostility" that each side harboured against the other (Eph. 2:14), Jesus Christ has acted through the cross to "create one new humanity in place of the two, thus making peace" (2:15).

Pheme Perkins, writing in *The New Interpreter's Bible*,[1] examines the role of the cross in Ephesians 2:16:

> The cross has achieved what no human ever could: reconciliation of a sinful humanity with God… By dying on the cross, God breaks down a wall that separated humanity from God. Humans are too trapped in the deadly effects of sin to return to God on their own – or even to notice the wall that is keeping God out. Why is the cross important to Christians today? People still need to be convinced of God's unconditional love for them.

In the English language, the cross has come to be understood in terms of the Christian doctrine of "atonement." The word *atone* originates in the two words "*at one*" – so that the cross is seen as God acting in Christ to overcome past divisions and bring about the possibility of reconciliation.[2]

The vision in Ephesians is of a congregation, a local community of believers redeemed by the cross of Jesus Christ and living as subjects of the kingdom of God. In this community, each member has equal "access in one Spirit to the Father" (2:18). People of different origins – once "strangers and

---

1. P. Perkins, 'The Letter fo the Ephesians', *NIB* vol. 11 (Nashville: Abingdon, 2000), 405.
2. Cf. 2 Corinthians 5:19-21. Atonement with God enables the community itself to be "at one" (Eph. 4:4-5).

aliens" to one another – will, in the end, find unity as fellow "citizens with the saints and also members of the household of God" (2:19).

Dividing Walls of Hostility

In the ancient world, cities were surrounded by walls. Towering rows of stone served as a recognition of the hostility that existed between peoples. There was normally a sense of security in being snugly inside the walls; on the opposite side, being shut out of the city marked one's exclusion from the community within.

Today we find walls, both literal and figurative, in the world around us.

A "separation barrier" mars the landscape of Palestine and Israel. The demilitarized zone (DMZ) divides the Korean peninsula. High fences defend borders between some countries, with camps nearby for the detention of would-be migrants. Baghdad with its "green zone," Famagusta in northern Cyprus and Belfast in northern Ireland are among the cities of our world demarcated by "blast walls" and barbed wire, keeping one group of inhabitants from easy interaction with neighbouring groups.

In more towns and cities, less tangible barriers are erected between the rich and the poor, the native-born and the immigrants, persons of varying ethnicities, citizens of one faith and people of other traditions. Even when these boundaries are not patrolled by armed guards, the raw material most often used in their construction is mutual hostility.

Despite the many walls that remain, recent history provides at least one memorable example of the real possibility of establishing peace: the breaching of the Berlin Wall in November 1989 and its subsequent dismantling. Metaphorical walls have fallen, too, in events like the electoral defeat of the minority government in South Africa and the landmark presidency of Nelson Mandela.

The Unity of Christians in a Divided World

Ephesians speaks directly to the healing of divisions among Christians. Its teaching promotes equality within the church, calling for members of the faith to maintain "the unity of the Spirit in the bond of peace" (Eph. 4:3).

In the nearly two millennia since the New Testament was written, a number of divisions have arisen among Christians. Quite apart from theological disputes, instances of schism and denominationalism have frequently drawn strength from differences in ethnicity, race, nationality, geography. Do the ethnic rivalries reflected in Ephesians and other first-century texts offer a word to us regarding later cases of disharmony among Christians?

---

3. Michael Kinnamon and Brian Cope, eds., *The Ecumenical Movement: An Anthology of Key Texts and Voices* (Geneva/Grand Rapids: WCC Publications/Wm. B. Eerdmans, 1997), 241.

And what responsibility do Christians bear regarding disunity in the world as a whole? Archbishop Desmond Tutu called for Christian unity in the South African struggle against political domination by one race. He famously observed that *apartheid* was "too strong for a divided church,"[3] and as a leader of the South African Council of Churches he inspired the *ecumenical* resistance to minority rule in his nation. In unity, Christianity found spiritual resources to make a difference in establishing justice and peace in the world. For the author of Ephesians, too, unity in Christ leads the believer to ministries beyond the boundaries of one's own community. Indeed, the purpose of church unity is conceived and presented in literally universal terms:

> Although I am the very least of all the saints, this grace was given to me to bring to the Gentiles the news of the boundless riches of Christ, and to make everyone see what is the plan of the mystery hidden for ages in God who created all things; so that through the church the wisdom of God in its rich variety might now be made known to the rulers and authorities in the heavenly places. [Eph. 3:8-10]

Members of the church of Jesus Christ on earth are called to unity as a stage on their journey outward into the world. They take what they have learned as "members of God's household" (*oikeioi*) and apply these lessons to the whole inhabited earth (*oikoumene*).

Ralph P. Martin has commented[4] on the passage under discussion:

> No passage of the New Testament could be more relevant... The world that we know and inhabit is fallen, divided, suspicious and full of the possibility and threat of self-destruction. The apostle's teaching holds out the hope and prospect of a reconciled, unified and amicable society, whose microcosm is seen in the church's worldwide, transnational and reconciling family.

It has been said that the church serves as "a provisional demonstration of what God intends for the whole world." Christian unity is essential so that the church may bear witness to the possibility of "one new humanity" (2:15) extending throughout the world, with access to God "in one Spirit" (2:18). Having once experienced the leveling of walls within the church, Christians will be enabled to bring a convincing "peace testimony" to rulers, authorities and all who long to overcome violence and put hostility behind them.

---

4. R.P. Martin, *Ephesians, Colossians and Philemon* in the Interpretation commentary series (Atlanta: John Knox, 1991), 32.

Christians who wish to witness "peace on earth" need first to establish peace in their churches.

Breaking Down and Building Up

In Ephesians 2:11-22 we are presented with an image of Christ as one who "breaks down" the dividing wall of hostility that separates peoples and nations (2:14), yet he is also revealed as the cornerstone of a new construction, a home to shelter and nurture all the community within "a dwelling place for God" (2:19-22).

Group Activities Based on Ephesians 2

Using images from printed publications or the Internet, construct a collage depicting "the dividing walls of hostility" in our world today – or depicting the overcoming of divisions.

Is there a group within your church or a nearby church whom you regard as "the others"? Describe examples of divisions within churches or in the whole church, and ways in which attempts are made to address suspicions and heal divisions among Christians.

Drawing on your own context, how do you see people of faith "building up"; i.e., contributing to peace among separate peoples or ethnic groups?

In seeking peace among the nations of the earth, what responsibility do you believe churches and church-related institutions have in the realm of lobbying, international diplomacy and peace-making?

Recalling Desmond Tutu's warning that apartheid was "too strong for a divided church," discuss where the churches' priorities lie: To what extent must we concentrate on being reconciled to brothers and sisters in Christ, and to what extent must we focus our time and energy working for peace and justice throughout the world?

Discuss the history, contemporary attitudes, misunderstandings and fears that contribute to hostility between different faith communities. Does religion play a major role in modern-day confrontations between nations? Give specific examples.

Meditate on the cross. Consider the dynamics of "atonement" – between God and humanity, among individuals, between one group and another, among nations.

What are the confrontations in church and world that bother you most? What can Christians do to "break down" walls of hostility still dividing people and nations?

"Christ is our peace!" What does this affirmation mean for you?

Sending Forth
into the Whole Inhabited World:

Go in Peace (2 Kings 6:8-23)

Once when the king of Aram was at war with Israel, he took counsel with his officers. He said, 'At such and such a place shall be my camp.' But the man of God sent word to the king of Israel, 'Take care not to pass this place, because the Arameans are going down there.' The king of Israel sent word to the place of which the man of God spoke. More than once or twice he warned such a place so that it was on the alert.

The mind of the king of Aram was greatly perturbed because of this; he called his officers and said to them, 'Now tell me, who among us sides with the king of Israel?' Then one of his officers said, 'No one, my lord king. It is Elisha, the prophet in Israel, who tells the king of Israel the words that you speak in your bedchamber.' He said, "Go and find where he is; I will send and seize him.' He was told, 'He is in Dothan.' So he sent horses and chariots there and a great army; they came by night, and surrounded the city.

When an attendant of the man of God rose early and went out, an army of horses and chariots was all around the city. His servant said, 'Alas, master! What shall we do?' He replied, 'Do not be afraid, for there are more with us than there are with them.' Then Elisha prayed: 'O Lord, please open his eyes that he may see.' So the Lord opened the eyes of the servant, and he saw; the mountain was full of horses and chariots of fire all around Elisha. When the Arameans came down against him, Elisha prayed to the Lord, and said, 'Strike this people, please, with blindness.' So he struck them with blindness as Elisha had asked. Elisha said to them, 'This is not the way, and this is not the city; follow me, and I will bring you to the man whom you seek.' And he led them to Samaria.

As soon as they entered Samaria, Elisha said, 'O Lord, open the eyes of these men so that they may see.' The Lord opened their eyes, and they saw that they were inside Samaria. When the king of Israel saw them, he said to Elisha, 'Father, shall I kill them? Shall I kill them?' He answered, 'No! Did you capture with your sword and your bow those whom you want to kill? Set food and water before them so that they may eat and drink; and let them go to their master.' So he prepared for them a great feast; after they ate and drank, he sent them on their way, and they went to their master. And the Arameans no longer came raiding into the land of Israel.

The Background of the Text

Despite vagueness of reference to the historical circumstances in this passage, the focus of the interest on the prophet and the element of the miracle in this narrative are to be noted, as these elements are important for interpretation.

The wider background is provided by the Aramean wars, but no precise historical information is provided. Neither king, of Aram nor of Israel, is mentioned by name. The author does not seem to be much interested in presenting the narrative in a historical perspective; rather, he seeks to exemplify the supernatural abilities of the man of God, Elisha.

It appears that a former narrative around Elisha was enlarged with the addition of vv. 15b-17 in which the theme of the mighty divinity fighting on the side of Israel is underlined. The specific type of war seems to be this: with a numerically small group of soldiers, one inimical king falls on the other nation, stealing and plundering the villages and towns without giving the impression of a full-fledged war. Such actions are not meant to defeat the enemy but to weaken it.

Here as well as in chapter 5 the Aramean king is not mentioned, and therefore accurate dating is impossible. A reference to "bands" of Arameans in the Hebrew text of v. 23 may suggest not full-scale war but border raids, as indicated also in 5:2 (an Israelite girl being taken away). Raids may be undertaken not by the army of Aram but by semi-nomad Arameans loosely federated with Damascus. Their frequency and the impression that the Arameans were regularly repulsed (v. 10) suggest raids on this scale rather than full-scale war, which otherwise would surely have left its imprint on Holy Scripture.

Raids and ambushes across the border are likely to have characterized the two nations' relations all through the 9th century BCE. Unlike the previous stories, now Elisha's ministry is in the arena of international politics during a time of war between Aram and Israel. There is suspicion of treason (v. 11). The Syrian king is presented as dispatching a large force (v. 14).

Scope of the Narrative

The point of attraction in the narrative is the capacity of the man of God to see beyond the senses on account of which Elisha can warn the king of Israel. The king of Aram is enraged by this action of the prophet of Israel. But he has been told by his own people that the prophet possesses supernatural powers. Even though the Syrian king commands him to be taken prisoner, the commandos sent for the purpose have themselves been taken prisoner.

The temporary blinding of the men sent for the purpose stands in contrast to the vision of the man of God. With his powers, the prophet succeeds in leading astray the whole army sent to capture him, delivering them into the hands of the Israelite king.

The Plot Development

Central problem – The incursion of Aramean raiding parties (seen also at the start of the Naaman stories in 5:2). As in chapter 5, Elisha is now known in the Syrian court circles.

vv. 8-10 - Introduction of the main characters - king of Syria (v. 8), Elisha (v. 9), and king of Israel (v. 10). The opening passage also introduces the motive of the Syrian king's action against the prophet.

vv. 11-14 - The complicating problem of the army being sent. The advisors use the logic of arguing from greater to lesser: if Elisha knows the words in the bedchamber, how much more what passes in the council of war. "Go and see" – the king's command has ironic implications.

vv. 15-17 - The development of the story plot is put on hold in vv. 15-17 which is a narrative aside foreshadowing what will come. When the servant sees that God's victory over the Syrian is really inevitable, he is no longer afraid.

Syria's horse (collective sing.) and chariots (Ps 69,17) surround Elisha (vv. 15.16). V. 17 is a proleptic climax anticipating the true climax of v. 20b with the repeated "opened the eyes" and "saw."

vv. 18-20 - In these verses there is much humour and irony as the story proceeds from the servant's seeing to the blindness of the army and its seeing once again. Syrian troops are literally dazzled. Elisha is aware of their orders and offers to help them find the one they seek. He fulfills their mission to "go and see" by causing them to go (3 times) and see (2 times).

vv. 21-23 - Consequences and reactions: the pardon and sending away of the prisoners. Elisha is in charge, even in the royal city. The king is anxious to kill, but Elisha is not. Here there is no holy war ban as in 1 Kings 20:31-42, and the rules of the civilized war are maintained. Elisha controls policy by offering a banquet instead of execution. The central problem of raids is solved in v. 23.

Explanations

v. 8 - At *such and such a place*. Indefinite pronoun is used here in Hebrew. The narrator avoids naming the place and may be abstracting, or generalizing certain specific facts. The reader/hearer need not know the place of the ambush site, also because there was more than one such attack.

v. 12 - In view of the Israelite prisoners such as the maid of Namaan's wife and others who perhaps became concubines of the king and his officers, there might well have been a leakage of secrets from the bedchamber, if not of the king, at least of the leaders of the raid. This could have been a regular source of information to the enemy in the wars.

v. 15 - *Naar* (the term used for Elisha's servant/companion) - could be a traditional title coming from pre-Israelite Canaan. *Naar* could refer to a man of rank, serving in various capacities: arms bearer (Judges 9:54; 1 Samuel 14:1), steward and estate manager (2 Sam 19,18), personal attendant in non-military contexts (Exodus 33:11; 1 Kings 18:43; Ruth 2:15).

v. 16 - *Fear not* – a formulaic opening of salvation prophecies found in all strata of biblical literature (Genesis 15:1; 26:24; Isaiah 41:10; Jeremiah 1:8).

v. 17 - *fiery horses and chariots*: Fire is a regular feature of divine manifestation (Exodus 3:2; 13:21; 19:18) and is of the divine essence (Deuteronomy 4:24). In 2 Kings 2:1, the vehicle seen by Elisha is of the Lord.

The blindness is to be seen correctly: the troops are not completely blinded, for they were able to follow to Samaria. Blinding light, Hebrew *sanwerim*, found also in Genesis 19:11, could be a Akkadian loan word from *sunwarum* meaning "to make radiant, to keep (the eye) sharp." One may distinguish between ordinary blindness and this numinous flash of light which temporarily disables.

Reflections

Elisha stands here in opposition to the murderous wish of the king and presents himself as the protector of life and of rights, precisely those of the enemies. The Syrians who would be fed in a banquet would become a testimony to the supernatural powers of the Israelite man of God. Based on their own experience they would be able to proclaim that any further attempt against Israel would meet failure due to the presence of the omniscient man of God who dwelt there.

1. There is satire at the expense of the ruling elite class. All officials are powerless; YHWH is one who gives victory. Elisha provides vital military intelligence. Only when he sends word (v.9) can the king send to protect himself (v. 10). YHWH's chariots neutralize those of the Syrians. It is he who helps them in the mission and also sets the royal policy about captives.

2. As in the whole of the books of Kings, this narrative part also shows that kings, of Israel, Judah, Assyria or of Babylon, were never in control of the history of God's people; God alone is in control. God gives victory to people. In the larger story depicted in 1-2 Kings, the people were to experience total, humiliating defeat at the hands of the Babylonians, but again under the power and control of God.

3. Here again the prophet's unique powers are at the centre stage and he shows himself to be the possessor of "second sight." He has the ability

to see hidden things: the ambush of the Arameans planned in the private quarters of the king (vv. 10-12), the fiery cavalry (v. 17). At his command the eyes of the enemies are closed and opened.

In the midst of general hostilities, Elisha stands out as adviser to the king, and through his foresight Israel regularly avoids entrapment. Since the Syrians were not royal prisoners, they had to be treated as invited guests and then sent home.

The paradoxical behaviour of the prophet is seen as an "act of clemency" and "general concern for the prisoners." This may have been refined later on (see the she-bears story in 2:23-24).

Why was there no more hostility? According to verse 23, the end of raids came about due to an act of reciprocity in response to Elisha's graciousness, or out of respect for the powers he displayed: with such a prophet on their side, how could Israel be overcome?

Conclusion

1. The prophet is involved in international politics here, working to thwart a naked aggression of the Arameans, on the one hand, and preventing violence on the part of the Israelites, on the other. What is the role of the people of God?

2. Against those who may be eager to annihilate their enemy, the narrator elevates a response of hospitality and kindness instead of violence. This passage offers a perspective that is different from the harsh demands of "holy war" ideology (1 Kings 20:31-42).

3. The very prophet they were sent to capture tells them that they were going in the wrong direction. When he volunteers to lead them to the man they seek to capture, they blindly follow him. There may not be anything more humiliating for the big invading army than to be fed and then sent on its way.

4. State power, totalitarian or democratic, is nothing when compared to the horses and chariots of YHWH, operative through the word of God's true spokesperson. The believing community proclaims: "Do not be afraid, for those who are with us are more than those who are with them."

VI.
"Reasoning"

Workshops

Reasoning **is a term used by Jamaica's Rastafari to denote their** ritual coming-together in a circular seating pattern to share divinely-inspired thoughts and insights about their faith, the affairs of the day and their hopes for repatriation and redemption. Nowadays, the term has entered folk culture to mean any form of intellectual discourse; this is the name that was chosen for the sharing and learning sessions at the International Ecumenical Peace Convocation (IEPC) – the Reasoning workshop programme.

In Kingston, Jamaica, these workshops provided a space for reflection, formation and sharing of best practices through practical examples related to peace-making with a special focus on youth. Over 100 workshops offered an opportunity for IEPC participants to grow and to learn, to meet people from diverse cultural, confessional and regional backgrounds and to discern together how to be agents of God's transforming presence in the world for peace.

From the healing of memories to the Christian presence in the Middle East, from ecological theology and the work of reconciliation to interfaith dialogue as a tool for building peaceful societies, the IEPC Reasoning workshops were designed to engage participants while guiding them through an in-depth exploration of issues. While most workshops consisted of a one-off session, others were provided as a series of workshops covering a particular issue. Workshops were related to the theme of the day and although there was some overlap, most followed the daily sequential order:

- Peace in the Community
- Peace with the Earth
- Peace in the Marketplace
- Peace among the Peoples

The following selection of workshop reports gives a "taste" of the richness of contributions and learnings gained from the encounter. As the World Council of Churches (WCC) moves toward its next Assembly in Busan,

Korea, in 2013, there is much to take forward in the programmatic work, especially as churches have highlighted ongoing needs for further work and reflection.

Workshops on Peace in the Community

Living in Dignity and Sacredness in the Great House of Our Mother Earth

This workshop offered information about the present practices of the Aymara culture and in particular, how the Ayllu Indigenous community seeks to affirm the dignity of all its members, recognizing the sacredness and interconnectedness of the whole of creation.

Overcoming Armed Violence by Addressing the Supply and Demand for Small Arms and Light Weapons

This workshop drew on experience from the Caribbean civil society network to demonstrate how social concern for the rampant supply and demand for small arms was being creatively addressed through development programming and disarmament efforts.

Enhancing Urban Peace

Using case studies in Guatemala city, Mexico city and Port-au-Prince, this workshop presented practical experiences in reducing urban violence and enhancing reconciliation and peace among urban divided communities.

The Call to Peace-making: Training Programmes for Young People

Educating young people on basic principles for peace-building and conflict transformation is an effective method to overcome violence and foster peace in communities. This workshop presented two training programmes drawn from the project "Youth Becoming Peace-makers" and "Peace-makers: Youth with a Peace Mission" which offer skills in peace-building for youth and community leaders in the effective handling of conflict situations in a non-violent way. The focus was on how best practices could be adopted in other contexts and the conditions necessary for churches to involve youth in creating peaceful communities.

Engaging Conflict Well: Religion and Conflict Transformation

Learning to engage conflict well means the development of a theology, theory and practice of faith-based conflict transformation. This workshop carried this thought into the realm of the public square with reference to national and international conflict. It sought to lay out important components of what might be termed a ministry of reconciliation, shaping theological education around the demands of forgiveness, restorative justice, reconciliation and community formation.

Gender Training Using a Manual (2 workshops)

Participants in this workshop were taken on a journey of exploration regarding what socially has informed their concept of who a man or woman is supposed to be and to do, and the role of families, schools, churches, male and female models play in this socialization process. The workshop shared the Gender Training Manual (from hegemony to partnership) as a resource for gender-awareness and training.

Peace-building and Conflict Transformation: The Jos, Nigeria, Experience

This workshop focused on the history and impact of violence on the people of Jos, Nigeria, the current situation and the intervention of key stakeholders to restore calm. How far have we gone and what needs to be done in the search for sustainable peace and development in the state?

From Ashes to Hope: From Brokenness to Healing

This workshop enabled the exchange of Asian experiences (e.g., Timor Leste, Cambodia and Myanmar) of creative peace-building of healing and reconciling communities and individuals in the context of violence and brokenness, especially evolving from Asian women's spirituality of resilience and just peace.

For the People, by the People: A Jamaican Example

This workshop was offered by the Jamaican Baptist Union and was facilitated by Psychiatrist and Consultant in church-based health ministries, Dr E. Anthony Allen. It brought the motto "Glory to God and Peace on Earth" into focus and shared the premise that "there will be no peace without health and no health without peace." The basic question posed was: "How can the local congregation become a healing community for health and peace-building?"

The experience of the Bethel Baptist Church "Whole Person Congregation-based Healing Ministry" that has operated in a participatory and sustainable manner to minister to underserved areas of Kingston over the past 37 years was shared. The example sought to provide insights into how a community and spiritually based comprehensive initiative in health care can be started and run with the resources available within communities.

Empowerment for Just Peace (2 workshops)

Following on from the recommendation of the WCC convocation in Seoul 1990: an ecumenical programme "to develop and coordinate justice and peace ministries including a global nonviolent service which can advance the struggle for human rights and liberation and serve in situations of conflict, crisis and violence," this workshop offered an opportunity for continued planning and discussion around empowerment for Just Peace, and how best to enable local people to prevent escalation of conflicts and to be agents for nonviolent change.

Women, Peace and Security: A Roadmap to UN Resolution 1325

This workshop raised awareness and discussed the role of women in peace-building in Europe and internationally. The UNSCR 1325 stresses women's active role as peace agents and the workshop highlighted the resolution and introduced a Swedish model of training of how to be a peace agent.

Peace-making: Solidarity and Undoing Racism— A Journey toward Listening

Christian Peacemaker Teams (CPT) partners with communities from a variety of faith backgrounds in Colombia, Palestine, Iraq and North America that are working to build lasting peace and justice in and around their homes. However, too often, organizations based in North America have approached their work expecting others to fit into the North American mould under the guise of "colour blindness." CPT believes that recognizing privilege is critical in rooting out the systemic structures of oppression that feed and breed violence. This workshop explored how CPT are working to develop best practices for peace-making that puts partners at the centre of peace-making and that listens to the voices of those on the margins.

Growing Up without Violence: Ending Legalized Violence against Children

The workshop discussed how the WCC Decade to Overcome Violence and recommendations of the United Nations World Report on Violence against Children can continue to inspire people of faith to work ecumenically with their communities and with the wider society to address the problem of violence against children.

Call to Mission, Call to Peace-making: The Transformative Power of the "Gospel of Peace" (2 workshops)

This workshop discussed how Christian witness through mission work and the sharing of the Gospel of Peace, becomes a pacifying presence within troubled communities and amid distressed peoples, juxtaposing the challenges with successful paradigms of peace-making practices.

To Claim One's Own Power and Dignity: Sharing the Liturgical Practice of the Church's Resource Centre against Sexual Abuse

This workshop enabled other churches to start the work of developing a liturgical practice, where the abused soul can find God in the Church and among fellow worshippers without feeling guilty about what has happened to him/her. We want to create a liberating liturgy which has room for the experiences of abused people. What is special about the Resource Centre's liturgical practice and way in which it differs from the traditional one is the focus on actions and participation as a way of regaining one's own sense of personal value in society. The issue of violence and sexual abuse is universal, and in order to have peace in our communities, we must create spaces to express and name also the difficult experiences, and to also share the experience of hope and dignity.

Seeking Peace and Wholeness through Pain and Death

This workshop provided insights into palliative care and issues that congregations and communities can deal with in situations associated with suffering, death and dying. The session provided a possibility to discuss and reflect on these important issues.

Local to Global Protection

This workshop shared key experiences with community-based protection of civilians from ongoing research and activities in different parts of Myanmar, Sudan and Zimbabwe. The workshop also explored the real-life dynamics between actual local protection efforts and efforts by external actors (national authorities, armed groups, United Nations, international & national non-governmental organizations etc.) and how this all relates to the wider international frameworks such as The Responsibility to Protect & International Humanitarian Law.

Learning Skills for Building Peace (2 workshops)

This series of workshops gave participants new tools for working with conflicts and building peace in their families, communities, countries and globally. The skills are those taught at Eastern Mennonite University's Centre for Justice and Peace-building and included: active listening; peace-making circles; analyzing conflicts; breaking cycles of violence and finding paths to healing.

Ecumenical Advocacy for Peace in the Community

The workshop sought to explore the specific nature and practice of 'ecumenical advocacy' – though the experiences of the Ecumenical Advocacy Alliance in addressing the issues of HIV-AIDS and food – and considerd the role of ecumenical advocacy in challenging injustice, stigma and discrimination so as to contribute to true peace in the community.

Peace between Religions: A Delicate Plant

Conflicts between young people are an everyday occurrence in all cultures. In Germany, mediators are trained for schools in order to be able to resolve conflicts between pupils and work on finding solutions together. With the Ecumenical Center of the Protestant Church in Hesse and Nassau and their partner church in Ghana (Presbyterian Church of Ghana), the workshop demonstrated the forms of conflict management used by the young mediators and reported on what they had achieved.

Women with Disabilities in Violent Situations: Seeking Peace and Reconciliation

This workshop explored the situation of women with disabilities with specific reference to disabled women in the Democratic Republic of Congo and the Republic of Korea, who suffer from violence and abuse. The workshop offered a space for the exchange of experiences, and proposed and adopted actions and commitments for inclusion, nonviolence, peace and reconciliation.

Promoting Inclusion and Prominent Roles for Persons Living with Disability in Communities

This workshop shared best practices in creating good partnerships in order to promote the inclusion and role of persons living with disability in society. The workshop focused on ecumenical and inter-religious dimensions.

Training for Nonviolent Conflict Resolution (3 workshops)

In this series of three workshops, training was offered in non-violent conflict resolution for everyday life, including best practices/positive experiences with networks of trainers and alumni, as an example for ongoing work at a grass-roots level.

Diversity in Unity: Sexual Orientation as Challenge and a Living Example of the Ecumenical Dialogue

The aim of this workshop was to share personal stories about experiences of being gay/lesbian in the Christian faith and to present the 'Safe Space' ecumenical training project, which was developed by the European Forum of Lesbian, Gay, Bisexual and Transgender Christian Group.

Living Faithfully in a Violent World: When Will the Stones Speak? (2 workshops)

This workshop explored how people can live faithfully in a violent world. Participants were guided by a written resource and committed to actions that would lead to making a real difference in building a culture of peace.

Steps against Violence: Anti-Racism and Violence Prevention

This workshop gave an introduction to "Steps against Violence" – an anti-racism and violence prevention programme developed for students (Gr.8 and above) with an ecumenical background. In South Africa, it is conducted through theatrical communication tools/skills; in Germany it is carried out as a nonviolence training within a formal school curriculum. It has been the connecting bond between the "Peace to the City" partner cities of Durban and Braunschweig and continued in "Peace Train" projects between South Africa and Germany within the Decade to Overcome Violence.

Violence against Oneself: Prevention and Postvention of Suicide Prevention

The five pillars of suicide prevention:

1. Methodical Prevention (constraining the availability of suicidal means)
2. Dealing with crises (specific prevention for high-risk groups)
3. Involvement of multiplicators
4. Media (prevention of acts of imitation)
5. Persons concerned, high-risk groups (claim for help in crises)

Postvention: guided self-help groups, supervision and networking: introduction to self-help groups for people who lost a parent or spouse or another close person through suicide.

Meeting for people on how have to deal with suicide in their profession.

The Heart of Peace: Women and Children's Health and Welfare

This workshop gave a global overview of the situation of women and children's health and shared strategies and the actions taken by faith communities in addressing this key concern from specific contexts.

Children's' Contributions to Peace

Young people are normally very active in peace processes implemented in their communities when they are given the opportunity to participate and lead. Conflicts sometimes are handed down from one generation to the next and children and young people do not always have the opportunity to reassess the situation and look at it from other perspectives. Churches and religions need to value the contributions of children and young people. These four workshops provided a space for children and young people for: (i) learning tools and methodologies on how to contribute to peace; (ii) reflecting on the IEPC from their own theologies, values and backgrounds, (iii) sharing their best practices through concrete examples related to peacemaking. A mix of music, art and dialogue were used to explore these issues.

Healing of Memories: Training of Facilitators (4 workshops)

The need for healing and reconciliation in our broken world cannot be overemphasized. The pain and burden of memories – of ongoing, recent and past conflicts haunt and hamper normal life and progress. This training programme conducted a series of four workshops designed to train facilitators to advocate, develop and promote healing of memories and other healing and reconciliation processes in churches and faith communities, so as to be channels of hope, healing and reconciliation in our world today. The training oriented the group on 'healing of memories' and promoted the theological and ethical dialogue surrounding the issue.

Human Security and Human Dignity: Violence and Persons with Disabilities

This workshop addressed the issue of violence and persons with disabilities, exploring ways in which churches and communities need to work together to promote human security and dignity for all.

Immigration in the 21st Century

The objectives of this workshop were looking at the issue of migration from a theological perspective; seeking peace and wellbeing for migrants, showing the drama of forced migration and exposing the discriminatory laws of first-world countries. The issue of Indigenous migrants and their traditions facing the interculturality trauma was also tackled.

Peace: Beyond Dialogue

This workshop explored the 'Dialogue of Life' peace-building tools used by the National Council of Churches in India as they work in conflict situations going beyond the traditional 'faith-based dialogue among communities' to life-based dialogue amidst peoples' as the locus for conflict transformation and peace-building.

Fostering Peace: The Approach and Practice of the Uniting Church in Australia

The Uniting Church holds that a Christian responsibility to society is fundamental to the mission of the church. Therefore it is involved in a range of peace-building activities. The experience and strategies of the Uniting Church in Australia were explained as an example of how one church is seeking to engage in peace-building in its region. Various practices are being used to influence government and foster peace among people in the area. In particular the Young Ambassadors for Peace workshops held in the Asia and Pacific region were described. In the workshop these approaches were outlined and the accounts and experiences of others involved in peacemaking were invited.

Reflecting on Peace Practices

'Reflecting on Peace Practices' is an initiative about reflection and practice. An introduction of 'Reflecting on Peace Practices' contains the sharing of experience and lessons learnt from peace processes since 1999 up to now, conducted by actors like faith communities, agencies, United Nations and governments. By analyzing these experiences through 26 case studies and consultations with over 1000 practitioners, the initiative was able to clarify why some things work and others do not. This workshop was about sharing these core findings.

Start Dancing, Stop AIDS

HIV/AIDS doesn't discriminate against people according to religious denominations, colour or age, nor does it have any boundaries. It requires collective and uncompromising voices of principle to prevent it from further spread. This workshop explored how faith traditions compel us to achieve universal access to HIV treatment, care, support and prevention, and how networks with people of faith involved in the global response to HIV and AIDS can inspire others on the need to be advocates for this issue. The workshop shared the 'Dance Drill' methodology used to promote this community work in Uganda.

Reconciliation and Restorative Justice

Pax Christi International derives its inspiration from the biblical call to live in a just and peaceful world. The movement is driven by its basic value which is reconciliation among peoples. This workshop shared the experience of Pax Christi in the area of reconciliation and restorative justice.

Church's Efforts for a Permanent Peace Treaty in the Korean Peninsula

This workshop dealt with peace issues in Korea and suggested a world petition campaign for a permanent peace treaty between the two Koreas. Dialogues and exchanges between the two Koreas have been suspended for the last three years and political and military tension is high. Koreans need world churches' and people's support for the peace treaty and at the same time, pressure on the South Korean government to build sustainable peace.

Experiences and Challenges to Peace in Colombia

The main purpose of this workshop was to share experiences in the context of the armed conflict of Colombia and the peace-building initiatives set up by churches and social organizations, while making a call to enhance solidarity and support to peace initiatives to which some churches in Colombia are contributing.

Accompaniment: A Model for Peace-making in Colombia

This workshop showed how for the last five years the Colombia Accompaniment Program had represented a unique example of international ecumenical cooperation in an active ministry of witnessing to peace in the face of violence. The churches and communities involved are agents of peace-building. It is a programme that has made a significant difference in the lives of the people and churches in Colombia and in the United States.

Youth, Culture and Peace

This workshop was an opportunity to share methodologies for sociocultural work in churches and protection centres, in the context of rehabilitation processes for Colombian youth who face different conflicts such as forced recruitment, delinquency, drug addiction or prostitution.

Overcoming Hidden Violence: A Spirituality of Survival

The British Methodist Church (BMC) has done ground-breaking work with the issue of domestic abuse, through research and reflection of key Christian theological themes. This work was carried out collaboratively with Churches Together in England and other ecumenical partners. The British Methodist

Church has also funded domestic abuse work in overseas partner churches. This workshop offered opportunities to share experiences of this work within the group, reflect on the deceit of abuse and its incompatibility with the Christian life and deepen participants' reflective practices.

Training for a Prophetic Church

The workshop acknowledged the gulf that often exists between the stated position of our churches on peace and justice and the engagement with the mainstream of church members. Participants were offered case studies in prophetic action and shared their own stories and experiences. In so doing, the workshop aimed to affirm participants in counter-cultural prophetic action and explored how churches at all levels might develop greater confidence in supporting action by members.

Partnering in Mutuality in Mission toward Reconciliation and Peace

This workshop addressed important themes of peace-building and reconciliation, through initial exchange of particular experience and evaluative reflection and then in creative collaboration with participants. It also related to the Ecumenical Call to Just Peace through the conceptions and practices of reconciliation and restorative justice.

Deconstructing Power and Creating Peace

Unchecked and unconstructive power is a form of violence. The misuse of power can create disharmony and structural inequities. This workshop aimed to look at how best to deconstruct power and create peace. As such, one part of workshop focused on: defining power, personal power and unearned privilege. A second part focused on racism. This workshop ended with the inclusion of an ecumenical component, and particularly focused on the work around transformative justice in the World Council of Churches, and the work of the Canadian Ecumenical Anti-Racism Network.

Garrisons into Communities: Empowerment through the Arts

This workshop explored how a culture of violence is growing in Jamaica. It has brought an epidemic of homicides. From a human and Christian perspective, the solution lies in ending the social exclusion that has created a process of criminalization driving youth into criminal gangs. This means tackling unemployment, giving opportunities for training and development, ending police brutality, correcting a court system that allows murder to be committed with impunity. Only these and similar steps will bring the justice on which peace can be built.

Ecumenical Women Addressing Disarmament and Gender-Based Violence in Pastoralist Communities

This workshop shared a project of peace-building from the perspective of gender-based violence. Women from rural communities embarked on a training programme to raise awareness of the status of women in their communities and to look at how to best address issues of gender-based violence. The workshop explored their best practices in the training undertaken and especially in how they have been able to multiply and transfer the training in neighbouring communities.

Securing Safe Spaces: HIV & Human Sexuality

Resistance to providing information and a forum for honest dialogue on issues related to human sexuality and HIV — either in faith communities or in secular settings — often comes from people's unwillingness to question firmly held beliefs and to step outside our comfort zones of feigned ignorance. The workshop shared different churches' experiences in preparing safe spaces in their congregations with well designed material and training programmes (for different age groups) in dealing with human sexuality and HIV. The experience of Christian Conference of Asia in bringing clear policies to the fellowship of churches to provide a safe space for HIV and Sexuality was also a clear offering from a diverse regional ecumenical context.

Building Together a Pastoral Response to Care for the Elderly: Toward a Society Which Includes All Ages

The workshop called for the recognition of the right of elderly to age with dignity in a context of a rapidly increasing elderly population in Peru, as well as in other poor regions of the world. The workshop presented an ecumenical and interfaith dimension seeking to move forward in building a pastoral response to care for the Elderly.

Models of Christian-Muslim Dialogue in Theological Education as a Contribution to Peace-building: An Inter-Regional Dialogue

The interfaith component is essential for many contexts in world Christianity with regard to peace-building and conflict resolution. Theological education plays a major role to prepare attitudes, values and theological reasoning and capacity building for people active in peace work in today's multi-religious world. How is Christian-Muslim dialogue reflected, practiced and built into current programmes for theological education in different contexts? What are the innovative models for Christian-Muslim dialogue in theological education which contribute to peace-building today? The two workshops offered case-studies on different models of Christian-Muslim dialogue and peace-building in theological education and shared helpful resources in this regard. The workshop was aimed at representatives coming from networks and institutes on interfaith dialogue as well as regional associations of theological schools.

Peace, Mission and Evangelism: Exploring the Implications of the 'Code of Conduct on Conversion'

The workshop offered participants a brief overview of how the Code of Conduct came about and aimed to draw them into thinking about difficulties that arise in the mission context when it is done without proper consideration of people's religions, cultures and contextual realities. The Code itself – used as a basis for inter-religious dialogue - can serve peace-making practice, since it provides for meaningful discussion and dialogue about the expectations and acknowledgement of past failures. The Code of Conduct has also served as a success story in ecumenical cooperation and has encouraged participants to think together about their own witness and the witness of their communities, whether these are located in a Christian minority or majority context.

Historic Peace Church Continental Consultations during the Decade to Overcome Violence

This workshop shared the results of a series of conferences convened with the theme on the evolving theology and practice of peace. Each of the conferences involved the participation of Mennonites, Quakers and the members of the Church of the Brethren. The workshop highlighted the outcomes of the conferences and other activities of the historic peace churches over the past decade.

Life under Occupation: The Impact of Occupation in the Daily Life of Palestinians

Since 1967, each Israeli government has invested significant resources in establishing and expanding settlements in the Occupied Territories, resulting in approximately 500,000 Israeli citizens now living in settlements in the West Bank. This workshop presented the hardships of life under occupation as experienced by Palestinians and tackled a crucial question: Can there be peace between these communities while Israel continues the occupation of Palestinian land?

Contextual Bible Study (2 workshops)

How do we read biblical texts that are otherwise difficult to deal with – texts that we usually do not find in the liturgical calendar yet that narrate realities that are still part of endemic issues of concern in today's communities? How do we read those texts that actually help us to talk about taboo issues of sexual violence and other related violence against women that most churches tend to have a conspiracy of silence? This workshop helped train readers of Scriptures to be able to read for gender – just peace for the process of building just communities of women and men.

Peace-making as Witness and Friendship: Local Practices, Global Implications

This workshop addressed the practice of peace-making and reconciliation as a necessary and inherent aspect of the Christian gospel. 'Peace' is part of the good news in the Hebrew Scriptures as well (Isaiah 52:7) and it is this ministry that has been given to the Church (2 Cor. 5). Within this context, this workshop examined how the Church bears witness to this task and how this witness happens "on the ground" in local, personal practices of peace-making and friendship. Through a closer look at these stories, the workshop explored both the implicit and the explicit connection between Christian peace-making and evangelism and demonstrated an ecumenical dimension drawing on the experiences of its participants in both the ecumenical movement and in interreligious dialogue.

World Student Christian Federation Contribution to Peace-making

This workshop explored the contribution of the World Student Christian Federation to peace-making within their global youth network.

Creating an Atmosphere for Racial Justice through the Ecumenical Movement from an Ecumenical and Interfaith Context

One of the pernicious issues facing the ecumenical movement is that of creating structures that adhere to the mandates of racial justice. Facing the need for racial justice within our church structures and our societies is critical to the quest for unity. This workshop explored the ways in which racism hinders community-building and strategies for eradicating racial discrimination.

To Become a Church of Peace?

The churches and the ecumenical movement played a significant role during the intense years of political transformation and the peaceful revolution in the German Democratic Republic (GDR). What can we learn from these experiences? How can the ideas, hopes and actions evolved from the churches in the GDR help to develop a spirituality and theology of peace today? Grounded on various perspectives from East and West and from different generations, the workshop provided the opportunity to reflect on the peace movement of the 1980s in the GDR and to transfer some of these ideas and hopes into our contexts and our time.

Dialogue for Peaceful Change (4 workshops)

From early childhood, we face the challenge of living and working with each other, in the playground, at home, at school, in the community and at the office. Conflicts are opportunities to help us grow and learn. However, conflicts can also seriously hamper relations or development if they becomes a trap where we stay with our opposing positions and there seems to be no way out. In a series of four workshops, participants explored the Dialogue for Peaceful Change (DPC) methodology. DPC is a model for peace-building which creates a setting and provides a pathway for overcoming division. DPC is not the goal but the instrument in a process which seeks to build creative and practical skills for peaceful change. It's about analyzing conflict situations and facilitating the road to solutions, found and agreed by the people who are in conflict or experience opposite interests.

A Forum for Pursuing Peace

The Decade to Overcome Violence (DOV) has sought to intensify and resource the church's peace witness through Living Letters visits and the Annual Focus. It has identified leading peace-makers in churches around the world and encouraged them in their efforts. There is a need to continue to offer these groups and individuals an opportunity for ecumenical collaboration on a global level, beyond regional and denominational structures. This workshop was an opportunity to have a conversation reflecting on the DOV and to look to the future for potential forums that could enhance the exchange of theological and practical resources for peace and justice among churches around the world.

For the Healing of the Nations

In a broken world of strife, greed, injustice and pain, we look for signs of hope for a better world. This workshop gave two specific examples which showed how communities can promote justice, healing and reconciliation. The first example dealt with violence and hope in the Great Lakes Region (Central Africa): how basic communities struggle for healing of little girls accused of witchcraft. The second example was from Egypt, with the church-related programme 'Freedom' which has striven to free the society from drug dependence and HIV.

Weaving Pacific Women's Voices against Violence

This workshop explored the issue of gender-based violence in the Pacific region. Participants also discussed the role of the churches in advocating and educating for the dignity of all – identifying critical issues and concerns in the issues of violence against women.

Christian Women's Presence, Role and Participation in the Churches in the Middle East: The Case of Lebanon

This workshop dealt with the status and role of Christian Women in the Middle East, with a special focus on Lebanon. It tackled several issues pertaining to them, such as the challenges that face women in church and their position in the personal status laws. In addition, the workshop focused on the recommendations which resulted from workshops and conferences in which women from different countries participated, especially those related to 'women as peace-makers', 'ecumenism' and 'dialogue.'

Workshops on Peace with the Earth

Green Theology: The Armenian Church and its Nature-Friendly Projects

This workshop explored the 2004-initiated project of 'Green Theology,' a project to test and implement a new course in the educational curriculum of future clergy, trying to link 'the science of ecology with the deep wisdom of theology' and to re-think the relationship of Christian faith and nature and better understanding of God's Creation.

Ecological Theology and the Work of Reconciliation

The theological approaches of the ecological problem have pointed out its deep anthropological and cosmological roots. By not accepting the creation as a donation of God, the human person fails to realize the ontological foundation of the world; the earth may be easily regarded as the field of a merciless struggle between egocentric individuals. In its workshop, the Orthodox Academy of Crete (OAC) wished to present the eucharistic way of behaving toward the creatures and the ontological framework which, according to the Orthodox tradition, should inspire human relations as relations between beings created in the image and likeness of God; the OAC shared its over-40-years-old experience of work in the fields of ecology and reconciliation and referred to its initiatives for establishing peace and justice, as these have been realized in a great series of ecumenical conferences organized by the Ecumenical Patriarchate. Since a serious part of its work is youth-oriented, it also provided proposals for the engagement of young people for the IEPC goals.

Just Water

This workshop shared the JUST WATER initiatives of the first Congregational Church of Christ including:

How Community WASH Projects Contribute to a Comprehensive Just Peace; How Faith Communities can assist other Communities in Achieving Clean Water and Community Control of Water (inter-faith); How Community Control of Water can lead to Improved Governance in Fragile Developing Countries. JUST water requires that everyone in the world have affordable access to the water they need for drinking, cooking, bathing, domestic animals, and subsistence farming and livestock -- as well as sanitation and health promotion education. It also requires community control of water and other common resources. If we fail to provide JUST water, wars in the 21st century may well center on availability of clean water for drinking and community development. Community efforts to provide just water can create the basis for community development, effective community governance, and community leadership and influence on regional and national policy.

From Ecological Debt to Ecological Justice: Churches Need to Side with the Poor! (2 workshops)

The two-tiered workshop explored (i) concepts of ecological debt and ecological justice as part of overcoming violence; (ii) analyzed the violent root causes of the earth-destroying western civilization and collected resources for an inter-cultural, inter-religious new culture of life; (iii) shared stories from around the world of communities that have been violently displaced from their land and dispossessed of their sources of sustenance by multinational and state actors, often in the name of development and (iv) highlighted successful examples of how churches have worked or are working together with affected communities on actions to halt harmful extractive industries, exploration and development projects as well as to demand restoration and reparations for the ecological debt owed to them.

Empowering Women and Youth for Sustainable Benefits with Mother Earth

This workshop explored the sustainable use of natural resources; the equitable distribution and access to natural resources for all; and the representation and participation of women and youth groups in decision-making for environmental conservation.

Land Rights and Rights to Peace

The aim of the workshop was to generate a reflection on the role of the Christian church in Indigenous communities and how to engage them in peace-making in a context of struggles for land rights. This struggle is against the dominant powers which also take the control over the land. The case study built on the experiences of the struggles of the Mapuche peoples in Chile.

Bringing Together *Ubuntu* and *Sangsaing*: In search for Theology and Spirituality for Making Peace with the Earth

It is widely accepted today that ecological crisis has its origin in Western civilization and, along with it, the Christian worldview has been a major contributor to ecological destruction. In face of this situation, many efforts for re-orientation of theological thinking in the face of ecological crisis have been made over the last many years. However, such efforts are still being made within the framework of traditional theology that has been developed on the basis of a Western worldview. For a substantial response to this crisis, a radical re-orientation of theology and spirituality is needed. In 2007 a theological consultation was organized in Changseong, Korea, to explore a more interrelated and organic worldview by studying *Ubuntu* and *Sangsaeng* concepts. A follow-up consultation was held in 2010. This workshop further explored the results of this work.

There Is No Way to Peace: Peace Is the Way

Pax Christi International began a new project on the development of peace spirituality and peace theology. The theme is "There is no way to peace, peace is the way – Our life is a journey in peace – a peace-making journey." Justice and peace activists worldwide have been invited to participate in the project. This is an open process wherein we first listen to and capture the lived experiences of Pax Christi individuals and groups from diverse situations of war, violence and conflicts. Bringing together the human stories of grassroots people – individuals and communities – we aim to provide a space for the expression of experiences of hope and despair, joy and suffering, light and darkness – experiences that often change with different situations. During the workshop, the first results of this project were presented and new witnesses will be given and further reflections considered.

After the Flood

Natural disasters harm more than the physical environment, they destroy community. Churches can work together with government agencies, NGO's and local communities themselves to heal and bring peace. Taiwan's Christians have experienced this kind of disaster and recovery several times between 1999 and 2010. Their experience may serve to guide others who are confronted with disaster. Many churches around the world refrain from this kind of intervention. In this workshop, the Presbyterian Church in Taiwan wished to demonstrate how the church's role is critical in holding the government to account and that such a partnership with the government is a very practical way of bearing witness to God's love for all people especially those in desperate need.

Empowering Churches in North and South to Advocate for Climate and Environmental Protection

This workshop shared concrete examples of how churches respond to the challenge of climate change and environmental destruction (giving different perspectives from North and South). It encouraged and empowered others in their efforts to address the issue from a theological/ spiritual, human rights and development perspective. These examples also showed that churches can act locally and globally, and that their actions can make a difference and raise awareness within communities and societies.

As Long as We Have Our Land

This workshop explored the doctrine of discovery and Indigenous peoples, the secularization of Indigenous sacred spaces, exploring Indigenous spiritual resources for peace in a global context rooted in soil and the land and identity of Indigenous peoples.

Kairos Palestine

The "Moment of Truth: A word of faith, hope and love from the Palestinian suffering" is the Christian Palestinian word to the world about what is happening in Palestine. The document is not a theoretical theological study or a policy paper, but is rather a document of faith and work. Its importance stems from the sincere expression of the concerns of the people and their view of this moment in history that we are living through. It seeks to be prophetic in addressing things as they are without equivocation and with boldness. In addition it puts forward ending the Israeli occupation of Palestinian land and all forms of discrimination as the solution that will lead to a just and lasting peace. This workshop examined the context of the elaboration of the document and the many responses by churches and several other partners that were received. It also tried to make an analysis of the impact it had on the local Christian communities in Palestine, and on theological debate ecumenically.

Water and Just Peace

Water is the very source of life, yet it is also increasingly becoming a source of conflict. The Ecumenical Water Network (EWN) strives to promote the preservation, responsible management and the equitable distribution of water for all, based on the understanding that water is a gift of God and a fundamental human right. In this session, partners involved in the Ecumenical Water Network from around the explored, together with the participants of the workshop, the links between water, struggles, and building just peace.

The Moana Declaration: The Witness of Pacific Churches on Climate Change

This workshop explored the Pacific churches' concerns for the rights of the marginalized and vulnerable in the Pacific region in relation to climate change and their current involvement in advocacy, education and resettlement.

Under the Catastrophe of Nuclear Meltdown in Japan

This workshop discussed the recent nuclear power plant crisis in Fukushima, Japan, following the earthquake and tsunami in March, 2011. The workshop presenters shared stories and experiences of these tragic events and discussed the churches' response to the crisis.

Workshops on Peace in the Marketplace

Arms Trade, Fair Trade?

The Gothenburg Process has worked on involving churches in a public discourse on the Arms Trade by raising awareness and promoting ethical considerations. Four church-based and Christian organizations are behind the initiative. Several international seminars or workshops have been arranged. This workshop discussed the implications of the arms trade and how it relates to Christian ethics.

Selling Justice for a Pair of Sandals: Fenestration of Justice in the Market

This workshop helped raise issues of how courts of law get manipulated in favour of the 'market' and in the name of 'development'. From the Democratic Republic of the Congo to Macambini Traditional community area, from Colombia to India, Indigenous poor communities get evicted from their land in the name of 'development'.

Combating Human Trafficking: Churches' Role in Tackling Emerging Vulnerabilities

This workshop discussed conceptual understandings of the issue of human trafficking with special reference to South Asia. It shared a model of combating human trafficking in India through the "just" engagement of the Church of North India (which has pushed the agenda of combating human trafficking in the South Asian region and globally in partnership with the Council for World Mission and UNIFEM) together with success stories of churches' and communities' effective roles in restoring the dignity of survivors. Therefore, the workshop looked at churches' engagement in overcoming violence, especially against women and children; discussed the challenges faced; celebrated the successes achieved and shared effective tools of prevention, social re-integration and restoration of justice and peace.

Solidarity Economics: Focal Point, Turning Point, Future of the Ecumenical Movement (2 workshops)

This workshop explored the ongoing international debate on Solidarity economics. Nowadays, it becomes more and more obvious what some key speakers of the social movement had ever since pointed out: You have to offer alternatives to the current dominant neo-capitalism governed by the financial markets. To achieve this, it is essential to mobilize political will and pressure. This workshop aimed to contribute to this by sharing guidelines, experiences and strategies, originated from the last 18 months of work in the Academy of Solidarity Economics in the German ecumenical grassroots network.

Our Economy Is a Violent One: The Theology and Practice of Moving toward "God's Economy"

Wendell Berry calls our dominant economic system "industrialism" and says it has been, since its inception, in a "constant state of riot" against that which gives life, against the health of creation. Viewed from the eyes of those whose voices are not powerful, the violence of this economy is particularly clear. The church community is called to speak out for those voices in word and deed, prophetically and practically. Creating a peaceful world by definition requires understanding and implementing a peaceful economy. This workshop provided a model/diagram of our current dominant human economy and a more sustainable economy, discussed the worldview and theology behind those economies, and reflected on the violence embodied within our dominant economy. The workshop also included discussion and stories of what churches in the United States particularly are doing to be more sustainable, describing some practical ways individuals and congregations, particularly those in "the global North," are practicing sustainability.

The Palestinian Economy: From Exploitation to Strangulation (2 workshops)

Since the 1967 occupation, more than three-quarters of the occupied Palestinian territories' exports and imports of goods and services have been to and from Israel. This workshop tackled the complex web of economic links between Palestine and Israel, the essential asymmetry of that relationship and the impact that boycotting, divestment and economic sanctions may have on both communities.

Overcoming the Violence of Global Imperial Capitalism (2 workshops)

This workshop:

- offered a biblical foundation for overcoming the violence of imperial capitalism;
- analyzed the institutional mechanisms of global capitalism and their violent effects in six continents, esp. the linkage between private property and capital accumulation ("possessiveness creates violence," Gandhi);
- detected a possible "greed line" for wealth, discussing greed as the general change in human subjectivity through the money economy as interpreted by Buddhism;
- gave practical examples of how people at local/regional levels can transcend capitalist economy by forms of solidarity economy, thus showing that a non-violent, cooperative economy is possible;
- gave practical examples of how people can build alliances against privatization, liberalization and deregulation for the common good, diminishing the violence of capitalism.

Health Care for All in the Marketplace

This workshop explored health care and peace in the marketplace, highlighting the struggles and successes of providing health care to resource – poor communities in a highly commercialized environment such as in the United States of America. It highlighted the mobilization of societal assets in bringing about health to the community from the congregational level, with excellence, participation and professionalism. The workshop shared some of the key experiences of the venture and suggested ways of adapting and applying this strategy in different contexts.

Ending Poverty Locally, Nationally, and Globally: Linking Ministries of Local Congregations with Broader Ministries

This workshop looked at how to link poverty ministries of local congregations with national (and global) poverty ministries. It worked from a case study of the First Christian Church of Omaha, Nebraska, United States, and its connection with the domestic poverty initiative of the National Council of Churches.

Interreligious Cooperation and Advocacy for Economic Justice in Extractive Industries

What role can and should religious leaders play in this arena? What is the scope for South-South and North-South cooperation? This workshop gave a recent example of how religious leaders and Faith-Based Organizations (FBOs) can play an important and transformative role in the struggle for economic justice in developing countries. In many countries in the South, religious leaders and FBOs are the only organizations with a wide enough reach and legitimacy with people able to challenge companies and authorities. The workshop was based on the experience of the Christian Council of Tanzania, Tanzania Episcopal Conference and the Muslim Council of Tanzania against the mining practices of companies in Tanzania.

Religion and Violent Radicalization

Peace processes over the world are undermined by the presence of radical religious groups. Although a minority, they often have a detrimental influence on sustainable peace-building processes. Military responses to the challenge of growing violent radicalization have proven to be insufficient at best and counterproductive at worst. Civil society organizations such as Pax Christi International have more flexibility in dealing with these issues and can play a different role. They are in a unique position to engage with the reality of violent radicalization in a non-militaristic and non-exclusive way. This workshop aimed to develop practical approaches and methods to deal with manifestations of violent radicalization in a non-violent way. As such, it aimed to help countering and preventing the negative impact of growing radicalization on sustainable peace-building.

Dalits in the Context of Economic Globalization

This workshop addressed the issue of how Dalits are negotiating economic globalization. Dalits are those who belong to formerly untouchable communities and who continue to be at the very bottom of the caste hierarchy. This workshop spoke of the ambiguous promise that globalization holds for Dalit communities, where on the one hand it serves to break down feudal ties while on the other, it reinvents the nature of Dalit subjugation and co-opts the caste system as a whole. The workshop looked at the situation of Dalits in traditional employment as well as those Dalit entrepreneurs that have apparently benefitted from the changes that globalization has made in modern India. Specifically, the workshop raised the issues of social discrimination and economic justice and how these interphase with each other.

"Sans-Papiers" – Undocumented Migrants

The workshop showed the living conditions of people without a residence authorization in the European-Swiss context. It included information on the help desk for "Sans-Papiers" (French for "without papers") in Bern/Switzerland. What are the key questions concerning the work with and for "Sans-Papiers" at present? And what are the positions of our churches? In particular, it welcomed people from Southern countries to this workshop. They were invited to depict their situation and their view on "Sans-Papiers." Together, they searched for a meaningful and Christian engagement.

Building Human Security through the Economics and Economies of Care

This workshop had the objective of (1) bringing to fore, via feminist analytical lenses, critical connections between security, gender relations and the economy as well as (2) identifying possibilities for collaborative interventions between and among women's movements and churches toward developing an economics of care as well as economies of care that build socio-economic security. What lessons can be gleaned from those who work at the intersection of these struggles for peace and socio-economic justice, and how can churches in solidarity with women's movements jointly strengthen these efforts? It was envisaged that the workshop would not only sharpen theoretical frameworks but also contribute toward the realization of a different kind of multilateral cooperation that can produce practical alternatives to the often violent measures being implemented in the name of security and development.

Workshops on Peace among the Peoples

The Responsibility to Witness: The Historical Peace Church Testimony toward Peace-building (2 workshops)

The workshop highlighted practical examples of peace-building as expressions of faithfulness to Christ from within the Peace Church tradition. It showed how members of the Mennonite, Quaker and Brethren faith communities conceive of the nature of the Church in terms of living for and testifying to the peace of Christ. This has led to active engagement in peace and reconciliation in many parts of the world, at local, national and international levels. Particular attention was paid to efforts they have made toward getting conflicted parties to enter into dialogue for the sake of conflict reduction, working for reconciliation after conflicts have been quelled and the lobby work of the Peace Church tradition with important international organizations like the European Union and the United Nations.

World without Nuclear Weapons

The workshop discussed 'Peace for Life in a World Free of Nuclear Weapons' from the perspective of people, peoples movements and from the perspective of non-nuclear states vis-à-vis states that possess nuclear weapons.

In Our Lifetime: Overcoming Nuclear Weapons' Deadly Connections

This workshop had three dimensions. With background presentations and through discussion it provided 1) an opportunity to learn about the little known history and the continuing dangers of the use of nuclear weapons, 2) background about religiously-based opposition to nuclear weapons and work for disarmament, 3) an overview of and ways to engage with local, national and international initiatives and campaigning for the elimination of nuclear weapons.

Youth in Action: Promoting Dialogue for Peace-building and Regional Reconciliation

Encouraging youth involvement and boosting of regional peace and reconciliation was the proposed topic for discussion and experience – sharing at the workshop. Breaking negative stereotypes of the "other" side and the image of enemy, preparing a ground for more perceptive ideas for peace and reconciliation on grassroots' and public level is a key objective of an ecumenical Armenia Round Table (ART) Foundation's Regional Peace and Reconciliation Programme.

Dignity, Freedom, Human Rights: A Christian Perspective (2 sessions)

This workshop explored questions regarding freedom, dignity and human rights ideas from a Christian-Orthodox perspective, and how these can contribute to building peace in the community.

How to Mobilize in Campaigning on Peace-related issues: Changemaker Norway's Experiences

Changemaker has experience in both mobilizing people in relation to the churches of Norway and outside. This workshop used the Changemakers peace campaign as an example of good practice and gave some tools on campaigning peace work in civil society. In June 2009, Changemaker launched a campaign to get a stricter arms export regime in Norway. The success of this campaign was a direct result of lobbying politicians, doing stunts in the streets, collecting signatures and getting media attention all over Norway. The workshop used this campaign as an example on how best to develop and implement political strategy, campaigning and mobilizing.

Healing and Reconciliation

The workshop focused on peace-building and reconstruction in a post-conflict Sri Lanka. The workshop shared best practices, including the creative handling of conflict situations which require ecumenical and interfaith responses.

Interfaith Dialogue as a Tool for Building Peaceful Societies

The primary aim of this workshop was to present cases of good practices in the field of interfaith dialogue, and how strengthened relationships created through dialogue can contribute to conflict resolution and peace-building. Another important aspect to be covered in this workshop was how dialogue can have a normative impact on different groups in society and through this contribute to the building of peaceful communities. The case presented was that of the Contact Group between the Council of Ecumenical and International Relations in the Church of Norway (MKR) and the Islamic Council of Norway (IRN).

Christian Mission and the Struggle for a World without Empire (2 workshops)

A workshop in two sessions, it offered biblical and theological foundations for resistance against empire and becoming prophetic communities of solidarity and peace through Christian mission and working with people in struggle. It situated the global context by providing an analysis of the nexus between imperial power and global capital and presenting the experiences of resistance by communities, churches, and social movements in Palestine/Israel, Colombia, and the Philippines.

Conscientious Objection to Military Service and Asylum

This workshop on conscientious objection to military service and asylum recalled and explored the WCC Central Committee Minute on conscientious objection, taking into account the national and international experience and the role of religious groups and communities in promoting and protecting conscientious objection for those in their own country and those fleeing persecution and seeking asylum in other countries using different examples.

Developing Strategic Education on Peace-making: An Orthodox Christian Contribution

This workshop was designed to build upon the WCC-Decade to Overcome Violence's work and leadership in peace-making. It focused specifically on how to strategically apply Orthodox Christian resources to the development of local and international justice, international relations theory, international diplomacy, ecumenical and interfaith collaboration in peace-making and reconciliation, as well as to the development of an integrative peace education of the future religious leaders and policymakers. The workshop also 'harvested' the findings from two international pan-Orthodox expert consultations jointly developed by ecumenical partners.

Whose Priorities? Military Spending vs. Spending to Achieve the Millennium Development Goals

This workshop looked at nuclear disarmament: ethical, political, economic and ecological dimensions. The workshop aimed to share experiences of campaigning for a shift in perspectives, especially among nuclear weapons states toward a human security approach that does not require reliance on weapons of mass destruction. The workshop also explored the current state of negotiations on disarmament and the situation one year after the 2010 Non-Proliferation Treaty review. A particular focus was work on creating a zone free of nuclear weapons in the Middle East – an area in which faith communities play an especially important role.

Peace: The Lens for Re-visioning Christian Theology and Mission

This workshop explored how some main themes of Christian theology have often been expressed in ways that can support violent oppression of other peoples and religions, and gave a proposal for formulating these themes, through the lens of peace, in ways which strongly critique this orientation and provide a very different Christian vision.

Korean Church's Vision for Peaceful Reunification in the Korean Peninsula

This workshop explored the issue of reunification in the Korean Peninsula as an urgent call for peace and security in the whole of North East Asia and not only in the two Koreas.

A Christian Understanding of War in an Age of Terrorism

The churches have struggled to find a central voice on the reality and permissibility of war. Appeals to 'just war' theory are not sufficient in this age of unbridled terror and conflict. Examples of individual and state-sanctioned terror were explored following an assessment of how the churches have responded to the violence of war and terror in the past two thousand years. This workshop explored a major paper developed in the fall of 2010 by the National Council of Churches in the United States. The paper was titled 'A Christian Understanding of War in an Age of Terror(ism)'. The challenge to the churches across the globe is to reach consensus on how they will emerge in the pluralistic and interreligious 21st century with one, unified voice on war and terror in the world.

Religions for Peaceful Co-existence

Using Ethiopia as a case study, this workshop shared how different faith groups teach and influence their wider constituencies and act together for peace. This workshop also gave wider perspectives on how people understand conflict and turn threats into an opportunity.

Promoting Peace and Reconciliation in the Great Lakes Region of Africa

This workshop developed how a concept of just peace could be promoted in a region that has suffered and is still suffering from heavily violent conflicts by promoting reconciliation and development. The workshop introduced the approach of the German organization EIRENE, which supports "peace-alliances" by sending experts to local initiatives that focus on peace-journalism, gender-equality and training in civil conflict management.

Faith into Practice: Seeking Peaceful Change at the Global Level

Building a more peaceful, just and sustainable world demands change at all levels: from the personal to the global. This particular workshop drew on the now more than 60 years of experience of the Quaker United Nations Office in working at the global policy level. It sought to demonstrate how issues and methods are discerned for that work, choices made, and tensions between ultimate values and practical engagement are resolved. It l also demonstrated how we work with others — including governments and other organizations, including religious ones — in the pursuit of global change. The workshop sought to show how the Religious Society of Friends, one of the historic peace churches, seeks to live out its faith at the interface of international politics and the issues and dilemmas it faces in trying to do so.

Just Peace and Global Advocacy: Setting the Compass in Kingston (2 workshops).

In the first quarter of the 21st century, what are the four key global public goods on which churches committed to Just Peace must advocate together globally? (Global issues they cannot address adequately or effectively on their own.) This workshop was intended to challenge and engage a cross-section of church and other participants including resource people. With those participants, it (a) examined premises for the question, (b) assessed a range of possible answers, (c) discussed goals related to possible 'answers', (d) drew on ecumenical heritage, and (e) explored collective advocacy strategies and capacities with reference to the above.

The Codification of the Human Right to Peace (3 workshops)

The main objective of the workshop was to share the Santiago Declaration on the Human Right to Peace with civil society representatives and to identify and explore how intercultural and inter-religious dialogue is a component of the human right to peace. It was anticipated that the workshop would also encourage peace activists and movements to become part of the Global Alliance for the Human Rights to Peace Declaration.

Healing Trauma, Building Peace

The Church's Foundation Wings of Hope is a "child" of the Decade to Overcome Violence. It was founded in 2003 in München with the aim of helping children and young people in troubled regions to overcome their violence-related trauma to help. The work of Wings of Hope is interreligious, and the traditions of religions and their scriptures are valued as an important part of healing and reconciliation processes.

The Role of the Orthodox Church in Peace-building

Recent research demonstrates that the Orthodox Church has been struggling when responding to situations of war, conflict or persecution of Christians.

As an important part of the society, the Orthodox Church can develop initiatives to address the roots of violence before the escalation of conflict by means of negotiations aiming at mediation. The Orthodox Church needs to maintain independently a careful analysis of any conflict in which it finds itself involved; this analysis focuses on parties involved, dynamics of a particular conflict and the cultural context. Certainly, the church may not be able to provide such an analysis, but it must be aware of its importance and have a resource group to help with such research. The workshop aimed at involving participants in a panel discussion on this topic by representatives of the Orthodox Church(es) in Kingston.

Models for Peace-building

This workshop discussed the "Ecumenical Accompaniment Programme in Palestine and Israel" (EAPPI) and why this particular way of accompaniment was chosen versus other types already existing and the added values of the churches in forming such a programme. Participants were invited to discuss how EAPPI has the potential for being used in other conflicts.

No Peace without Justice: Challenges for Churches to Strive for Human Rights against Impunity and Absence of the Rule of Law

The workshop shared concrete examples of how churches respond to different forms of violence, using examples which show how important international solidarity is and what can be achieved by local and international lobby and advocacy work making use of international standards and mechanisms to protect human rights. The workshop especially focused on marginalized people in conflict areas e.g., Indigenous people, children and women.

Philip Potter Chair in Ecumenism: Challenges for Peace, Justice, Liberation and Reconciliation (4 workshops)

This series of four workshops shared the inspirational and effective work of Philip Potter in ecumenism, and other ecumenical issues in the region. In light of the re-launching of the United Theological College of the West Indies Philip Potter Chair and the need to establish a new awareness of ecumenism in our classrooms and church relationships in the Caribbean region, the historical, sociological, religious and theological dimensions were important projections for the purpose of the workshop.

Health for the People, by the People: A Jamaican Example

This workshop shared the experience of the Bethel Baptist Church, which has developed the 'Whole Person Health and Church-based Health Ministries' in a participatory and sustainable manner, ministering underserved areas of Kingston, Jamaica over the last 35 years. The workshop provided insights into how the community and a spiritually-based comprehensive initiative in health care can be established and run with the resources available within communities.

Haïti: Gender, Peace and Communication

This workshop was an invitation to think together about the unbalanced representation of women in the media and its negative impact in the processes of resolution of conflicts and preservation of the peace. From the particular case of Haiti, the presenters invited participants to find general propositions together that can promote countries to adopt measures to apply the resolution 1325 of the United Nations relating to the participation of the women in the resolution of conflicts.

Theology of Life: Overcoming the Violence of HIV

HIV can be interpreted as a state of violence experienced by individuals and communities, causing suffering accentuated by societal discrimination and theological misinterpretations. This workshop was led by experienced theologians and presented innovative ecumenical and inter-faith reflections and experiences, based on contextual Bible studies and a sound theological curriculum. The workshop discussed how to further bring lamentation, healing of memories, forgiveness and reconciliation to the concerned people. The basis of the work is to try to mend the injustices and to bring healing processes into the centre of the churches and the hearts of our leaders.

A Peace Theology: An Orthodox View

Given the urgent necessity for peace all over the world, a new ethos, based on a fresh and dynamic interpretation of the common biblical sources and tradition was offered by this workshop, aiming to give practical solutions to burning issues, rendering the concerns for peace, justice and reconciliation, that is the essential task of Church's mission in the world today. This workshop (i) addressed an Orthodox understanding of the word peace and just peace, (ii) developed an Orthodox proposal for cultivating a theology of peace in the community, with earth, in the marketplace and among peoples, and (iii) discussing the necessity of ecumenical cooperation and common good practices in promoting an ethos of peace and reconciliation.

The Cuban Five: A History of Solidarity

The Cuban FIVE are five Cuban men who have been incarcerated in the US prisons for more than 11 years after being wrongly convicted in a federal court in Miami. During all these years, there are two wives of the Cuban

FIVE who have not been able to see their husbands. These workshops offered first-hand information of this case, which is not portrayed in the mass media, sharing stories and promoting solidarity and peace among the peoples. It was hoped that reconciliation would be further promoted among the two countries.

Pilgrimages for Transformation

Palestine is a unique country from all perspectives: history, religion, landscape and culture. It is known around the world as the home of the three monotheistic world religions: Christianity, Islam and Judaism. The Alternative Tourism Group (ATG) invited IEPC participants to join a workshop that sought to suggest how transformational pilgrims to Palestine can be justice tourists, seeking to understand and make a positive difference in the lives of people by visiting Palestinian families, witnessing the effects of occupation, learning about the history, religions, conflicts, cultures of this region and, thus, bring hope to the people.

Youth Voices for Peace in Israel and Palestine

This workshop was based on a visit of a youth delegation of the United Church of Canada to Israel and Palestine, which focused on solidarity, witness and exposure to the situation of conflict. Drawing on the stories and experiences of communities we visited in the region, this workshop encouraged the call to understanding, peace and solidarity among religious groups and solidarity within the wider community of nations as we work together for just peace.

Mission, Power and Peace

Mission and evangelism are theologically grounded in God's power. The experience of power and conflict of those sent out have always been crucial issues for mission. So some, especially in the North, connect mission with manipulation and conflict, while others connect mission with experience of the Holy Spirit. At this International Ecumenical Peace Convocation, it is essential in our deliberations to bring different views of mission on a scale between power and powerlessness, peace-making and peace-destroying energy into a real dialogue with one another.

Empire and Religious Violence: Imperative of Interfaith Solidarity (2 workshops)

This workshop (i) analyzed the nexus of empire-building and religious wars along with the nature of and reason for the rise and spread of violence identified as motivated by religious belief; (ii) demonstrated the role of religious doctrines (of the world's major religions) in perpetuating structural violence, economic exploitation, wars, various forms of social stratification etc and (iii) developed approaches to building interfaith solidarity against the instrumentalization of religion for empire-building and militarized globalization.

Christian Presence in the Middle East

Recent developments and appraisals in the Middle East might bring some hope for the populations in different countries. But at the same time, several attacks against Christians in their places of worship have raised fears and concerns among churches everywhere. This workshop made an analysis of the situation in different countries of the region, focusing on the role of Christians in building just societies, based on respect of human dignity, human rights, and diversity.

Gen Rosso – International Performing Arts Group

This workshop shared its work with educating young people toward peace and violence prevention through different disciplines of stage performing arts: instrumental music, dance, singing, acting etc. The Gen Rosso projects have already been experienced in different parts of the world and in various religious contexts.

VII.
"Innerstandings"

Seminars

The "Innerstandings" seminars embodied the process of theological reflection on the four IEPC themes and the response to the Ecumenical Call to Just Peace (ECJP). They were facilitated by theologians and a team of 50 church community-rooted theologians who led participants on a journey of life to bring to consciousness the tensions experienced as they explored existing traditions of peace. Each afternoon, one seminar was based on the theme of the day and the other focused on the Ecumenical Call – the first and last from a Christian perspective and the second and third from an inter-faith perspective.

Thursday 19 May; 14.00-15.30
Peace in the Community
- Gender and just peace
- Racial, caste and Indigenous justice
- Just communities of peace

Thursday 19 May; 15.45-17.15
Christian Perspectives on the ECJP

Friday 20 May; 14.00-15.30
Peace with the Earth
- Theology of interconnectedness/interdependence
- Water of life
- Climate justice

Friday 20 May; 15.45-17.15
Inter-Religious Perspectives on the ECJP
- Hindu religious perspective
- Buddhist religious perspective
- Muslim religious perspective
- Sikh religious perspective
- Rastafarian religious perspective

Saturday 21 May: 14.00-15.30
Peace in the Marketplace
- Economic-related violence
- Theology of enough
- Globalization, migration and justice

Saturday 21 May: 15.45-17.15
Inter-Religious Perspectives on the ECJP

Monday 23 May: 14.00-15.30
Peace among the Peoples:
- Ethical analysis of rape as weapon of war
- Turning swords to plowshares
- Just war to Just peace

Monday 23 May: 15.45-17.15
Christian Perspectives on the ECJP

VIII.
An Ecumenical Call to Just Peace (ECJP)

"Guide our feet into the way of peace" (Luke 1:79)

Preamble: This call is a concerted Christian voice addressed primarily to the worldwide Christian community. Inspired by the example of Jesus of Nazareth, it invites Christians to commit themselves to the Way of Just Peace. Aware that the promise of peace is a core value of all religions, it reaches out to all who seek peace according to their own religious traditions and commitments. The call is received by the Central Committee of the World Council of Churches and commended for study, reflection, collaboration and common action. It is issued in response to a WCC Assembly recommendation in Porto Alegre, Brazil, 2006, and builds on insights gained in the course of the ecumenical "Decade to Overcome Violence, 2001-2010: Churches Seeking Reconciliation and Peace."

Just Peace embodies a fundamental shift in ethical practice. It implies a different framework of analysis and criteria for action. This call signals the shift and indicates some of the implications for the life and witness of the churches. A resource document, the Just Peace Companion, presents more developed biblical, theological and ethical considerations, proposals for further exploration and examples of good practice.

It is hoped that these materials, together with the commitments arising from the International Ecumenical Peace Convocation in Kingston, Jamaica, in May 2011, under the theme "Glory to God and Peace on Earth," will assist the forthcoming Assembly of the WCC to reach a new ecumenical consensus on justice and peace.

1 Justice embracing peace. Without peace, can there be justice? Without justice, can there be peace? Too often, we pursue justice at the expense of peace, and peace at the expense of justice. To conceive peace apart from justice is to compromise the hope that "justice and peace shall embrace" (Ps. 85:10). When justice and peace are lacking, or set in opposition, we need to reform our ways. Let us rise, therefore, and work together for peace and justice.

2 Let the peoples speak: There are many stories to tell—stories soaked with violence, the violation of human dignity and the destruction of creation. I f all ears would hear the cries, no place would be truly silent. M any continue to reel from the impact of wars; ethnic and religious animosity, discrimination based on race and caste mar the façade of nations and leave ugly scars. Thousands are dead, displaced, homeless, refugees within their own homeland. Women and children often bear the brunt of conflicts: many women are abused, trafficked, killed; children are separated from their parents, orphaned, recruited as soldiers, abused. Citizens in some countries face violence by occupation, paramilitaries, guerrillas, criminal cartels or government forces. Citizens of many nations suffer governments obsessed with national security and armed might; yet these fail to bring real security, year after year. Thousands of children die each day from inadequate nutrition while those in power continue to make economic and political decisions that favor a relative few.

3 Let the Scriptures speak: The Bible makes justice the inseparable companion of peace (Isaiah 32:17; James 3:18). Both point to right and sustainable relationships in human society, the vitality of our connections with the earth, the "well-being" and integrity of creation. Peace is God's gift to a broken but beloved world, today as in the lifetime of Jesus Christ: "Peace I leave with you, my peace I give to you." (John 14:27). Through the life and teachings, the death and resurrection of Jesus Christ, we perceive peace as both promise and present—a hope for the future and a gift here and now.

4 Jesus told us to love our enemies, pray for our persecutors, and not to use deadly weapons. His peace is expressed by the spirit of the Beatitudes (Matthew 5:3-11). Despite persecution, he remains steadfast in his active nonviolence, even to death. His life of commitment to justice ends on a cross, an instrument of torture and execution. With the resurrection of Jesus, God confirms that such steadfast love, such obedience, such trust, leads to life. This is true also for us.

5 Wherever there is forgiveness, respect for human dignity, generosity, and care for the weak in the common life of humanity, we catch a glimpse—no matter how dim—of the gift of peace. It follows therefore that peace is lost when injustice, poverty and disease—as well as armed conflict, violence, and war—inflict wounds on the bodies and souls of human beings, on society and on the earth.

6 Yet some texts in the scriptures associate violence with the will of God. O n the basis of these texts, sections of our Christian family have legitimized and continue to legitimize the use of violence by themselves and others. We can no longer read such texts without calling attention to the human failure to answer the divine call to peace. Today, we must interrogate texts that speak of violence, hate and prejudice, or call for the wrath of God to annihilate another people. We must allow such texts to teach us to discern when, like the people in the Bible, our purposes, our schemes, our animosities, passions and habits reflect our desires rather than the will of God.

7 Let the church speak: As the Body of Christ, the church is called to be a place of peacemaking. In manifold ways, especially in the celebration of the Eucharist, our liturgical traditions illustrate how God's peace calls us to share peace with each other and with the world. Yet, more often than not, churches fail to live out their call. Christian disunity, which in many ways undermines the churches' credibility in terms of peacemaking, invites us to a continuous conversion of hearts and minds. Only when grounded in God's peace can communities of faith be "agents of reconciliation and peace with justice in homes, churches and societies as well as in political, social and economic structures at the global level" (WCC Assembly, 1998). The church that lives the peace it proclaims is what Jesus called a city set on a hill for all to see (Matt. 5:14). Believers exercising the ministry of reconciliation entrusted to them by God in Christ point beyond the churches to what God is doing in the world (see 2 Cor. 5:18).

The Way of Just Peace

8 There are many ways of responding to violence; many ways of practicing peace. As members of the community that proclaims Christ the embodiment of peace, we respond to the call to bring the divine gift of peace into contemporary contexts of violence and conflict. S o we join the Way of Just Peace, which requires both movement toward the goal and commitment to the journey. We invite people of all worldviews and religious traditions to consider the goal and to share of their journeys. Just Peace invites all of us to testify with our lives. To pursue peace we must prevent and eliminate personal, structural and media violence, including violence against people because of race, caste, gender, sexual orientation, culture or religion. We must be responsible to those who have gone before us, living in ways that honor the wisdom of our ancestors and the witness of the saints in Christ. We also have a responsibility to those who are the future: our children, "tomorrow people." Our children deserve to inherit a more just and peaceful world.

9 Nonviolent resistance is central to the Way of Just Peace. Well-organized and peaceful resistance is active, tenacious and effective – whether in the face of governmental oppression and abuse or business practices which exploit vulnerable communities and creation. Recognizing that the strength of the powerful depends on the obedience and compliance of citizens, of soldiers and, increasingly, of consumers, nonviolent strategies may include acts of civil disobedience and non-compliance.

10 On the Way of Just Peace the justifications of armed conflict and war become increasingly implausible and unacceptable. The churches have struggled with their disagreement on this matter for decades; however, the Way of Just Peace now compels us to move forward. Yet, to condemn war is not enough; we must do everything in our power to promote justice and peaceful cooperation among peoples and nations. The Way of Just Peace is fundamentally different from the concept of "just war" and much more than criteria for protecting people from the unjust use of force; in addition to silencing weapons it embraces social justice, the rule of law, respect for human rights and shared human security.

11 Within the limitations of tongue and intellect, we propose that Just Peace may be comprehended as *a collective and dynamic yet grounded process of freeing human beings from fear and want, of overcoming enmity, discrimination and oppression, and of establishing conditions for just relationships that privilege the experience of the most vulnerable and respect the integrity of creation.*

Living the Journey

12 Just Peace is a journey into God's purpose for humanity and all creation, trusting that God will "guide our feet into the way of peace" (Luke 1:79).

13 The journey is difficult. We recognize that we must face up to truth along the way. We come to realize how often we deceive ourselves and are complicit with violence. We learn to give up looking for justifications of what we have done, and train ourselves in the practice of justice. This means confessing our wrong-doings, giving and receiving forgiveness and learning to reconcile with each other.

14 The sins of violence and war divide communities deeply. Those who have stereotyped and demonized their adversaries will need long-term support and accompaniment in order to work through their condition and be healed. To reconcile with enemies and to restore broken relationships is a lengthy process as well as a necessary goal. In a process of reconciliation there are no longer powerful and powerless, superior and inferior, mighty and lowly. Both victims and victimizers are transformed.

15 Peace agreements are often fragile, temporary, and inadequate. Places where peace is declared may still be filled with hatred. Repairing the damage of war and violence may take longer than the conflict that caused it. But what exists of peace along the way, though imperfect, is a promise of greater things to come.

16 We journey together. The church divided about peace, and churches torn by conflict, have little credibility as witnesses or workers for peace. The churches' power to work for and witness to peace depends on finding a common purpose in the service of peace despite differences in ethnic and national identity, and even in doctrine and church order.

17 We travel as a community, sharing an ethic and practice of peace that includes forgiveness and love of enemies, active nonviolence and respect for others, gentleness and mercy. We strive to give of our lives in solidarity with others and for the common good. We pursue peace in prayer, asking God for discernment as we go and for the fruits of the Spirit along the way.

18 In loving communities of faith that journey together, there are many hands to unburden the weary. One may have a witness of hope in the face of despair; another, a generous love for the needy. People who have suffered much find the courage to keep on living despite tragedy and loss. The power of the gospel enables them to leave behind even the unimaginable burdens of personal and collective sin, of anger, bitterness and hatred, which are the legacy of violence and war. Forgiveness does not erase the past; but when we look back we may well see that memories were healed, burdens were set aside and traumas were shared with others and with God. We are able to travel on.

19 The journey is inviting. With time and dedication to the cause, more and more people hear the call to become peacemakers. They come from wide circles within the church, from other communities of faith, and from society at large. They work to overcome divisions of race and religion, nation and class; learn to stand with the impoverished; or take up the difficult ministry of reconciliation. Many discover that peace cannot be sustained without caring for creation and cherishing God's miraculous handiwork.

20 Sharing the road with our neighbours, we learn to move from defending what is ours toward living generous, open lives. We find our feet as peacemakers. We discover people from different walks of life. We gain strength in working with them, acknowledging our mutual vulnerability and affirming our common humanity. The other is no longer a stranger or an adversary but a fellow human being with whom we share both the road and the journey.

Signposts on the Way of Just Peace

21 Just Peace and the transformation of conflict. Transforming conflicts is an essential part of peacemaking. The process of transformation begins with unmasking violence and uncovering hidden conflict in order to make their consequences visible to victims and communities. Conflict transformation aims at challenging adversaries to redirect their conflicting interests toward the common good. I t may have to disturb an artificial peace, expose structural violence or find ways to restore relationships without retribution. The vocation of churches and religious communities is to accompany the victims of violence and be their advocates. I t also includes strengthening civic mechanisms for managing conflicts and holding public authorities and other perpetrators accountable–even perpetrators from within church communities. The "rule of law" is a critical framework for all such efforts.

22 Just Peace and the use of armed force. Yet there are bound to be times when our commitment to Just Peace is put to a test, since peace is pursued in the midst of violence and under the threat of violent conflict. There are extreme circumstances where, as the last resort and the lesser evil, the lawful use of armed force may become necessary in order to protect vulnerable groups of people exposed to imminent lethal threats. Yet, even then we recognize the use of armed force in situations of conflict as both a sign of serious failure and a new obstacle on the Way of Just Peace.

23 While we acknowledge the authority of the United Nations under international law to respond to threats to world peace in the spirit and the letter of the UN Charter, including the use of military power within the constraints of international law, we feel obliged as Christians to go further – to challenge any theological or *other* justifications of the use of military power and to consider reliance on the concept of a "just war" and its customary use to be obsolete.

24 We acknowledge the moral dilemma inherent in these affirmations. The dilemma is partially resolved if the criteria developed in the just war tradition may still serve as a framework for an ethic of the lawful use of force. That ethic would allow, for example, consideration of "just policing," the emergence of a new norm in international law around the "responsibility to protect" and the exercise in good faith of the peacemaking mechanisms enshrined in the UN Charter. Conscientious objection to service in armed forces should be recognized as a human right. Much else that is antithetical to peace and the international rule of law must be categorically and finally rejected, starting with the possession or use of all weapons of mass destruction. Our common life invites convergence in thought, action and law for the making and building of peace. As Christians we therefore commit to a transformed ethical discourse that guides the community in the praxis of nonviolent conflict transformation and in fostering conditions for progress toward peace.

25 Just Peace and human dignity. Our scriptures teach us that humanity is created in the likeness of God and is graced with dignity and rights. The recognition of this dignity and these rights is central to our understanding of Just Peace. We affirm that universal human rights are the indispensable international legal instrument for protecting human dignity. To that end we hold states responsible for ensuring the rule of law and guaranteeing civil and political as well as economic, social and cultural rights. However, we observe that abuse of human rights is rampant in many societies, in war and in peace, and that those who should be held accountable benefit from impunity. In response we must reach out in friendship and cooperation to all partners in civil society, including people of other religions, who seek to defend human rights and strengthen the international rule of law.

26 Just Peace and caring for creation. God made all things good and has entrusted humankind with the responsibility to care for creation (Gen. 2:4b-9). The exploitation of the natural world and the misuse of its finite resources disclose a pattern of violence that often benefits some people at the expense of many. We know that all creation groans to be set free, not least from the abusive actions of humans (Romans 8:22). As people of faith, we acknowledge our guilt for the damage we have done to creation and all living things, through action and our inaction. The vision of Just Peace is much more than the restoration of right relationships in community; it also compels human beings to care for the earth as our home. We must trust in God's promise and strive for an equitable and just sharing of the earth's resources.

27 Building cultures of peace. We are committed to building cultures of peace in cooperation with people of other religious traditions, convictions and worldviews. I n this commitment we seek to respond to the gospel imperatives of loving our neighbours, rejecting violence and seeking justice for the poor, the disinherited and the oppressed (Matthew 5:1-12; Luke 4:18). The collective effort relies on the gifts of men and women, the young and the old, leaders and workers. We acknowledge and value women's gifts for building peace. We recognize the unique role of religious leaders, their influence in societies and the potentially liberating power of religious wisdom and insight in promoting peace and human dignity. At the same time, we lament the cases where religious leaders have abused their power for selfish ends or where cultural and religious patterns have contributed to violence and oppression. We are especially concerned about aggressive rhetoric and teaching propagated under the guise of religion and amplified by the power of media. While we acknowledge with deep humility Christian complicity—past and present—in the manifestation of prejudice and other attitudes that fuel hate, we commit ourselves to build communities of reconciliation, acceptance and love.

28 Education for peace. Education inspired by the vision of peace is more than instruction in the strategies of peace work. It is a profoundly spiritual formation of character that involves family, church, and society. Peace education teaches us to nurture the spirit of peace, instil respect for human rights, and imagine and adopt alternatives to violence. Peace education promotes active nonviolence as an unequalled power for change that is practiced and valued in different traditions and cultures. Education of character and conscience equips people to seek peace and pursue it.

Seeking and Pursuing Just Peace Together

29 The Christian pilgrimage toward peace presents many opportunities to build visible and viable communities for peace. A church that prays for peace, serves its community, uses money ethically, cares for the environment and cultivates good relations with others can become an instrument for peace. Furthermore, when churches work in a united way for peace, their witness becomes more credible (John 17:21).

For Peace in the Community

So that all may live free from fear. (Micah 4:4)

"What does the Lord require of you but to do justice, and to love kindness…?"
"Love your neighbor as yourself." "Pray for those who persecute
you." (Micah 6:8; Luke 10:27; Matthew 5:44)

30 Global challenges. All too many communities are divided by economic class, by race, color and caste, by religion and gender. Homes and schools are plagued by violence and abuse. Women and children are violated physically, psychologically and by cultural practice. Drug and alcohol abuse and suicide are forms of self-destruction on a large scale. Workplaces and houses of worship are scarred by conflicts within the community. Prejudice and racism deny human dignity. Workers are exploited and industries pollute the environment. Health care is inaccessible for many and affordable for only a few. There is a widening gap between the rich and the poor. Traditions that bind communities together are weakened by commercial influences and imported lifestyles. Media, games and entertainment that promote violence, war and pornography distort community values and invite destructive behaviors. When violence occurs, young males will generally be perpetrators as well as victims and women and children will find themselves at greatest risk.

31 Main directions. Churches become builders of a culture of peace as they engage, cooperate and learn from one another. Members, families, parishes and communities will be involved. The tasks include learning to prevent conflicts and transform them; to protect and empower those who are marginalized; to affirm the role of women in resolving conflict and building peace and include them in all such initiatives; to support and participate in nonviolent movements for justice and human rights; and to give peace education its rightful place in churches and schools. A culture of peace requires churches and other faith and community groups to challenge violence wherever it happens: this concerns structural and habitual violence as well as the violence that pervades media entertainment, games and music. Cultures of peace are realized when all, especially women and children, are safe from sexual violence and protected from armed conflict, when deadly weapons are banned and removed from communities, and domestic violence is addressed and stopped.

32 If churches are to be peacemakers, Christians must first strive for unity in action for peace. Congregations must unite to break the culture of silence about the violence within church life and unite to overcome habitual disunity in the face of the violence within our communities.

For Peace with the Earth
so that life is sustained

God created the world and made it whole, offering humanity life in all its fullness. Yet sin breaks relationships between people and with the created order. Creation longs for the children of God to be stewards of life, of justice and of love. (Gen. 2:1-3; John 10:10; Romans 8:20-22)

33 Global challenges. Human beings are to respect and protect creation. But greed at many levels, self-centeredness and a belief in unlimited growth have brought exploitation and destruction on the earth and its creatures. The cries of the poor and vulnerable echo in the groans of the earth. Excessive consumption of fossil fuels and other limited resources is doing violence to people and the planet. Climate change as a consequence of human lifestyles poses a global threat to just peace. Global warming, the rise of sea levels and the increasing frequency and intensity of droughts and floods affect especially the most vulnerable populations in the world. Indigenous people are exemplary in sustainable living and, along with inhabitants of coral atolls and impoverished coastal communities, they are among those who contribute the least to global warming. Yet they are the ones who will suffer the most.

34 Main directions. To care for God's precious gift of creation and to strive for ecological justice are key principles of just peace. For Christians they are also an expression of the gospel's call to repent from wasteful use of natural resources and be converted daily. Churches and their members must be cautious with earth's resources, especially with water. We must protect the populations most vulnerable to climate change and help to secure their rights. 35 Church members and parishes around the world must self-critically assess their environmental impact. Individually and in communities, Christians need to learn to live in ways that allow the entire earth to thrive. Many more "eco-congregations" and "green" churches are needed locally. Much ecumenical advocacy is needed globally for the implementation of international agreements and protocols among governments and businesses in order to ensure a more inhabitable earth not only for us but also for all creatures and for future generations.

For Peace in the Marketplace

so that all may live with dignity

In wondrously creating a world with more than enough natural riches to support countless generations of human beings and other living things, God makes manifest a vision for all people to live in fullness of life and with dignity, regardless of class, gender, religion, race or ethnicity. (Ps. 24:1; Ps. 145:15; Isaiah 65:17-23)

36 Global challenges. Even as tiny global elites accumulate unimaginable wealth, more than 1.4 billion humans subsist in extreme poverty. There is something profoundly wrong when the wealth of the world's three richest individuals is greater than the gross domestic product of the world's 48 poorest countries. Ineffective regulation, innovative but immoral financial instruments, distorted reward structures and other systemic factors exacerbated by greed trigger global financial crises that wipe out millions of jobs and impoverish tens of millions of people. The widening socio-economic chasms within and between nations raise serious questions about the effectiveness of market-oriented economic liberalization policies in eradicating poverty and challenge the pursuit of growth as an overriding objective for any society. Over-consumption and deprivation are forms of violence. Global military expenditures—now higher than during the Cold War—do little to enhance international peace and security and much to endanger it; weapons do not address the main threats to humanity but use vast resources that could be rededicated to that end. Such disparities pose fundamental challenges to justice, social cohesion and the public good within what has become a global human community.

37 Main directions. Peace in the marketplace is nurtured by creating "economies of life." Their essential foundations are equitable socio-economic relationships, respect for workers rights, the just sharing and sustainable use of resources, healthy and affordable food for all, and broad participation in economic decision-making.

38 Churches and their partners in society must advocate for the full implementation of economic, social and cultural rights. Churches must promote alternative economic policies for sustainable production and consumption, redistributive growth, fair taxes, fair trade, and the universal provisioning of clean water, clean air and other common goods. Regulatory structures and policies must reconnect finance not only to economic production but also to human need and ecological sustainability. Deep cuts in military spending should be made in order to fund programs that advance the goals of sufficient food, shelter, education and health for all people and that provide remedies for climate change. Human and ecological security must become a greater economic priority than national security.

For Peace among the Peoples
so that human lives are protected

We are made in the image of the Giver of Life, forbidden to take life, and charged to love even enemies. Judged with equity by a righteous God, nations are called to embrace truth in the public square, turn weapons into farm implements, and not learn war any more. (Exodus 20:17; Isaiah 2:1-4; Matthew 5:44)

39 Global challenges. Human history is illuminated by courageous pursuits of peace and the transformation of conflict, advances in the rule of law, new norms and treaties that govern the use of force, and now judicial recourse against abuses of power that involve even heads of state. History is stained, however, by the moral and political opposites of these—including xenophobia, intercommunal violence, hate crimes, war crimes, slavery, genocide and more. Although the spirit and logic of violence is deeply rooted in human history, the consequences of such sins have increased exponentially in recent times, amplified by violent applications of science, technology and wealth.

40 A new ecumenical agenda for peace today is even more urgent because of the nature and the scope of such dangers now. We are witnesses to prodigious increases in the human capacity to destroy life and its foundations. The scale of the threat, the collective human responsibility behind it, and the need for a concerted global response are without precedent. Two threats of this magnitude—nuclear holocaust and climate change—could destroy much life and all prospects for Just Peace. Both are violent misuses of the energy inherent in Creation. One catastrophe stems from the proliferation of weapons, especially *weapons of mass destruction*; the other threat may be understood as the proliferation of *lifestyles of mass extinction*. The international community struggles to gain control of both threats with little success.

41 Main directions. To respect the sanctity of life and build peace among peoples, churches must work to strengthen international human rights law as well as treaties and instruments of mutual accountability and conflict resolution. To prevent deadly conflicts and mass killings, the proliferation of small arms and weapons of war must be stopped and reversed. Churches must build trust and collaborate with other communities of faith and people of different worldviews to reduce national capacities for waging war, eliminate weapons that put humanity and the planet at unprecedented risk, and generally delegitimize the institution of war.

* * *

42 A people born to longing. Our home is not what it might and will be. While life in God's hands is irrepressible, peace does not yet reign. The principalities and powers, though not sovereign, still enjoy their victories, and we will be restless and broken until peace prevails. Thus our peace building will of necessity criticize, denounce, advocate, and resist as well as proclaim, empower, console, reconcile, and heal. Peacemakers will speak against and speak for, tear down and build up, lament and celebrate, grieve and rejoice. Until our longing joins our belonging in the consummation of all things in God, the work of peace will continue as the flickering of sure grace.

IX.
Continued Work since IEPC

Toward the 10th Assembly

Between the International Ecumenical Peace Convocation (IEPC) in Kingston, Jamaica and the publication of the present report, over a year has elapsed. What has happened since May 2011?

In preparing for its 2013 Assembly in Busan, Korea and beyond the Assembly, the WCC has continued its efforts to carry forward the development of a common understanding of Just Peace. This section of the IEPC Report attempts to share some important elements of this "work in progress." It contains reports and summaries of

- a second edition of the *Just Peace Companion* and its use as a resource for building ecumenical consensus on Just Peace;
- a February 2012 consultation on "Peace and Security in the Emerging Global Context" and an IEPC Reference Group meeting on follow-up;
- ongoing post-IEPC WCC programmes and projects relating to the four Convocation themes;
- Assembly Planning Committee decisions and WCC Central Committee guidelines on incorporating Just Peace into the Busan Assembly agenda.

Revised *Just Peace Companion*

A resource document, the *Just Peace Companion*, offers material from an initial (2009) draft "Ecumenical Declaration on Just Peace" and presents other biblical, theological and ethical background material, plus proposals for further exploration and examples of good practice. A second edition of the *Just Peace Companion* was published in early 2012 to incorporate key insights, reflections and experiences from the International Ecumenical Peace Convocation (IEPC) in Kingston, Jamaica.

The documentation presented in the *Companion* is meant to be used alongside the *Ecumenical Call to Just Peace*; it largely follows the structure of the *Call* and intends to provide necessary background information as well as basic biblical, theological and ethical considerations to support and unfold its basic message.

The principal changes in the new edition are as follows. A new section at the beginning of "Vision for Just Peace" (Chapter One) introduces the *Companion* as an ecumenical resource. The section outlines how the concept of Just Peace has grown out of debate and engagement for justice and peace since the earliest days of the ecumenical movement. The *Companion* locates the *Ecumenical Call to Just Peace* as a current invitation to a common journey within the long-standing ecumenical pursuit of peace.

A new Chapter Three, "Contexts of Just Peace," develops the four themes of the IEPC addressing the community, ecological, economic and political-international dimensions of peace. The completely revised chapter offers insights and discernment on how best to respond to climate change, dominant economic models, the Responsibility to Protect and mass violence.

Chapter Five, "Just Peace Practices," includes a new section based on IEPC workshops. Highlights from 21 workshops are given – from Christian-Muslim contributions to peace-building, "Healing of Memories" and "Women, Peace and Security," to "Military Spending versus the Millennium Development Goals," Christian mission under today's empires, and "Just Peace and Global Advocacy." The *Companion* ends with a select bibliography of church statements related to the concept of Just Peace.

On 30 May 2012, copies of the revised edition of the *Companion* were sent to all members of the WCC Executive Committee, Assembly Planning Committee, Reference Group on IEPC Follow-up and participants at the February 2012 Consultation on Peace and Security (see below) with an invitation to them to make the fullest possible use of it in their respective contexts.

"This revised version includes many of the insights, experiences, understanding and wisdom garnered at the IEPC on Justice and Peace," said CCIA Director Mathews George Chunakara in an accompanying letter. "It paves the way toward the 10th Assembly and will be a precious document for its preparation, enabling member churches to reflect more meaningfully about the Assembly theme as well as helping them to be involved in all aspects of Just Peace as a basic frame of reference for coherent and integrated ecumenical engagement."

Follow-up Meetings of the IEPC Reference Group

Members of the IEPC Reference Group met in Geneva, Switzerland on 9 February 2012 for a one-day consultation on "Peace and Security in the Emerging Global Context." The consultation was followed by two days of reflection and discussion by the Group on the effectiveness, impact and results of the IEPC, and on its follow-up.

The consultation provided space for much fruitful and creative thinking. This helped shape the work of the Reference Group, which at their two-day meeting reviewed the IEPC, provided guidelines for the planning process toward the Assembly and made a number of related recommendations.

The WCC General Secretary was requested to transmit the Group's report to the Assembly Planning Committee (APC) and to convey the ethos and content of its deliberations to the WCC Executive Committee meeting from 14 to 17 February 2012. The Group would then report to Central Committee in August 2012, and the end result would be included in a "Porto Alegre to Busan" report.

Consultation on "Peace and Security in the Emerging Global Context"

Presentations on the consultation theme, a history of the WCC's peace and security endeavors and the theological basis for its engagement over the years provided the impetus for rich and creative discussion among IEPC Reference Group members at this one-day consultation on 9 February 2012.

Mr Kees Nieuwerth from the Religious Society Friends (Quakers) in the Netherlands emphasized the interconnectedness of the crises – food, financial, environmental – facing the world today and highlighted "the multi-polar, shifting nature of the world, increasingly fierce competition for resources, and the growing independence of capital from political control."

A Christian response to these realities would include:

- campaigning to abolish and declare war illegal;
- intensifying the campaign to abolish weapons of mass destruction;
- strengthening the campaign against the arms trade and the proliferation of small arms; and
- reopening dialogue on the Responsibility to Protect (R2P).

The ensuing discussion focused on the need to shift the frame of reference and discourse on peace and security from its current focus on national (military) security to a focus on inter-relational safety for all human beings in interdependence with the environment and the economy. Similarly, the concept of food security also needed a new reference framework that included the right to food and the principle of shared food sovereignty, the consultation said. In regard to the R2P, the consultation called for greater emphasis on early warnings of potential conflict and on the foreign policies, manufacture and arms sales of nations not directly involved in the conflicts.

With war an ever-present reality and the growing influence today of the military-industrial complex over economic, political and even spiritual life, former WCC Commission of the Churches on International Affairs (CCIA) Director, Mr Dwain Epps, suggested that past ecumenical statements and actions held important lessons for contemporary efforts to outlaw and abolish war.

Beginning from the 1937 World Conference on Church and Society which rewrote sections of the UN charter on peaceful democratic relations, Epps' review of the WCC's peace and security endeavors highlighted the Council's contribution to building international institutions.

The Fourth WCC Assembly in Uppsala, Sweden in 1968 had reflected on the war in Vietnam, the Cold War and East-West tensions, the civil rights struggle in the US and student rebellions in Europe. New WCC programmes had been created after Uppsala and CCIA had become less diplomatic and more action-oriented, addressing the militarization of Latin American countries for example, Epps reported.

The 1974 Central Committee had begun to link human rights and economic and ecological threats to peace, and had dealt with them in an inter-related fashion from that time on. Consultations on human rights over the following decade had led to work on militarization and disarmament, which had then fed into the WCC's 1983 Vancouver Assembly.

While the churches' public statements had only the weight of their inherent wisdom, their influence had nevertheless been considerable, Epps judged. If the churches act together, changes are possible.

The discussion following this presentation noted that basic presuppositions had changed and that little of the ecumenical movement's early vision could be translated into the contemporary context. The consultation noted that while the WCC and the ecumenical movement had helped in the creation of the UN and its bodies, these had changed over time. Multilateralism was a threat and some bodies were taking decisions that should be taken by the UN. Reforms had not delivered. So, while the ecumenical movement continued to support the UN, it needed to see what could be done on security issues; a new chapter needed to be opened.

The third consultation speaker, former WCC General Secretary Rev. Dr Konrad Raiser, presented several theses on the understanding and praxis of peace, of security and of justice. These built on theological and ethical reflection in the context of preparing the "Ecumenical Call to Just Peace" (ECJP) and presented in more developed form in the *Just Peace Companion*. Work on the "Call" had led to the conviction that the concept of "Just Peace" signalled a potential "paradigm shift" in the ecumenical approach to issues of peace, security and justice, Raiser said.

The IEPC and the ECJP had reaffirmed the long-standing ecumenical understanding that the biblical *shalom* was much more than the normal use of the word "peace". It included wholeness, sufficiency, justice, right relationships and the integrity of creation. It was nevertheless unclear to what extent this framework had been appropriated by the churches. To find out could be a task for the Busan Assembly, Raiser asserted.

On security, he affirmed that churches had made great efforts to move from concepts of national security to that of human security in sustainable communities. Security, he said, should be sought within a framework of shared and acknowledged vulnerability. Nonviolence was dependent on vulnerability; active nonviolence affirmed human dignity, broke the cycle of enmity and violence and sought to transform these into partnerships.

Reactions to this presentation included the observation that "After DOV and IEPC, if we still see a tension between justice and peace, we have not understood them." Commenting on the concept of vulnerability, consultation participants said that the key element was *who* was talking about it, and that those who were not at risk should not decide the parameters of vulnerability for those who were.

The discussion affirmed that while the purpose of the R2P had been to shift emphasis to preventive action, the debate had now moved back into intervention and regime change. "This is so much about treating the woes of someone else without looking at our own part in it. We have a long list of vulnerable countries. We know their problems. We know who is supporting them. We know who is profiting from them. If we were very serious about prevention, we would turn the picture around and fix our part of the problem – by non-violent means." The use and misuse of R2P had demonstrated the importance of working on prevention in the long term, consultation participants said.

A final paper from an International Consultation on Peace and Security in Africa held in Kigali, Rwanda on 1 February 2012 was presented by WCC/CCIA Director Dr Mathews George Chunkara. The "Kigali paper" ended with the concept of *shalom*. It argued that Article 25 of the Universal Declaration of Human Rights, which acknowledges well-being in terms of education, housing, employment, etc., was a key indicator of peace and security in today's world. Internal advocacy on these issues was needed among churches, based on ecumenical solidarity, Chunkara suggested. There was a lot each church could do; all could call their governments to greater account, and know that others were responding in their contexts.

Follow-up Meeting of the IEPC Reference Group

At the beginning of the 10-11 February 2012 meeting of the Reference Group on follow-up, a quantitative evaluation of the IEPC was shared with members of the Reference Group; the evaluation had shown appreciation for the IEPC's spiritual life, particularly the Bible studies, as well as a high level of commitment to networks among the respondents and their many creative follow-up actions.

The Group heard a report on the work of the Message Committee. The many changes proposed to the draft Message had put a great deal of pressure on the Message Committee. Its adoption by spontaneous applause had nevertheless been a clear sign of the discipline and sensitive spirit of the whole meeting.

The Group then proceeded to consider the peace agenda of the ecumenical movement beyond the Assembly as reflected in WCC programme plans. It explored Just Peace as a basic frame of reference for coherent and integrated ecumenical engagement, emphasized a strong need for contextualization, and said that Just Peace should integrate the ecological, economic and social dimensions of life.

Different non-exclusive approaches were emphasized, including

- personal conversion and morality: the search for peace in one's heart;
- mutual support and correction among and between persons and groups; and
- involvement in civil society via public witness and networking.

Further theological reflection and biblical studies were needed in order to anchor Just Peace more securely within a Trinitarian theology, the Group said. Moreover, a deeper, common understanding of the terms "justice," "peace" and "reconciliation" needed to be developed to steer away from the limited dichotomy of Just Peace as opposed to Just War.

"Greed" as the root cause of violence needed to be identified, named and exposed and this called for an interfaith approach, the Group said. It emphasized that churches and Christians needed to confess their complicity and display repentance in order to be able to move forward in a credible and coherent way and to hold governments responsible.

In its efforts to develop a methodology that might address the concerns raised and allow Christians and churches to live, grow into and practice Just Peace, the Reference Group suggested that the Assembly should be understood as an invitation on the way of a Just Peace Ethos, anticipating Just

Peace as an eschatological reality. This was a methodology that gets people inspired to approach conflict not by avoiding but by transforming it and by allowing themselves to be transformed, the Group said.

The Just Peace ethos and methodology should be used at the Assembly as an overall approach rather than as an "extra," the Group emphasized. Thus, the Assembly should:

- be dialogical and participatory rather than proclamational;
- inspire and empower;
- help delegates to get into the flow of the argument rather than just react to positions put forward;
- carefully select examples of good practice of living Just Peace;
- look for issues where social, ecological and economic dimensions come together as a joint challenge to Just Peace;
- keep Korea and the East-Asian context as the primary focus;
- make the most of the fact that the language of Just Peace communicates well in interreligious relation-building;
- show that many do just peace-making at tremendous risk and cost.

WCC Programmatic Work since the IEPC

Post-IEPC WCC programmatic work on the four Convocation themes is summarized in the following brief and non-exclusive review.

Peace in the Community

On the theme of Peace in the Community, the final IEPC Message noted "the intersection of multiple injustices and oppressions that are simultaneously at work in the lives of many" and called on churches to promote human rights and combat their abuse. "The church is called to go public with its concerns, speaking the truth beyond the walls of its own sanctuary," this part of the Message said.

According to a report to the February 2012 WCC Executive Committee meeting, there is "a constant request to continue the accompaniment of churches in their struggle for the defense of human rights and human dignity and to continue supporting and facilitating their active participation at the UN Human Rights Council."

There is also a request from partners from Asia, Latin America and Africa for the WCC to continue its capacity-building activities on defense of human rights.

Since May 2011, the WCC has actively pursued such international advocacy and capacity-building on peace and human security in a number of ways.

Indigenous Peoples

The Council organized an Indigenous Women's Global Caucus and a Global Caucus of Indigenous Peoples prior to the UN Permanent Forum on Indigenous Issues taking place in May 2011 in New York.

The WCC was present at and participated in the 18th session of the UN Human Rights Council in September 2011, providing accreditation to Indigenous people from the Amazon, organizing side events, drafting written and oral interventions and participating in the International Day of Peace organized by the UN. "The WCC continues to be a relevant stakeholder at the UN Human Rights Council, well known and respected as a credible faith–based organization by both UN officers and permanent missions," an International Affairs, Public Witness and Global Advocacy programme report noted.

Rights of migrant workers

Meeting in Kingston, Jamaica on 25-26 May 2011 just after the IEPC, the Commission of the Churches on International Affairs (WCC/CCIA) Working Group on Rights of Migrant Workers and Stateless People recommended a visit to the United Arab Emirates to assess and understand the human rights situation of migrant workers there. In September 2011, CCIA Director and Middle East Council of Churches (MECC) Justice Unit Director Ms Seta Hadeshian travelled to Dubai and Sharjah, where they visited the Sonapur labor camp in Dubai and met with representatives of different churches, church centres and NGOs and migrant workers.

Also decided by the CCIA Working Group on Rights of Migrant Workers and Stateless People in May 2011, a consultation on Rights of Stateless People was organized in Dhaka, Bangladesh in December 2011. The consultation was an opportunity to reflect on the fundamental human rights to nationality and citizenship that are denied in various countries and to evolve strategies for advocacy, especially for ratification of international instruments protecting stateless people and uprooted people in general.

Training, advocacy, solidarity visits, freedom of religion

Part of a three-year project with the European Commission, a Workshop on "Human Rights Defenders in Africa," was organized by the WCC in

Freetown, Sierra Leone in October 2011. This second human rights training workshop was designed to provide human rights training to church leaders and representatives from faith-based organizations to enhance their cooperation with local civil society actors actively involved in the field of human rights.

In January 2012, a strategic meeting in Nairobi with African partners on human rights defenders evaluated the workshops organized within this project in the DRC and Sierra Leone, identified existing challenges and explored ways of enhancing cooperation and coordination on issues related to human rights, peace and security between the different ecumenical partners at national, regional and international levels.

The Ecumenical Accompaniment Programme in Palestine and Israel (EAPPI) is another ongoing WCC-related activity to promote and protect human rights via advocacy *and* direct action. Since the IEPC, Ecumenical Accompaniers (EAs) from Argentina, Brazil, Colombia and the Philippines have joined the programme. EAPPI has increasingly strengthened cooperation with other organizations providing material such as photos, checkpoint and gate logs and EAPPI Incident Reports to other organizations and UN agencies. EAPPI organized a second lobby tour at European Union headquarters; the EU Commission was subsequently questioned on many of the subjects discussed during the tour.

A consultation on "The Christian Presence in the Middle East – Theological and Political challenges" was co-organized by the WCC with the Volos Theological Academy in Volos, Greece, in June 2011 to discuss the theological and political challenges facing Christians in Palestine and the Middle East today. Participants affirmed the importance of bridging gaps between different ecumenical families, including the need for greater dialogue among the churches in the Middle East and between Christians in the East and West.

Solidarity visits relating to human rights issues were organized to Ivory Coast, Nepal, Bangladesh and Pakistan in November - December 2011. The visits were undertaken by international ecumenical solidarity teams composed of delegates from the WCC, member churches and ecumenical organizations at the request of churches in each of the countries.

Other human rights-related events organized by the WCC after the IEPC included a conference on "Caste, Religion and Culture" in Kochi, India in April 2011, and a conference on Racism in the Experience of Afro-Descendent Communities in Latin America in Managua, Nicaragua, in June 2011.

A December 2011 International Study Consultation on "Freedom of Religion and the Rights of Religious Minorities" organized by the WCC/Commission of the Churches on International Affairs (CCIA) and hosted by the Ecumenical Patriarchate of Constantinople in Istanbul adopted a communiqué that advocated international standards of protecting religious minorities' rights to freedom of religious expression.

The last study by CCIA on the subject of freedom of religion dates back to 1981. With political developments following the cold war and the rise of religious extremism, the picture has changed considerably since then, and CCIA was seeking a mandate for further follow-up actions. A WCC statement on "freedom of religion and rights of religious minorities" is to be presented at the upcoming 10th Assembly of the WCC in Busan, Korea in 2013.

Peace with the Earth

On the theme of Peace with the Earth, the final IEPC Message made a strong connection between ecological and economic justice: "Our concern for the Earth and our concern for humanity go hand in hand. Natural resources and common goods such as water must be shared in a just and sustainable manner. We join global civil society in urging governments to reconstruct radically all our economic activities toward the goal of an ecologically sustainable economy."

Since the IEPC, WCC advocacy work at the Conference of Parties of the UN Convention on Climate Change, a Youth for Eco-Justice training programme and several consultations including Ecology and Climate conferences in India and an Ecumenical Water Network (EWN) Global Forum have highlighted this link.

A consultation of African Faith Leaders representing Christian, Muslim, Hindu, African traditional religions, Baha'i and Buddhist communities from thirty countries across Africa was organized ahead of the 17th Conference of the Parties (COP17) to the UN Framework Convention on Climate Change scheduled to take place 29 November-9 December 2011 in Durban, South Africa. The consultation drafted a strong message to world leaders, the international community and African political leaders on how to address climate change issues and negotiate with polluters to compensate African farmers and citizens.

A WCC delegation of 15 people attended COP17. The delegation brought the voices of climate change victims, organized seminars and an interfaith side event and delivered a statement at the high-level segment. Although the outcome of the UN Conference did not come up to expectations, ecumenical participation from Africa and overall interfaith advocacy were enhanced.

A Youth for Eco-Justice training programme for thirty young Christians was organized jointly during the COP17 by the WCC's Eco-Justice team and the Lutheran World Federation. Participants communicated their experiences, learnings and aspirations by posting texts, photos and videos in social media, writing articles and making themselves available for interviews. They all also developed outlines for follow-up projects in their national and local contexts.

The WCC also played an active role in the two major events that took place in Rio de Janeiro, Brazil in June 2012: a UN Conference on Sustainable Development (UNCSD, also known as Rio+20) and a People's Summit. The Council and its ecumenical partners helped build an ecumenical and interreligious platform called "Religions for Rights" at the Summit and organized a series of activities in the "Religions for Rights" tents. The platform represented more than seventy different religious expressions, churches and specialized ministries.

Near the close of Rio+20, the co-founder of Latin American liberation theology Professor Leonardo Boff joined a chorus of critics of the UN conference. "Renowned environmental scientists are saying that practically nothing happened between 1992 and 2012 in terms of public policy and global commitment," Boff observed. With WCC Central Committee Moderator Rev. Dr Walter Altmann, Boff co-chaired a People's Summit event on "the ethical and theological basis for climate justice."

Twenty-five participants and partners of the Ecumenical Water Network (EWN) gathered in Nairobi, Kenya in October 2011 for a EWN Global Forum, bringing to a conclusion a strategic development process started at the beginning of 2011. Success stories were shared, lessons identified, a common vision and mission statement was adopted, and a strategic framework including key objectives as well as a work plan for the next two years were finalized.

Sponsored by the Council for World Mission, the World Communion of Reformed Churches and the WCC, Oikotree is an ecumenical space open to people of all faiths in which a movement of those seeking to live faithfully in the midst of economic injustice and ecological destruction can take shape. An Oikotree facilitating group meeting met in November 2011 in Singapore to prepare a three-year strategic plan on eco-justice.

Poverty Wealth and Ecology hearings for North America and a Global Forum on Poverty, Wealth and Ecology in Bogor, Indonesia also made the link between ecology and economy. These consultations are summarized under "Peace in the Marketplace," below.

Peace in the Marketplace

On the theme of Peace in the Marketplace, the final IEPC Message urged churches to advocate more effectively for full implementation of economic, social and cultural rights as the foundation for "economies of life" and address more effectively irresponsible concentration of power and wealth as well as the disease of corruption.

Decent work

"Decent work" in the context of a values-based response to globalization was at the core of an April 2011 international inter-religious seminar hosted by the WCC and co-organized with the International Labour Organization (ILO) in partnership with the Islamic Educational, Scientific and Cultural Organization (ISESCO), the Pontifical Council for Justice and Peace and Globethics.net.

Working toward a goal of preserving human dignity, eradicating poverty and promoting peace and social justice, the seminar looked at spiritual teachings and doctrines in order to develop ethics and convergences relating to decent work. Participants identified convergences between Christian, Muslim, Jewish and Buddhist religious traditions and the ILO agenda to guarantee decent work for all.

The seminar was the first in a series on inter-religious perspectives on decent work organized by the ILO in different regions of the world ; a second ILO-WCC workshop was held in Dakar, Senegal in December 2011.

A joint ILO-WCC Policy handbook entitled *Convergences: Decent Work and Social Justice in Religious Traditions* was published in 2011. The handbook explains the commitments of various religious traditions, showing that spiritual values are essential in the quest for fair globalization. In the book, the WCC and ILO encourage policy-makers to work with faith communities for social protection and security for all, especially in the area of labour.

Eco-justice

A Global Forum on Poverty, Wealth and Ecology was organized by the WCC in Bogor, Indonesia in June 2012. With more than one hundred participants from around the world, the forum concluded with a strong "Call for Action" to evolve "transformative congregations" with the moral courage to build an "economy of life" that focuses on eradicating poverty, challenging wealth accumulation and safeguarding ecological integrity.

The Call for Action is an outcome of the WCC's 2007-2011 AGAPE (Alternative to Economic Globalization Addressing Peoples and Earth) study process. The Call points out that "greed and injustice" are the root causes of the intertwined economic and ecological crises, and goes on to say that the "crisis is therefore a deep moral and existential one. The challenges ... are not first and foremost technological and financial, but ethical and spiritual."

Addressing the Forum, Rev. Dr Konrad Raiser, former General Secretary of the WCC shared results of an AGAPE "Greed Line Study Group," and said that "Institutionalized greed with structural consequences demands counter measures at the structural level if we are to overcome pressing problems of poverty, socio-economic disparities and ecological destruction."

Events relating to eco-justice organized by the WCC *ahead* of the June 2012 Forum in Indonesia included

- a small meeting of economists, sociologists and theologians in Crete in March 2011 to discuss conceptual and methodological approaches to developing a "wealth/greed line" as a counterpart to "poverty line" indices;
- a meeting of experts co-organized with the All Africa Conference of Churches in Nairobi, Kenya in June 2011 to discuss a research proposal on European Union and Chinese investments in Africa and how they address poverty eradication and ecology; and
- November 2011 Poverty Wealth and Ecology hearings for North America in Calgary, Canada, focusing on the extraction of tar oil sands in Canada. After hearing testimonies on issues of social, financial, migrant labour, Indigenous and climate justice, the hearings participants issued a call to action that ends with the injunction: "It is the 11th hour. Make haste. The cry of Earth and the cry of the poor are one."

Peace among the Peoples

On the theme of Peace among the Peoples, the final IEPC Message signaled that commitment to Just Peace "requires moving from exclusive concepts of national security to safety for all. This includes a day-to-day responsibility to prevent, that is, to avoid violence at its root."

Peace and human security

The post-IEPC programme thrusts of the Commission of the Churches on International Affairs (CCIA) have emphasized peace and human security, which covers areas related to increasing militarization, the arms race, widespread proliferation of small arms which intensifies ethnic and political violence; human trafficking, forced migration and statelessness. Responding to conflict situations and accompanying churches was also an area on which CCIA concentrated during the period. A series of consultations on peace and human security in the emerging geo-political context were organized with regional foci on Asia in Bangkok, Thailand (August 2011), Africa in Kigali, Rwanda (January 2012), and Latin America in Antigua, Guatemala (November–December 2012). A fourth in the series with a focus on peace and human security in Europe is scheduled to take place in the Balkans in early 2013. These regional consultations focused on the deteriorating situation of human rights, democratic governance, rule of law, border conflicts, a growing trend of religious intolerance, freedom of religion and rights of migrant workers and of Indigenous peoples, privatization of security and military forces, etc. Priority issues and countries were identified for ecumenical engagements to accompany churches in conflict situations.

The "day-to-day responsibility to prevent, that is, to avoid violence at its root" invoked in the IEPC Message led the CCIA to organize several consultations and team visits to promote Just Peace after the IEPC. Among them were:

- An April 2011 meeting of the South Asia Ecumenical Forum on Peace and Security (SAEFPS) attended by national councils of churches general secretaries and selected WCC Central Committee members from six South Asian countries. The main focus of this meeting was on accompanying churches in conflict situations and advocacy strategies and initiatives on such issues as misuse of blasphemy laws in Pakistan, and freedom of religion and religious intolerance that threatens peace and security in all South Asian countries.

- A meeting of the working group of the Ecumenical Forum on Peace, Security and Development on the Korean Peninsula in June 2011 at which issues related to North and South Korea peace talks, de-nuclearization and ecumenical responses were discussed.

- An international ecumenical consultation on peace and reconciliation in Myanmar in which Nobel Peace prize laureate Aung Saan Su Kyi also participated. Since November 2010 elections, Myanmar is slowly evolving toward more democracy, but new conflict situations had erupted after a cease-fire in Kachin State broke down in June 2011 and ethnic violence erupted in Rakhaine state. Several thousands were displaced and faced serious food insecurity as well as disease as a result. Advocacy and ecumenical engagement for peace and reconciliation were discussed for follow-up at the global level.

- A meeting of the Strategy Group of the Sudan Ecumenical Forum at the All-Africa Conference of Churches headquarters in Nairobi, Kenya, discussed outstanding issues including the Abyei referendum situation and the popular consultation of South Kordofan and Blue Nile States before the declaration of independence on 9 July 2011. Ecumenical efforts to limit and eliminate certain lethal weapons have an impact that is measured mostly via treaties and their enforcement. Following the IEPC, the WCC has continued to work on building an ecumenical campaign and lobby for the Arms Trade Treaty (ATT) and on anti-nuclear advocacy strategy. The ATT ecumenical campaign led by the WCC provided a focal point, experience in advocacy and the strength in numbers needed to make an impact on how this issue would be settled. With governments unable to reach agreement on international regulation of arms exports, the adoption of the global treaty was called off after four weeks of negotiations at the UN Conference. Expressing concern for "people and communities waiting for protection from the unregulated arms trade," a WCC statement affirmed that "For decades, churches around the world have been calling for an Arms Trade Treaty that would protect people from irresponsible arms transfers. We will not let go of this demand."

- A regional consultation in Africa on "Proliferation of Small Arms and Light Weapons" was organized in Addis Ababa, Ethiopia in November 2012. It urged African churches to be equipped for ecumenical advocacy on the proliferation of small arms.

- Ecumenical solidarity visits to conflict-affected areas and situations were organized with a message of peace and reconciliation. These visits included countries such as Nigeria, Sudan, South Sudan, Ivory Cost, Liberia and Malawi in Africa; Sri Lanka, Myanmar and Cambodia in Asia; Guatemala in Latin America.

- As part of strengthening inter-religious relations, the WCC General Secretary visited conflict-affected situations, communities and regions in countries such as Pakistan, Nigeria, Indonesia, Lebanon, Palestine and Israel. A November 2011 WCC workshop in Edinburgh, Scotland afforded partners from Europe, the Middle East, Africa and Asia with an opportunity to discuss nuclear strategy and advocacy. And the WCC urged a May 2012 NATO summit in Chicago to "lead by example" and withdraw NATO nuclear weapons still deployed in Europe more than two decades after the close of the cold war.

Assembly Planning Committee Decisions and Central Committee Guidelines

The theme of the next, 10th Assembly of the WCC in Busan, South Korea from 30 October to 8 November 2013 is "God of Life, lead us to justice and peace."

Meeting in Geneva in July 2012, the Assembly Planning Committee (APC) addressed a request to the WCC Central Committee, due to meet from 28 August to 5 September 2012, that it "confirm that the Assembly be prepared so as to encourage discernment on what it means to be the church together in the world today as a witness to justice and peace for all creation."

The APC saw Bible study at the Assembly as "a space to experience fellowship and transformation on the common journey with the God of life toward justice and peace and the promise of abundant life for all." Texts for daily Bible study should thus "focus on moments in biblical history where life was threatened, yet justice and peace prevailed, through God's grace," the APC suggested.

Along with the Theme Plenary session itself, other Assembly Plenaries should also be designed around the theme of justice and peace, the APC said. The Asia plenary, for example "should focus on the assembly theme as it is understood within Asia, i.e., the urgency of the theme in view of the struggles for life, justice and peace and the religious plurality of Asia."

The current Assembly plan envisages twin plenaries on Justice and on Peace. These "should be closely inter-related," the APC said, thus seeking to carry forward the IEPC vision of an intrinsic link between the two. "The two plenaries should be prepared in such a way that they mutually address the challenges of injustices, i.e., economic, ecological, gender and racial injustices that threaten peace and life for all God's creation. The titles of the two plenaries should reflect this inter-relatedness." Furthermore, they "should not only present what has been done but present possible ways forward."

As is customary, the Assembly will be preceded by a number of pre-assemblies – for women, youth, the Ecumenical Disabilities Advocates' Network (EDAN) and Indigenous Peoples. An important objective of the EDAN Pre-Assembly is to "challenge the churches to take action in advocating for the full participation of people with disabilities"; for the Indigenous Peoples Pre-Assembly, a key objective is to "Give visibility to the struggles of Indigenous Peoples for justice and rights, and against displacement and dispossession with a view to facilitate global solidarity," the APC said.

The concept of Just Peace was amply addressed during the meeting of the WCC Central Committee that took place from 29 August to 5 September 2012 in Crete. Indeed the tone was immediately set with a substantial part of General Secretary Rev. Dr Olav Fykse Tveit's report being devoted to this theme.

The IEPC Reference Group on IEPC follow-up had requested that calls and contributions to Just Peace become "a bloodstream running through the whole Assembly and the work we do now and in the future as a Council," the General Secretary reported.

The IEPC itself had provided "ample material for the Council to give leadership in ecumenical contributions to justice and peace," he noted. This assessment was confirmed by the Central Committee's Programme Committee's decision to designate the major documents of the Convocation – the *Ecumenical Call to Just Peace*, the *IEPC Message* and the *Just Peace Companion* as preparatory material for all Assembly delegates.

The IEPC's wider understanding of peace was "clearly expressed through focus on the four realms: peace among the peoples, peace in the marketplace, peace with the earth and peace in the communities," Fykse Tveit noted. Yet, in the absence of "a settled terminology of Just Peace," "different ways of expressing the proper interrelation between justice and peace" were still needed, and those who might listen for guidance in difficult processes of decision-making in conflict situations should be offered arguments and principles that can be used and made operational in such situations.

Fykse Tveit cautioned that "We should avoid developing a counter-concept to the concept of just war [...]; we should aim at something more." The danger of the "just war" paradigm being used to legitimate the use of military means without taking moral and political criteria into consideration was a very real one, he warned.

Further, "The concepts of international law have, to some extent, been [...] used by the powerful to claim their 'rights' to control or colonize other territories." We should thus "avoid a new concept that can easily (and wrongly) be understood as a reflection of imperial language." The term of "Just Peace" must be given its "proper and dynamic meaning" and be made "a reality for those who need peace so desperately," he said. The Assembly will be a privileged opportunity to pursue conceptual and contextual reflection on this theme.

Encouraging continued reflection, the Central Committee mandated the Commission of the Churches in International Affairs (CCIA) to prepare a statement on Just Peace for consideration at the Assembly as part of the its public issues actions.

Thus, the WCC continues to work with the ethos and tenets of the DOV and IEPC as it goes toward the Assembly and beyond, ensuring their enduring impact on the life, mission and witness of the World Council of Churches.

Bible Study Groups

Workshops

Theology, Mission Peace

A World without Nuclear Weapons

A workshop led by Dr Samuel Lee at the IEPC, with Dr Mathews George Chunakara (WCC), Bishop Dr Martin Schindehütte (EKD), Vakhtang V. Kipshidze (Russian Orthodox Church)

Plenary Peace among People

Panel discussion from left: Moderator Rev. Kjell Magne Bondevik, Norway; Dr Christiane Agboton-Johnson, Senegal/Benin; Archbishop Avak Vazken Asadourian, Iraq

Left: Prof. Lisa Schirch, USA Iraq during panel discussion. Center: Dr Patricia Lewis, UK/Ireland. Right: Dr Christiane Agboton-Johnson, Senegal/Benin

WCC president Rev. Dr Ofelia Ortega, Cuba and former bishop of Lübeck Bärbel Wattenberg-Potter dance to the sound of Bethel Steel Orchestra

Peace Concert at Emancipation Park

Peace Concert in the Emancipation Park in Downtown Kingston

Peace Concert in the Emancipation Park in Downtown Kingston

Untraditional launch of a new book by the WCSF and WCC "When Pastors and Priests Pra(e)y" lead by Dr Valli Batchelor

Closing Plenary

Left: Ms Derri Ann Palmer, Jamaica. Center: Simone Poortman, Netherlands, Ecumenical Disability Advocates Network (EDAN). Right: Prof. Dr Fernando Enns, moderator of the Decade to Overcome Violence reference group

Left: Ms Kanan Kitani, Japan. Center: Prof. Dr Heinrich Bredford-Strohm, Germany. Right: Bp Ivan Manuel Abrahams, S. Africa

Conference participants line-up with suggestions and proposals for amendments to the message

Stewards

Kingston, Jamaica, May 24, 2011. International Ecumenical Peace Convocation "Glory to God and Peace on Earth". Stewards

Closing Plenary

Metropolitan Prof. Dr Gennadios of Sassima

Rev. Dr Olav Fykse Tveit, WCC General Secretary

Sanna Eriksson, Church of Sweden, spoke on behalf of the young IEPC participants at the closing plenary. "We rejoice that young people participated in this meeting in a wide variety of roles," she said. "We thank those churches and organizations who sent young people as their representatives."

IEPC Closing Plenary

WCC moderator Rev. Dr Walter Altmann receives a gift from the Jamaica Council of Churches, as WCC general secretary Rev. Dr Olav Fykse Tveit looks on

Appendices

Appendix 1. Pre-IEPC Visits in Jamaica

The International Ecumenical Peace Convocation (IEPC) formally opened on Tuesday 17 May 2012 in Kingston, Jamaica, as some 1,000 participants from more than 100 countries gathered together on the Mona campus of the University of the West Indies.

Ecumenical Delegation's Visit

Before the official opening and following a Saturday 14 May 2012 meeting of the WCC officers, an ecumenical delegation representing WCC churches and church councils visited Kingston in coordination with the Jamaica Council of Churches (JCC) and the Caribbean Conference of Churches (CCC). During their two-day (15-16 May) visit, the delegation met with several public officials. The delegation was led by the WCC General Secretary Rev. Dr Olav Fykse Tveit.

The aim was to gain insight into the realities of life in Jamaica, particularly in relation to violence and, at the same time, to highlight the need to work in partnership with the churches in order to build a culture of just peace at all levels.

Accompanying Rev. Dr Fykse Tveit were: Rev. Dr Walter Altmann, Moderator of the WCC Central Committee; Metropolitan Prof. Dr Gennadios of Sassima (Limouris), Vice Moderator of the WCC Central Committee; Rev. Dr Margaretha Hendriks-Ririmasse, Vice Moderator of the WCC Central Committee; Mr Gerard Granado, General Secretary of the CCC; Dr. Oluwakemi Linda Banks, member of the IEPC Planning Committee and President of the CCC; Rev. Gary Harriott, General Secretary of the JCC; Rev. Garland Pierce, Senior Assistant to the General Secretary and Rev. Carlos Ham, WCC Programme Executive for Latin America & Caribbean.

On 14 May, part of the delegation attended Sunday worship at the Webster Memorial United Church, where Rev. Dr. Fykse Tveit preached on the theme, *The Church: God's Missional Community*, based on Romans 14.

Ecumenical Delegation Meets Government Officials

An intensive programme of visits with government officials in Kingston began on Monday 15 May. The purpose was threefold: to meet and greet the Jamaican authorities, announce the presence of WCC and CCC leadership in Jamaica, introduce the officials to the IEPC and invite them to participate.

The programme began with a visit to Jamaica's Prime Minister, the Honourable Bruce Golding, who welcomed the delegation to the country. The delegation shared information on IEPC preparations and thanked the churches, people and government of Jamaica for their support to holding the Convocation on the island. An interesting discussion took place on the notion of just peace in Jamaica, in the Caribbean and globally.

The next visit was to His Excellency, the Most Honourable Sir Patrick Allen, Governor General of Jamaica. A committed Seventh-day Adventist, Allen also reflected – among other topics – on the role of Jamaica's churches, which have been ecumenically promoting a culture of peace in the midst of a spiral of violence.

After the visit to the Governor General, the delegation met with the Leader of the Parliamentary Opposition and former Prime Minister, the Most Honourable Portia Simpson-Miller. The country's first woman Prime Minister, Simpson-Miller mentioned that Jamaica's churches are playing an active role in attempting to overcome violence, in partnership with the Violence Prevention Alliance (VPA).

After laying a wreath at a shrine dedicated to children who died traumatically or violently, the delegation met with the Honourable Zaila McCalla, Chief Justice of Jamaica, who shared information on the work of the judiciary in facing crimes, restoring justice and working toward the prevention of corruption and wrongdoing.

The WCC General Secretary presented packages of IEPC material to each leader.

A dinner offered by the WCC General Secretary to the CCC officers ended the delegation's programme on Tuesday 16 May. Other dinner guests included CCC Presidium President, Rev. Dr Lesley Anderson, and CCC Associate General Secretary, Ms Allison Bidaisee.

The visit provided an excellent opportunity for members of both church councils to get to know each other, and their respective programmes, better as well as to strengthen historical ties. The meetings with public officials before the Convocation were felt by both sides to be a great privilege and a strongly positive experience.

Local Initiatives Visited by IEPC Participants

The following projects opened their doors to IEPC participants on the morning of 17 May 2012.

Agency for Inner-City Renewal

The Trench Town-based Agency for Inner-City Renewal (AIR) is a non-governmental organization run by business consultant, pastor and self-described "social entrepreneur" Dr Henley Morgan. It brings the promise of sustained economic activity to depressed Trench Town and its neighbours.

Area Youth Foundation

The Area Youth Foundation use the arts, drama and culture to change the lives of young people and to build bridges of friendship between the divided, marginalized communities of Kingston. Presentations in many counties have showcased this docu-drama approach, successful in turning around high-risk youth.

Boys' Town

Boys' Town is a multi-service faith-based complex embracing education from early childhood to all age levels, sports clubs, and certified youth skills training centre and social centre activities. In its 15-18 Youth Development Programme, Boys' Town uses personal development and life skills programmes (sports, music & culture); communication skills (including remedial education); skills development; mentoring and computer literacy to engage at-risk inner-city youth.

Children's First

Children's First is a unique community organization providing life-changing programmes for children and adolescents. Children's First is internationally recognized for its creative participatory approach building resilience by a long-term developmental process that involves integration of neighbouring schools, mental health services, church and community organizations.

Programme development is guided by the children at every level of the organization's approach to community outreach.

Child Resiliency

Child Resiliency is an outreach programme of the Hope United Church. It is a collaborative effort between the church, schools, families and health services in order to build a broad network of protection for Jamaica's young people. It seeks to meet the needs of pre-adolescents and build on their

competencies as the most effective strategy for preventing multiple problems and school dropouts. It also focuses on promoting physical, social, cog-
nitive, vocational and moral competence.

City Mission

City Mission wants to remind people that despite the challenges around
them, God is in their midst and can take them through all these challenges.
Many church members still suffer from residual trauma and require support; congregations focus on bringing healing to communities by offering
hope amid the pall of death, destruction and despair.

C-SALT

C-Salt teaches boys life-skills through sports and community service, workshops and summer camps. C-SALT partners with parents, schools and communities to help to develop the whole boy, spiritually, physically, mentally
and socially to become an ethical and compassionate servant-leader.

Dispute Resolution Foundation

Dispute Resolution Foundation aims to achieve nonviolent relationships
between citizens, corporations and other organizations within a democratic
and restorative justice framework, by strengthening and expanding the use
of mediation and other effective methods of preventing and resolving disputes. Located in Trench Town, this centre offers "walk-in" peace-building
and mediation services to community residents.

Grace and Staff

Grace and Staff has provided educational and financial assistance for children in need for the past 31 years. The foundation has also initiated a number of projects including job shadowing, outreach work to gang members
and other high-risk youth, parenting education, school fee support and
homework centres. Financial sustainability is ensured by worker contributions matched with company donations.

Grants Pen Community Consultative Committee

Grants Pen Community Consultative Committee is a ministers' fraternal
which along with other community stakeholders, teachers and businessmen
coordinate activities to cater to disadvantaged youth. Community pastoring
activities include church lunches, football games and dances. These activities have helped secure community-wide involvement in the peace-building
process.

Holy Networks

Reaching out to window-washer children from the juvenile court, their mission is youth empowerment, violence prevention and the promotion of healthy lifestyle choices through arts-based, spiritual and remedial educational activities. It aims to provide youths from inner-city Kingston with social and life skills, to effect attitudinal and behavioural change and impart useful skills - in particular literacy - which enhance opportunities for employment and healthy living.

Hope for Children

Hope for Children Development Company (HCDC) promotes the well-being of children and families in extremely difficult circumstances in three politically polarized Kingston inner-city communities. The primary activities include: institutional capacity-building of grassroot groups and organizations; parenting training and family support services; public education and awareness; child rights advocacy; education and training; leadership training; violence mitigation interventions and community governance. Hope for Children works in partnership with over fifty community-based formal and informal organizations.

Jones Town

The Jones Town community plans to turn dusty unoccupied land into vegetable gardens in keeping with the idea of eating what you grow. The project's goals include providing employment, lessening poverty and encouraging self-development in Jones Town. The programme includes Life/Survival Skills Training, and Environmental Awareness Management.

Joy Town

The Covenant Community Church (CCC) is a group of five churches born out of the Deeper Life/Charismatic Renewal Movement of the 1970's and early 1980s which has produced several charismatic churches in Jamaica over the last three decades. These churches are currently active in outreach to inner city youth.

KYMCA

This street boy programme uses mentorship, remedial education, sports and leadership training to change the lives of these high-risk youth. The programme builds values of caring, honesty, respect and responsibility. It promotes the equality of opportunity for all members of the community, regardless of age, race, gender, religion, ability or economic circumstances.

Mel Nathan Institute

Providing holistic education and community empowerment, the Mel Nathan Institute is a human and community development agency of the United Church in Jamaica and the Cayman Islands. Community leaders are encouraged and enabled to take a hold of their lives so that they, in turn, can influence others to become agents of change and development.

Missionaries of the Poor

Missionaries of the Poor centres span four countries: Jamaica, Philippines, Uganda and Haiti. In Jamaica, the mission is to bring hope and peace to the most disadvantaged members of the inner-city community. The ministry is guided by music and musical productions which are a highlight of the Jamaican calendar.

Mona Baptist Church's Help Ministry

Mona Baptist Church's Help Ministry is serving the spiritual, physical, emotional, educational and economic needs of many communities. The outreach gives particular support to those who are weak, sick, poor, and disenfranchised. The men's programme targets the most-at-risk-groups in the communities, including drug-users.

Mustard Seed Community

Mustard Seed Communities operate 14 residential homes in Jamaica, Dominican Republic, Nicaragua and Zimbabwe, caring for over 500 children with varying degrees of disability, many abandoned and some affected with HIV and AIDS. Situated in impoverished, violence-prone, marginalized inner-city communities of Kingston, St Andrew and St Catherine, MSC seeks to empower and uplift community residents through the application of caring capital practiced with the children. The main ingredients of the outreach strategy include, for example, education in Little Angels Basic schools, introduction to computerization through Zinc Link Internet Cafes, material support for "golden agers" and positive message-building through the community radio station ROOTS FM. Frequent community governance consultations involving CBOs and shareholders in partnerships lead to the adoption of a communications strategy through ROOTS FM interactive on-air panel discussions and outside broadcasts that publicize how communities overcome challenges, including violence prevention, thereby learning from each other.

Park Lane

Spearheaded by the Bethel Baptist outreach ministry, Park Lane seeks to provide jobs, skills, education, financial help, housing and spiritual uplifting to the community torn apart by violence. The opening of a new Skill Training Centre will become a focus for skills training, on-line literacy, homework classes, sporting activates, social support, counselling and conflict resolution classes. Special outreach to meet the spiritual needs of the community continues with weekly Sunday School, Vacation Bible School, Prayer and Counselling as needed.

Pentecostal Assembly Rehboth

Pentecostal Assembly Rehboth offers a Community Good News Club programme aiming to evangelize, disciple and introduce children to church. Members of the church volunteer as outreach teachers, helpers and prayer partners. Good News Clubs meet once a week in neighbourhoods, homes, community buildings or churches. A Child Evangelism Fellowship (CEF) provides training for all club volunteers, teaching materials, mentoring encouragement and staff support. The church finances the club, snacks/refreshments, follow-up of children/families, and a church home for children.

Sistren Theatre Collective

Sistren Theatre Collective uses the creative arts as a tool of analysis and action to interrogate and implement its work nationally and internationally. SISTREN operates a multi-faceted popular education programme and a participatory approach to learning with students in schools, youth groups in schools and communities, parents, community-based organizations and unattached male youth. The organization provides psychosocial services for students in nine public schools within the Kingston Metropolitan Region, facilitates street theatre productions including Tek it to Dem gender-based violence prevention project.

Stella Maris Foundation

Stella Maris Foundation of the Stella Maris Roman Catholic Church "seeks to promote goodwill and secure sustainable social and economic development within the community by means of skills training and social programmes." Training programmes encompass counselling, life skills, leadership, parenting, grooming and etiquette and conflict resolution designed to enable them to function as complete productive citizens.

St Andrew Settlement

A community-based facility operated by the Anglican Church in an inner city community, the centre offers counselling, sporting and educational activities. Community support covers a range of programmes including housing support.

St Patrick's Foundation

The Foundation's mission is to impart relevant skills, offer opportunity and care to residents of the low-income communities served. This is an effort to enable the social and economic advancement of the beneficiaries, while providing a high sense of fulfilment on the part of those rendering the service.

The Nest

Th Nest is the home for the Salvation Army School for the Blind. The project visit will allow for community participation and opportunity to gain an insight to the challenges offered by violence and proposed solutions.

University Township Project

University Township Project seeks to foster a more symbiotic relationship between the University of the West Indies (UWI) and the community. This initiative has seen members of the August Town community benefitting from programmes in education, skills training, health and nutrition, culture and sports, economic development, as well as violence and crime reduction and prevention.

Whole Life Sports

Whole Life Sports offers Christian development, career guidance and skills upgrade referral and youth advocacy training through sports. The Whole Life Sports mandate is to be a catalyst for transformation and metamorphosis that is not confined to the spiritual but includes the overall belief in man's strengths. This transformation aims to reach not only the individual's home but his family, his community and, ultimately, the nation.

Woman Inc

Woman Inc provides a Crisis Centre, a 24-hour Hotline and a shelter for abused women and their children. Woman Inc advocates for women's human rights, peaceful families and communities, ending impunity through public education and legal reform, campaigns and projects. Issues of violence against women, human trafficking, gender-based violence and HIV AIDS are also addressed by this NGO at the local, regional and global level.

Women's Centre of Jamaica

Providing outreach to teenage mothers and their parents, this is a highly successful good practice programme achieving a high level of reintegration into high school and a low level of repeat pregnancy. The fathers' programme is a new addition that has shown tremendous results.

Youth Reaching Youth

Youth Reaching Youth empowers a team of youths, teaching them what they need to know to cope with their life at their stage and in the future. Visiting other youngsters, the peer counsellors distribute pamphlets and manuals on issues surrounding youths. They also use dance, drama, dub poetry and other creative expressions to get across their message to youth who are often non-Christians.

Appendix 2. Participants' Comments on the Message

Because of space limitations, Convocation participants were encouraged to contribute comments and recommendations that could appear as an appendix to the Message. Unlike the Message, the following comments were not endorsed by the Convocation as a whole.

The following collection of material, from individuals, small groups and larger discussion groups that met during the IEPC serves as a reflection of the many written contributions that were received by the Message Committee before the final day of the gathering in Jamaica. In some cases, two or more similar comments have been combined editorially.

Comments are divided into categories representing the four subthemes, followed by more general contributions on the IEPC content in general.

Peace in the Community

1. From a group of younger participants: "We commit ourselves to continue exploring and implementing different, creative ways of violence prevention, conflict transformation and peace-building at every level."

2. Peace begins with the way we treat children. Prohibiting and eliminating all forms of violence against children, including corporal punishment, is a key strategy toward preventing violence and establishing peace.

3. Empower women to participate in peace-making. Women often have the most profound insight into local situations and embody peace-making strategies of hospitality and collaborative resistance to violence.

4. It cannot be stressed enough that churches and their members bear a considerable responsibility in overcoming violence in their communities. Churches should take risks, while also recognizing God's option for the poor and vulnerable.

5. A number of suggestions were received calling on the churches to be more forthright in condemning the sin of homophobia and prejudicial conditions based on a person's sexual orientation.

6. We must recognize that a member of one family, neighbourhood or community may be a victim of violence, yet at the same time exercise violence over others.

7. We must promote healing by safeguarding the human rights of all. Consider endorsing the declaration of "The Right to Peace."

8. We view with dismay the plight of Christian communities in the Middle East. Their survival is at great risk. We call for the worldwide Christian community to stand by the churches in the Holy Land and all across that region.

9. Violence may be embedded in a culture. We need to challenge the negative aspects of our own cultures and ask how cultural values can contribute to the perpetuation of violence. We must confront those who utilize negative, abusive and unchecked forms of power and privilege.

10. Women and children are at particular risk of violence, and not only in war zones.

11. We offer the methodology of "dialogue tables" as an instrument to involve people in situations of conflict who are seeking solutions that serve the common good.

12. Churches should examine their liturgies and lectionaries to assure that themes of peace-making are raised up in worship.

13. Interreligious dialogue and cooperation should be sought out at the community level.

Peace in the Marketplace

1. We encourage the WCC to appeal to the International Monetary Fund, the World Bank and the World Trade Organization to be more just in their trade policies toward countries in the global South which experience high levels of poverty.

2. Too many resources are exploited for the benefit of the few.

3. We urge global corporations not to seek excessive profit by exploiting local people, denying their needs and ignoring their rights.

4. Many countries are affected by a financial collapse caused by greed, cheating and corruption. Markets need strong regulation, as do banks and other financial institutions.

5. From a workshop leader: "We reaffirm the judgment of the 2004 Accra Confession of the WARC (now WCRC), the 2003 Lutheran declaration on globalization and the 2006 Agape Call of the WCC. We as churches have to reject the structural violence of the global, neoliberal, capitalist economy and the values of the imperialist forces and disorienting media."

6. From participants from the Academy for Solidarity Economy of the Ecumenical Network in Germany:

A Message on Peace and Solidarity in the Marketplace

In light of a "theology of life" and a thorough commitment to a "live-giving civilization," the churches participating in the ecumenical movement convene at the close of their Decade to Overcome Violence. To reach out for peace in the marketplace, they connect with all that they represent, are and have to do with the concept of an economy in solidarity as it has taken shape in many parts of the world as a "people's movement" (Seoul 1990) and as it has been further developed in initiatives of economic solidarity in the global south as well as in the north.

As participants of the International Ecumenical Peace Convocation of the World Council of Churches, we recognize in this the culmination of our commitment to discipleship that has been highlighted by the conciliar process for justice, peace and the integrity of creation. Furthermore, we regard it as an active sign by the Holy Spirit in the middle of a profound "multi-polar crisis of life."

As a consequence, we encourage each other to act as motors and change agents for the "transforming grace" (Porto Alegre 2006) therein. Internally, our churches are called to this as employers and owners of land and capital. Externally, they shall act through decisive advocacy work to reach adequate political conditions.

In promoting this, we particularly aim to foster the self-organization of peoples' movements and the actors concerned. We will accompany the further development of the respective socio-cultural approaches in accordance with the Gospel and to publicly award best practices.

Participating in the "Missio Dei" our coming years' work shall concentrate on the sharpening and application of the concept of a solidarity economy of life. We aim to understand local and global phenomena of crisis in their respective interdependencies in order to be able to advance toward peace in the marketplace in a comprehensive way. The transformation of economy and society toward solidarity becomes possible as we commit ourselves to this transforming grace.

Peace with the Earth

1. It is essential to recognize the spiritual and practical relationships of Indigenous peoples and the Earth. The churches are called to support Indigenous populations, and to learn from them in an atmosphere of mutual respect and interdependence.

2. We offer support to family farms and small communities who work the land with love for the Earth. Agribusiness must not be allowed to abolish them.

3. The question of equitable distribution of existing food must be seriously and globally considered.

4. As Christians, we must consume less and share more widely so that every child of God has food to eat and clean water to drink.

5. We heard a powerful account of the bombing of Hiroshima. We urge all governments to eliminate nuclear weapons that put humanity and the planet at unprecedented risk.

6. Members of a workshop on nuclear energy in the aftermath of the catastrophe at Fukushima, Japan, strongly recommended that the churches take a stand in favour of the abolition of nuclear power plants.

7. The aftermath of recent earthquakes in Haiti, Aotearoa-New Zealand and the earthquake and tsunami in Japan raises urgent questions concerning the future regulation of nuclear energy.

8. We must work to overcome the irresponsible consumption of fossil fuels.

9. In one "reasoning" group, resource persons from Africa, Asia and Europe shared initiatives and experiences from churches in the North and South to advocate for climate justice and environmental protection.

    People from DR Congo, Switzerland, Jamaica, India, Barbados, the Philippines, Tanzania, Indonesia and Germany underscored the importance of paying attention to the impacts of climate change as well as environmental degradation. One participant also expressed the wish to extend partnership between the United Evangelical Mission and the island states of the West Indies. In relation to Africa, the topic of building consciousness was underlined. With respect to plantations, a number of comments expressed concern about the involvement of church-based institutions in palm oil production on a large scale.

    Participants in this reasoning workshop are convinced that the Tenth Assembly of the WCC in 2013 at Busan, Korea should take the decision that climate justice and peace on and with the earth be made a principal programme priority for the WCC in the years following the 2013 Assembly.

10. From a "buzz group" in the plenary tent: "We call upon members of the Body of Christ to take personal responsibility in stewardship for the Earth, all natural resources and all creatures."

11. In all deliberations on climate change, the WCC must give special emphasis to the human rights and testimonies of the poor and vulnerable throughout the Earth.

Peace among the Peoples

1. It is essential to continue upholding and supporting those who work to promote peace, including conscientious objectors to military service; in addition, we should underline the negative role of the military in relation to the use of the Earth and its resources, as well as the economic and social impacts of expenditures for the military.

2. The right to asylum also helps to protect conscientious objectors. Please consider the issue of asylum in general and asylum to conscientious objectors in particular. Globally, the number of people fleeing their countries of origin for a number of reasons, including conscientious objection and seeking asylum elsewhere, is increasing. This is a challenge to peace-building in countries both of origin and destination; therefore, addressing asylum and its root causes is timely.

3. The churches must raise their voices in support of a comprehensive Arms Trade Treaty.

4. We stand in solidarity with those who have been imprisoned for taking nonviolent direct action against state policies leading to violence and war.

5. Notice was taken of results from the July 2010 "Peace Among the Peoples Conference" in Elkhart, Indiana, USA. For further documentation, see: http://www.ambs.edu/programs-institutes/ims/consultations/peace-conference

6. A challenge to the churches: Develop and coordinate Just Peace ministries in conflict areas in order to prevent the escalation of conflicts into violence and war, and to build a sustainable culture of peace for all.

7. Increasing violence in Mexico must be a concern for the world's churches and the WCC. This poses a threat not only to one nation, but throughout the Americas. Recommendation: endorse the declaration "Por un México en paz con justicia y dignidad."

8. From a discussion group: "While we invoke peace at the IEPC, an entire people suffer from war in Libya. We refuse to believe that the only means of supporting their struggle for liberty is through military force. War descends in a spiral of ever-increasing violence until the situation no longer allows for dialogue or mediation. The war has resulted in the massacre of civilians and the flight of thousands of refugees. Yet war also offers advantages to the armaments industry and industrialists who wish to take control of territories and sources of energy. We demand that the churches press the United Nations and especially NATO to cease the bombardment of Libya and to seek other avenues to combat the regime in support of the rebels and the civilian population."

9. The WCC and its member churches continue to struggle with the concept of the "Responsibility to Protect" (R2P). How can innocent people best be protected from war and violence? How can we avoid "the violence of silence" when people are dying?

10. A statement endorsed by one of the reasoning workshops: *For a World of Peace: A World Free of Nuclear Weapons*: An Ecumenical Call from Hwacheon.[1]

The Hwacheon Call is addressed to the ecumenical community, its worldwide and regional organizations, member churches and all those willing to cooperate in the active pursuit of a world of peace – a world free of nuclear weapons.

The time has come for the churches to seek greater and stronger unity to address together the issues of nuclear weapons. This demands robust development of clear policy goals, close attention to the wisdom and values reflected in sixty years of ecumenical engagement for a world without nuclear weapons, plus disciplined pursuit by member churches, specialized ministries, church-related NGOs and Christians, active in wider peace movements of the actions and recommendations that the ecumenical community has made over the years.

The WCC should give the highest priority to nuclear disarmament and carry out its God-given and historic responsibility in clearly envisioning a nuclear-weapon-free world and actively working for it. This should form an important agenda of the WCC International Ecumenical Peace Convocation in Kingston in 2011 and the WCC Assembly in 2013 in South Korea.

While the theological positions of the WCC on nuclear issues have been clear, it is necessary to reformulate those positions taking into account new developments and new nuclear doctrines including pre-emption. The implications of nuclear-sharing and extended deterrence have to be taken into account. Such reformulation is necessary to form the basis for a new commitment by churches and Christians toward nuclear disarmament especially in view of the increasing propensity to the use of force to settle disputes between nations.

The dangers posed by the nuclearization of Northeast Asia with the background of division and continuing tension in the Korean peninsula

1. This is the final section of a statement by a group of 40 persons active in the ecumenical movement who met in Hwacheon, Republic of Korea, in 2009 and 2010 to seek ways to strengthen the ecumenical movement for urgent action on nuclear disarmament. Participants came from Canada, Fiji, Korea, Norway, Pakistan, the Philippines and USA. The Conference was organized jointly by the Asia Pacific Graduate School, Seoul, and the Korean YMCA, with support from the National Council of Churches in Korea, Presbyterian Church in Korea, the Christian Conference of Asia and the World Council of Churches. The meeting was hosted by the government of Hwacheon County, at a peace park near the Demilitarized Zone (DMZ).

should alert the ecumenical community for focused attention on the situation and for sustained support to the Korean churches and people in their continuing struggle for peace and reunification.

It is important to mobilize and consolidate latent majorities in all the churches opposed to nuclear weapons as part of the strategy. There should be coordination between international action and national level actions by the churches so that governments and inter-governmental bodies hear the same message from the member churches and their ecumenical organizations.

The United Nations and international organizations should be called upon to ensure steps by Nuclear Weapon States for disarmament, take steps for a Nuclear Weapons Convention and for security assurances to Non-Nuclear Weapon States.

In view of the increasing nuclear proliferation and nuclear tensions in the Asian region, the WCC and CCA should give high priority to the issue. In Asia, the nuclear threat has never been as high as it is today, stretching from West Asia through South Asia to North-East Asia. Nuclear disarmament should be treated by the WCC, CCA and member churches as a major faith concern and a test of discipleship. The 2013 WCC Assembly should be an occasion for such affirmation.

Inter-faith cooperation should be actively sought in dealing with the threat to humanity and the Creation from nuclear weapons and working for a word without nuclear weapons.

General Comments

1.   From a working group on arms, peace and security:

Our Security Challenge on the Way of Just Peace
We are all vulnerable and we all long for security. Indeed, our common vulnerability must inform our understanding of security. In our era it is clear: there is either security for all, or security for none.

The "security" so widely offered and promoted today is built on domination, violence, weapons and a culture of fear. Its promises are lies, yet we become conditioned to accept the use of force.

Genuine security is built upon just relations, mutual responsibility, interdependence, and shared vulnerability. Such security promotes the welfare of the other and nurtures the common hope of a shared future of all creatures.

To seek security for all requires allocation of skills and resources to meet basic human needs, reductions in spending on false forms of security and the adoption of strategies to prevent armed violence. This organization of peace will be as demanding as the organization of war. It requires of us all a mental and spiritual revolution. We must regard any use of violence as obstacles to a just peace and something to be replaced by a pro-active ethos of nonviolence for ourselves and our societies. Our common longing is for a world without weapons and a just peace.

2. From a group involved in the peace and reconciliation work of FinnChurchAid:

(1) Whereas the Message should speak mainly to the Christian brothers and sisters, it also needs to speak to the whole world, taking into account the context in which it is delivered. Interreligious perspectives are a cross-cutting theme at the IEPC and perspectives from other religions have featured well in the 'Innerstandings' as well as some of the workshops. Yet in Kingston, we are not able to engage in true dialogue with other religions on matters of Just Peace. The dialogue needs to take place post-Kingston, with the help of the message(s) that are sent from here. One way of engaging this would be to refer to the Golden Rule: One should treat others as one would like others to treat oneself, which has universal resonance within the world's religions, and which encompasses peace in the community (tolerance, indiscrimination, gender equality), peace in the marketplace (economic justice, fairness in distribution of wealth), peace with the earth (shared understanding of identifying the Creation with human beings) and peace among peoples (nonviolence, solidarity). A suggestion for a text:

'The pursuit for Just Peace is a call for all the peoples and religions across the globe. It is an inclusive journey, defined by interdependence and love for the neighbour. In building a shared and just peace among the peoples and communities, with the earth and in the marketplace, we are once more called to treat others as we would like others to treat ourselves.'

(2) The journey of peace, justice and nonviolence that began long ago, and of which the DOV and the IEPC are important milestones, will have its next brief 'stop' at Busan at the 10th WCC Assembly. Some participants at the IEPC have expressed their confusion over this journey that should take us from Kingston's 'Glory to God and Peace on Earth' and the message contained in the 'Ecumenical Call for Just Peace' to Busan's 'God of life, lead us to justice and peace'. The path of the journey needs to be clear, and thus the Message should be able to provide guidelines on our way from Kingston to Busan and, importantly, beyond.

(3) The Message should indicate that the churches and related organizations are addressing peace and just peace in the context of global politics and in timely manner. As of now, (Sunday), there has been very little

reference, at least in the plenaries, to the burning global (geographical) issues of peace beyond the Middle East. The events in the Arab world, for example, are something about which we cannot remain silent. The situation in the Sudan is very tense as we speak. And there are other examples."

3. In solidarity, let us provide food and drinkable water for all the people of the world, fight corruption and promote good governance in each nation.

4. Beware proposals for new military systems that are promoted as "defensive." This too often leads to escalation of the arms race and suffering in civilian populations.

5. "Christianophobia" is a reality worldwide for Christian communities living in both minority and majority situations. We think of militant secularization in some western countries, of the churches in the Middle East and of Christians in the northern part of Cyprus that is occupied by Turkey.

6. From a "buzz group" in the plenary tent: "We call the churches worldwide to initiate interfaith dialogue and action for peace at all levels – community, Earth, marketplace, peoples."

7. The churches need to renew their commitment to the healing of memories, and to develop interfaith ceremonies to underscore the spiritual dimension of this process.

8. We encourage the writing of letters making an appeal for Just Peace to leaders of COP 17, the G8, the G20, world religions and to members of the UN Security Council.

9. Youth in the IEPC called attention to the need for churches to support: peace education, both as a part of religious education and public education; communication initiatives by the churches on Just Peace, including a special website and other means of information-sharing; and significant advocacy work by the churches on behalf of Just Peace in the world.

10. "Too often we assume that the church in itself is not powerful. We do not sufficiently acknowledge the church's agency in the world, and its capacity to live as a witness to the world. We must hear the call to practice and action, acknowledging that we can practice Just Peace in concrete, local, congregational and personal ways. We can take action through non-participation in war, war profiteering, war taxes and through other expressions of conscientious objection. We can participate in nonviolent peace-making and direct action. Such witness,

lived out in the sight of all, speaks more loudly than any ecumenical statement.

11. The participants in the Convocation deeply appreciate the work of many women, youth and men in congregations, initiatives, networks and movements toward the overcoming of violence during the DOV decade, and we give our thanks to them. We invite you to continue your journey toward Just Peace and encourage you to deepen your commitment. We shall live in peace today!

Appendix 3.
Participants' Evaluation of the IEPC

At the close of the International Ecumenical Peace Convocation (IEPC), participants were invited to complete an evaluation questionnaire in which they could rate the IEPC's different elements (Bible studies, opening plenary session, thematic, and closing plenaries, seminars/"innerstandings," workshops "reasoning," and the IEPC venue/facilities) and indicate whether the Convocation had enabled them to gain new insights, establish new contacts and/or become aware of the need to focus on certain key areas. They were also asked to indicate whether or not they were involved in any of 21 possible follow-up steps listed on the evaluation form.

A total of 145 signed evaluation forms were returned with a majority (53) from Europe, followed by responses from Asia (29), North America (23), Africa, Latin America and the Caribbean (12 each), the Middle East (3) and the Pacific (1).

In terms of representation, 75 of the respondents were from WCC member churches, ten from the wider ecumenical constituency (Regional Ecumenical Organizations, Christian World Communions, International Ecumenical Organizations, the Roman Catholic Church and Specialized Ministries), and 60 from other, diverse, peace-related organizations.

Highlights of the responses to the quantitative questions included the following:

- Bible study was rated as the most appreciated element, followed by the opening plenary
- 93% of participants committed to sharing the IEPC message within their church, organization or network
- 90% committed to promote the "Ecumenical Call to Just Peace"
- 72% committed to link up ecumenically on the annual International Day of Prayer for Peace on 21 September.

Questions related to evaluating the different IEPC elements, and to follow-up steps, also gave participants the opportunity to note their explanations and comments. The response to these open questions was as follows:

- 85 people responded with overall explanations and comments
- 29 people explained that they had joined a network or initiative related to Just Peace and the four IEPC themes that was not already proposed on the form

- 29 people said they had started a new network, campaign or initiative related to Just Peace themes
- 48 people shared ways – other than those proposed on the form – in which they would share the collaborative approach and the common journey of peace as experienced in Kingston.

Examples of follow-up commitment included the following activities:
- developing peace resources and activities for worship and peace education;
- collaboration in developing an ecumenical theology of Just Peace during the lead-up to the WCC Assembly in 2013;
- assisting theological institutions or networks to study and address specific themes and topics of Just Peace;
- cooperation with other religions on issues of peace, including, for example, the United Nations' new World Interfaith Harmony Week;
- engagement of churches, ministries or networks in using the "Ecumenical Call to Just Peace," for example, applying the Just Peace approach as a framework for action and advocacy or to build cooperation between disciplines.

Appendix 4. IEPC Programme

Tuesday 17th: Arrivals — **Wednesday 25th: Departures**

Time	Wednesday 18th	Thursday 19th	Friday 20th	Saturday 21st	Sunday 22nd	Monday 23rd	Tuesday 24th
07:00-07:30				Morning Prayer			
07:30-08:15	Breakfast	Breakfast	Breakfast	Breakfast	Breakfast	Breakfast	Breakfast
08:15-08:45	Orientation for Community Visits	Morning Prayer	Morning Prayer			Morning Prayer	Morning Prayer
08:45-09:00		Move to Bible Study	Move to Bible Study	Move to Bible Study		Move to Bible Study	Move to Bible Study
09:00-09:30		Bible Study	Bible Study	Bible Study		Bible Study	Bible Study
09:30-10:00	Visits to local projects and initiatives						
10:00-10:30		Break	Break	Break	Ecumenical Prayer	Break	Break
10:30-11:00		Plenary: Peace in the Community	Plenary: Peace with the Earth	Plenary: Peace in the Marketplace		Plenary: Peace among the Peoples	Plenary: Weaving Ceremony
11:00-11:30							
11:30-12:00		Midday prayer	Midday prayer	Midday prayer		Midday prayer	Midday prayer
12:00-12:30							
12:30-13:00	Lunch and free time						
13:00-13:30		Lunch and free time	Lunch and free time	Lunch and free time		Lunch and free time	Lunch and free time
13:30-14:00							
14:00-14:30	Opening Prayer	Innerstandings and Reasoning	Innerstandings and Reasoning	Innerstandings and Reasoning	Caribbean Day Celebrations	Innerstandings and Reasoning	Closing Plenary IEPC message (re-)committment next steps
14:30-15:00							
15:00-15:30							
15:30-15:45		Break of 15 minutes	Break of 15 minutes	Break of 15 minutes		Break of 15 minutes	
15:45-16:00							
16:00-16:30	Break	Innerstandings and Reasoning	Innerstandings and Reasoning	Innerstandings and Reasoning		Innerstandings and Reasoning	Break
16:30-16:45		Break of 15 minutes	Break of 15 minutes	Break of 15 minutes		Break of 15 minutes	
16:45-17:15	Opening Plenary: greetings, DOV celebration, keynote address						
17:15-17:30		Evening Prayer	Break of 15 minutes	Break of 15 minutes		Break of 15 minutes	Sending Prayer
17:30-18:00			Evening Prayer	Evening Prayer		Evening Prayer	
18:00-18:30			Public Event	Dinner	Dinner	Dinner	and
18:30-19:00		Dinner	Dinner				
19:00-19:30	Dinner	Film: Pray the Devil Back to Hell	Evening Prayer	Youth Evening	Musical: Strong Without Violence	Film Evening	Celebration Dinner
19:30-20:00							
20:00-21:30							

Reasoning = workshops for sharing and learning

Appendix 5. Documents of the Convocation

Preparatory Documents

- Ecumenical Call to Just Peace: Aware that the promise of peace is a core value of all religions, the Call reaches out to all who seek peace, Ecumenical Call to Just Peace.

- Draft version of a **Just Peace Companion**: a complement to the Call, the document provides necessary background information as well as basic biblical, theological and ethical considerations to support and unfold its basic message.

- **Overcoming Violence: The Ecumenical Decade 2001-2010:** a report on ten years of work on reconciliation and peace and a call to move peace-building from the periphery to the centre of church life and witness Final report of the Decade to Overcome Violence.

- Bible Study Reflections: Reflections on each of the five texts used in the IEPC Bible Study sessions related to each of the four themes and the going forth on the last day from the Convocation, Bible Study reflections.

- **Telling the Truth about Ourselves and Our World:** A study guide to help individuals and churches continue to reflect and act together as the 2001-2010 Decade to Overcome Violence – Churches Seeking Reconciliation and Peace is celebrated at the IEPC.

Suggested Reading

- **Peace on Earth, Peace with the Earth:** a special issue of *The Ecumenical Review* providing diverse perspectives related to the IEPC's themes, Peace on Earth - Peace with the Earth.

- **New Routes:** spring 2011 issue of the Life and Peace Institute magazine dedicated to the IEPC, *New Routes*.

Information

- Handbook: A booklet with both programmatic and practical information for participants, including information about the many side-events that took place.

- Reasoning Workshops: A comprehensive list of workshops being offered with succinct descriptions to help participants plan their participation in each of the eight sessions

- Reasoning Booklet: workshops list and descriptions.

Worship Resources

- *Imagine: Peace:* contains suggestions for services on the four Sundays in Advent. It is the first part of a collection of Bible meditations, texts and songs from different regions of the world for the IEPC.
- *Telling Peace:* a collection of liturgical resources for the four Sundays of Advent. It is the second of a collection of worship materials from different regions of the world, prepared in the framework of the IEPC.
- *Singing Peace:* the songbook of the IEPC and third in the series after *Imagine: Peace and Telling Peace*, it is an encouragement to confess and multiply God's glory.
- *World Sunday for Peace*: a resource for use by churches around the world on 22 May 2011, it contains prayers, hymns and a biblical reflection.

Message and Follow-up

- IEPC Message: an expression of the unified experience of participants' exploration of a just peace and a path forward as they return to their homes and churches across the world.
- *Just Peace Companion, second edition.* The deliberations and experiences of the convocation have been incorporated into the the *Just Peace Companion*, ISBN 978-2-8254-1567-2, intended for individuals, churches and groups in studying and reflecting on the Ecumenical Call to Just Peace.

Appendix 6. IEPC Theme Song

2. Ours is a task in pro - gress, peace - mak - ers we've be - come. We're build - ing peace - ful bridg - es for gen - er - a - tions to come. Peace in the mar - ket - place, peace with the earth, peace in our com - mu - ni - ty and peace a - mong all rac - es. Glo - ry to God and peace on earth. We're stand - ing on the front line as bea - cons of peace. Our mis - sion will be long and re - sis - tance may be strong but peace will con - quer all. That's our cry and our song. Glo - ry to God and peace on earth. Sing glo - ry to God and peace on earth. 3. From the ris - ing of the sun to the set - ting of the

Appendix 7. Participants

Mr Adarsh Abraham, Mar Thoma Syrian Church of Malabar, United States of America

Bishop Ivan Manuel Abrahams, Methodist Church of Southern Africa, South Africa

Lic. Elias C. Abramides, Ecumenical Patriarchate, Argentina

Dr Agnes Abuom, Anglican Church of Kenya

Mr Andrea Acosta, Cuban Embassy, Cuba

Mr Stefan Adam, Media, Germany

Rev Deborah Lee Adams, Seminarian, United States of America

Ms Christine Ade-Gold, Media, Jamaica

Mr Joyanta Adhikari, Bangladesh Baptist Church Sangha

Dr. Christiane Agboton Johnson, Protestant Church in Senegal, France

Mrs Berit Hagen Agøy, Church of Norway

Ms Su Mara Akong, Medical team, Jamaica

Ms Loucille Alcalà, Roman Catholic Church - Official Delegation, France

H.E. Archbishop Nareg Alemezian, Armenian Apostolic Church (Holy See of Cilicia), Lebanon

Dr Gail Allan, United Church of Canada

Dr E. Anthony Allen, Whole Person Resource Centre Jamaica, Jamaica

Mrs Guro Almås, Church of Norway, Norway

Rev. Dr Walter Altmann, Evangelical Church of Lutheran Confession in Brazil, Brazil

Mrs Clare Amos, Nifcon (Network for Inter Faith Concerns), United Kingdom

Mr Aldo Raul Amuchástegui, Gen Rosso, Italy

Ms Hannah Eline Ander, Changemaker, Norway

Rev. Christoph Anders, Evangelisches Missionswerk in Deutschland, Germany

Ms Kamala Anderson, Medical team, Jamaica

Rev. Dr Lesley Anderson, Methodist Church in the Caribbean and the Americas, Trinidad and Tobago

Rev. Dr. Lenworth Anglin, Jamaica Umbrella Group of Churches

Ms Joycelyn Anima Osei, Presbyterian Church of Ghana

Ms Monica Arias Valverde, Centro intereclesial de Estudios Teologicos y Sociales, Nicaragua

Rev. Mrs Kirubai Kumari Aruldoss, Church of South India

H.E. Archbishop Avak Vazken Asadourian, Diocese of the Armenian Church of Iraq

Ms Semegnish Asfaw, World Council of Churches, Switzerland

Dr Deanna Ashley, Violence Prevention Alliance, Jamaica

Rev Nicole Ashwood, Caribbean and North America Council for Mission (CANACOM), Jamaica

Mr Nikolaos Asproulis, Volos Academy for Theological Studies, Greece

Ms Yvette Assem, Seminarian, United States of America

Mr David C. Atwood, Quaker United Nations Office (QUNO), Switzerland

Rev. Edgar Austen, EKD-Evangelical Lutheran Church in Brunswick, Germany

Mr Mervyn Austin, Methodist Church in the Caribbean and the Americas, Jamaica

Rev. Dick Avi, United Church in Papua New Guinea, Papua New Guinea

Ms Kyriaki Avtzi, Ecumenical Patriarchate, Switzerland

Archbishop Vicken Aykazian, Armenian Apostolic Church (Mother See of Holy Etchmiadzin), United States of America

Mrs Roberta Bacic, Stitching Peace, United Kingdom

Rev. Dr. Hyunju Bae, Busan Presbyterian University, Republic of Korea

Mrs Karine Baghdasaryan, Armenia Inter-Church Charitable Round Table Foundation, Armenia

Ms Maria Baile Rubio, World Council of Churches, Switzerland

Ms Valencia Bailey, Medical team, Jamaica

Mr Curt Baker, Local Volunteer, Jamaica

Rev. Fritz Baltruweit, EKD-Evangelisch-Lutherische Landeskirche Hannover, Germany

Ms Inger Bang Carlsen, The Church Resource Centre Against Violence and Sexual Abuse, Norway

Mr Cleveland Banks, Media, Jamaica

Dr Oluwakemi Linda Banks, Church in the Province of the West Indies, Anguilla

Ms Olufunmike Marjorie Banks Devonish, Volunteer, United Kingdom

Mrs Mercy Barends, Gereja Protestan Maluku (GPM), Indonesia

Rev. Thaddée Andrew Joseph Barnas, Media, Belgium

Ms Candy Barton, United Theological College of the West Indies, Jamaica

Ms Martina Basso, Vereinigung der Deutschen Mennonitengemeinden, Germany

Ms Muriel Victoria Bataclan, World Council of Churches, Switzerland

Mr Jean Rony Bataille, Baptist Convention of Haiti

Dr Valli Batchelor, WCC Movers of Gender Just Peace, Saudi Arabia

Mr Guillermo Ezekiel Batista, Fraternidad Baptist, Baptist Chruch Emmanuel, Haiti

Ms Damelia Baugh, Medical team, Jamaica

Rev. Liberato C. Bautista, United Methodist Church, United States of America

Mr John Baxter-Brown, World Council of Churches, Switzerland

Mr Jean-Nicolas Bazin, World Council of Churches, Switzerland

Mr Mark Beach, World Council of Churches, Switzerland

Prof. Dr Heinrich Bedford-Strohm, EKD-Evangelical Church in Germany, Germany

Ms Kadeen Bell, Media, Jamaica

Mr Mark Bell, Media, Jamaica

Mr Kenneth Tealava Ben, Cook Islands Christian Church, Cook Islands

Dr Harald Bender, Ecumenical Network in Germany

Ms Nadja Benes, Interpreter, Switzerland

Rev. Alvin Benguche, Methodist Church in the Caribbean and the Americas,

Rev. Abraham A. Berinyuu, Presbyterian Church of Ghana

Ms Verónica Biech, World Student Christian Federation - WSCF, Argentina

Dr Michael Biehl, Academy of Mission at the University of Hamburg, Germany

Ms Margrethe Bjernes, Ecumenical Disability Advocates Network, Norway

Mr Oddvar Bjørge, EAPPI, Norway

Rev. Steinunn A. Björnsdóttir, Evangelical Lutheran Church of Iceland

Mr Lancelot Black, Local Volunteer, Jamaica

Ms Natalie Blake, Local Volunteer, Jamaica

Mr Jordan Blevins, National Council of Churches of Christ in the USA

Rev. Kjell Magne Bondevik, Church of Norway

Rev. Dr Hyacinth Ione Boothe, Methodist Church in the Caribbean and the Americas, Jamaica

Rev. Sebastian Borck, EKD-North Elbian Evangelical Lutheran Church, Germany

Ms Lena Borgers, EKD-Evangelical Lutheran Church of Hanover, Germany

Mr Jec Dan Borlado, Convention of Philippine Baptist Churches

Very Rev. Archimandrite Iosif Leandro Bosch, Ecumenical Patriarchate, Argentina

Mr Ian Boyne, Media, Jamaica

Rev. Renke Brahms, EKD-Evangelical Church in Germany, Germany

Rev. Dieter Brandes, EKD-Evangelical Church of Württemberg, Germany

Ms Nan Braunschweiger, World Council of Churches, Switzerland

Profesor Oscar Bravo Castillo, Misión Urbana y Rural (MUR), Peru

Rev. Almut Bretschneider-Felzmann, EKD-Evangelische Kirche in Mitteldeutschland, Germany

Ms Rachel Brett, Quaker United Nations Office (QUNO), Switzerland

Rev. Perry Brohier, Church of Ceylon, Sri Lanka

Mr Mario Brown, Methodist (Inter-denominational), Jamaica

Ms Jessica Brown, Pax Christi International, Belgium

Ms Ingrid Brown, Media, Jamaica

Major Desmond Brown, Jamaica Baptist Union

Mr Hugh Brown, Local Volunteer, Jamaica

Mr Kirk Brown, Anglican (Episcopal) Diocese of Jamaica

Ms Angella Brown, Local Volunteer, Jamaica

Ms Karlene Brown Thompson, Media, Jamaica

Prof. Dr Pamela Brubaker, California Lutheran University, United States of America

Mrs Cheryl Brumbaugh-Cayfford, Media, United States of America

Ms Patricia Bruschweiler, World Council of Churches, Switzerland

Mrs Rita Bruvers, Evangelical Lutheran Church of Latvia

Ms Andrea Bryan, Media, Jamaica

Mr Durmutt Bryant, Media, Jamaica

Ms Fiona Elizabeth Buchanan, Church of Scotland, United Kingdom

Ms Racquel Buckley, Jamaica Baptist Union

Ms Omega Bula, United Church of Canada

Hegumen Filaret Bulekov, Russian Orthodox Church (Moscow Patriarchate),

Mr Zakaria Bulus, Seminarian, Nigeria

Mr Maurizio Burcini, Pax Christi Italy, Italy

Rev. Klaus Burckhardt, EKD-Evangelisch-Lutherische Landeskirche Hannovers, Germany

Mr Delroy Burley, Moravian Church in Jamaica

Rev. Theo Buss, Interpreter, Switzerland

Pastor Barry W. Bussey, General Conference of Seventh-day Adventists, United States of America

Rev. Msgr Gosbert Byamungu, Roman Catholic Church - Official Delegation, Vatican City

Rev. Phyllis Byrd Ochillo, Organisation of African Instituted Churches, Kenya

Rev. LaMarco Cable, Christian Church (Disciples of Christ) USA - Week of Compassion, United States of America

Ms La-Toya Cameron, Methodist Church in the Caribbean and the Americas, Jamaica

Mr Frantz Camille, Seminarian, Jamaica

Rev. Dr Sofia Camnerin, Mission Covenant Church of Sweden

Ms Evette Campbell, Seminarian, Jamaica

Ms Aretha Campbell, Presbyterian Church, Jamaica

Mr Desmond Campbell, Media, Jamaica

Ms Chevelle Campbell, Medical team, Jamaica

Ms Andrea Campbell, Media, Jamaica

Dr Ena Campbell, Moravian Church in Jamaica

Dr Oscar Franklin Canelos Castillo, Latin American Council of Churches, Ecuador

Mrs Shirley Carby, Jamaica Methodist District, Jamaica

Prof. Dr Nancy Cardoso Pereira, Land Pastoral Commission (Rio Sul) & Peace for Life, Brazil

Ms Els-Marie Carlbäcker, Mission Covenant Church of Sweden

Rev. Verna Cassells, United Theological College of the West Indies, Jamaica

Dr Björn Cedersjö, Christian Council of Sweden

Mr Nelson Fernando Celis Angel, Latin American Council of Churches, Ecuador

Mr Felipe Arturo Cesari Casas, Iglesia Evangelica Libre, Cuba

Ms Rose Chadderton, Medical team, Jamaica

Rev. Heawon Chae, Presbyterian Church in the Republic of Korea

Dr Byron Chambers, United Theological College of the West Indies, Jamaica

Ms Mary Chang, Senate of Serampore College, India

Mr Pascal Chang'a Ponsiano, Gen Rosso, Italy

Mr Jaroslaw Charkiewicz, Polish Autocephalous Orthodox Church

Mr Michael Charles, Local Volunteer, Jamaica

Rev. Ching-Fa Chen, Presbyterian Church in Taiwan

Rev Young-Cheol Cheon, World Association for Christian Communication (WACC), Republic of Korea

Rev. Rothangliani R. Chhangte, American Baptist Churches in the USA

Mr Douglas L. Chial, World Council of Churches, Switzerland

Ms Shina Chileshe, United Church of Zambia

Mrs Sofía Nicolasa Chipana Quispe, Religiosas Terciarias Trinitarias, Bolivia

Rev. Augusto Chipesse, Evangelical Congregational Church in Angola

Rev. Theresa Cho, Presbyterian Church (USA)

Ms Catherine Christ-Taha, World Council of Churches, Switzerland

Mr Mu-Jen Chu, Presbyterian Church in Taiwan

Dr Jujin Chung, Prebyterian Church in the Republic of Korea (PROK)

Mrs Clover Chung, Local Volunteer, Jamaica

Rev. Prof. Dr Emmanuel Clapsis, Ecumenical Patriarchate, United States of America

Ms Vanesa Clarke, United Church in Jamaica and the Cayman Islands, Jamaica

Ms Jaki Codner, Local Volunteer, Jamaica

Rev. Patrick Coke, Moravian Church in Jamaica

Mr Edwin Coleman, Religious Society of Friends (Quakers), Jamaica

Ms Meredith Coleman-Tobias, Lutheran School of Theology, United States of America

Ms Mairead Collins, Stitching Peace, United Kingdom

Rev. Sian Collins, United Reformed Church, United Kingdom

Dr. Paolo Colombo, Centro Ecumenico Europeo per la Pace, Italy

Mrs Elaine Commissiong, United Church in Jamaica and the Cayman Islands, Jamaica

Ms Tanya Conliffe, Seminarian, Jamaica

Bishop Dr Geevarghese Mor Coorilos, Syrian Orthodox Patriarchate of Antioch and All the East, India

Ms Mihaela Copot, European Forum of Lesbian, Gay, Bisexual and Transgender Christian Groups, Moldova

Rev. Terence Corkin, Uniting Church in Australia

Ms Georgia Llewellyn Corowa, Uniting Church in Australia

Mr Fabian Corrales Gutierrez, Ecumenical Disability Advocates Network, Costa Rica

Rev. Omar Cortés-Gaibur, Latin American Theological Fraternity, Chile

Dr. Oscar E. Corvalan-Vasquez, Iglesia Pentecostal de Chile

Rev. Dr Gordon Cowans, Ecumenical Disability Advocates Network, Jamaica

Mr Robert Craigue, Andover Newton Theological School, United States of America

Ms Chrys-Ann Crawford, Local Volunteer, Jamaica

Rev. Didier Crouzet, Reformed Church of France

Rev Dr Peter Cruchley-Jones, CWME Transformative Spirituality and Mission, United Kingdom

Rev. Tara Curlewis, National Council of Churches in Australia

Dr Teresa Cutts, Methodist Le Bonheur Healthcare Center, United States of America

Rev. Albino Da Costa, Protestant Church in Timor Lorosa'e, East Timor

Mr Odio Dacres, Religious Society of Friends (Quakers), Jamaica

Dr. Rev. Silfredo Bernardo Dalferth, Visitor, Germany

Rev. Malcolm Damon, Economic Justice Network of Foccisa, South Africa

Ms Sasha-Gaye Dandy, Local Volunteer, Jamaica

Mr Ronnie Daniel, Caribbean Conference of Churches, Saint Vincent

H.G. Bishop Daniel of Sydney, Coptic Orthodox Church, Australia

Archpriest Nikolai Danilevich, Russian Orthodox Church (Moscow Patriarchate), Ukraine

Ms Sanjana Das, Church of North India

Rev. Dr Richard M. Daulay, Communion of Churches in Indonesia (PGI)

Rev. Eniola Davis, United Church in Jamaica and the Cayman Islands, Jamaica

Bishop Sarah Frances Davis, African Methodist Episcopal Church, Jamaica

Rev. Lazree Davis, African Methodist Episcopal Church, Jamaica

Mr Javed Davis, Local Volunteer, Jamaica

Rev. Dr. Millard Davis, African Methodist Episcopal Church, Jamaica

Mr Sean Davis, Methodist Church in the Caribbean and the Americas, Jamaica

Fr. Wolde Dawit, Ethiopian Orthodox Church, Jamaica

Ms Dorothy Day, Religious Society of Friends: Friends General Conference, United States of America

The Right Reverend Francisco De Assis da Silva, Igreja Episcopal Anglicana do Brasil, Brazil

Rt. Rev. Duleep Kamil de Chickera, Church of Ceylon, Sri Lanka

Rev. Goyo de la Cruz Cutimanco, United Methodist Church, United States of America

Mr Kraig De Leon-Diedrick, United Church in Jamaica and the Cayman Islands, Jamaica

Mr Ralston H. Deffenbaugh, Lutheran World Federation, Switzerland

Dr Wanda Deifelt, Igreja Evangélica de Confissão Luterana no Brasil, United States of America

Ms Marie Dennis, Pax Christi International, United States of America

Ms Myrtha Deslume, Haitian/ Jamaican Society, Jamaica

Mr Geronimo Desumala, WCC United Nations Liaison Office, United States of America

Rev. Shirley DeWolf, Methodist Church in Zimbabwe

Mrs Sophie Dhanjal, World Council of Churches, Switzerland

Rev. Dr Moiseraele Prince Dibeela, Council for World Mission - CWM, South Africa

Ms Sylvia Dieter, Ökumenisches Netz Württemberg, Germany

Ms Maya Dietz, Seminarian, United States of America

Rev. Dr Gebre Georgis Dimtsu, Ethiopian Orthodox Tewahedo Church, United Kingdom

Rev. Jerda Djawa, Gereja Masehi Injili di Halmahera (GMIH), Indonesia

Ms Christine Dodd, Churches' Network for Nonviolence (CNNV), United Kingdom

Rev. Dr Andrew Donaldson, Presbyterian Church in Canada, Canada

Dr Hans-Joachim Döring, EKD-Evangelische Kirche in Mitteldeutschland, Germany

Rev. Margaret Downer-Messias, Disciples Ecumenical Consultative Council (Christian Churches), United States of America

Rev. Dr. Ulrich Duchrow, Kairos Europa, Germany

Ms Emily Duggan, United Church of Canada

Bishop Dr. Martin Dutzmann, EKD-Evangelical Church in Germany

Ms Torill Edoy, Ecumenical Disability Advocates Network, Norway

Mr Kelton Edwards, Church of God of Prophecy, Jamaica

Rev. Trevor Edwards, Jamaica Baptist Union

Rev. Helene Eichrodt-Kessel, Visitor, Germany

Prof. Barbara Einhorn, University of Sussex Department of Sociology, United Kingdom

Ms Charlotte Eisenberg, EIRENE - International Christian Service for Peace, Germany

Mr Peter Paul Ekker, IKV Pax Christi, Netherlands

Prof. Dr Amélé Ekué, World Council of Churches, Switzerland

Ms Fae Ellington, United Church in Jamaica and the Cayman Islands, Jamaica

Rev. Fr. Michael Elliott, Anglican Diocese of Jamaica

Mr Peter Emberson, Pacific Conference of Churches, Fiji

Dr Leonardo Emberti Gialloreti, Community of Sant'Egidio, Italy

Mr Benedikt August Enderle, Gen Rosso, Italy

Mr Irfan Engineer, Centre for Study of Society and Secularism, India

Prof. Dr Fernando Enns, Vereinigung der Deutschen Mennonitengemeinden, Germany

Mr Andre Enss Smith, Gospel Refuge Tabernacle, Jamaica

Mr Ciro Ercolanese, Gen Rosso, Italy

Ms Sanna Eriksson, Church of Sweden

Dr Faried Esack, University of Johannesburg, South Africa

Mrs Salpy Eskidjian Weiderud, Private Consultant on International Affairs, Cyprus

Mr Swaine Esson, United Church in Jamaica and the Cayman Islands, Jamaica

Mr Daren Evans, Anglican (Episcopal) Diocese of Jamaica

Mr Dwayne Fagan, United Church in Jamaica and the Caymen Islands, Jamaica

Mrs Veda Fagan, Methodist Church in the Caribbean and the Americas, Jamaica

Rev. Dr. Volker Faigle, EKD-Evangelical Church in Germany

Ms Lee Farrow, Seminarian, United States of America

Ms Solay Fearon, Church of God Prophecy, Jamaica

Mr Basil Ferguson, Medical team, Jamaica

Rev. Noel Osvaldo Fernández Collot, Ecumenical Disability Advocates Network, Cuba

Mr David Fernandez Puyana, Spanish Society for International Human Rights Law (SSIHRL), France

Mr Dhilanthi Fernando, Alliance of Baptists, Jamaica

Ms Robyn Fickes, National Council of Churches of Christ in the USA

Ms Sarah Finch, Gen Rosso, Italy

Rev. Dr. Thomas Finger, Mennonite Church USA

Mr Anthony Fischer, Media, Jamaica

Ms Donna Fitzpatrick-Lewis, Presbyterian Church in Canada

Ms Adrienne Fong, United Methodist Church, United States of America

Mr William Foster, CARA Communications, Jamaica

Mr Roy Foster, CARA Communications, Jamaica

Ms Kathryn Fournier, United Church of Canada

Mr Kevaughn Fraser, Local Volunteer, Jamaica

Ms Sharon Frater, Local Volunteer, Jamaica

Mr Jonathan Frerichs, World Council of Churches, Switzerland

Rev. Ulrich Frey, EKD-Evangelical Church in Germany

Mr Rudi Friedrich, Connection e.V. - Internationale Arbeit für Kriegsdienstverweigerer und Deserteure, Germany

Mr Henrik Frøjmark, Church of Sweden

Ms Julia Früh, Visitor, Germany

Mr Elroy Galbrath, Local Volunteer, Jamaica

Deacon Eva Alvalea Galimore, Bethel Baptist Church, Jamaica

Rt Revd Chad Nicholas Gandiya, Church of the Province of Central Africa, Zimbabwe

Mr Michael Garcia, World Student Christian Federation - WSCF, Philippines

Mr José Manuel García Lopez, Gen Rosso, Italy

Mrs Linnette Garcia Moodie, Religious Society of Friends (Quakers), Jamaica

Ms Carin Gardbring, Church of Sweden

Rev. Dr Paul Gardner, Moravian Church in Jamaica

Ms Beverley Garrick, Ethiopian Orthodox Church, Jamaica

Mr Gregg Gayle, Media, Jamaica

Rev. Daniel Wilhelm Geiser-Oppliger, Mennonite Church in Switzerland

Dr Magdi Gendi, Evangelical Theological Seminary, Egypt

H.E. Metropolitan Prof. Dr Gennadios of Sassima, Ecumenical Patriarchate, Turkey

Mr Valerio Gentile, Gen Rosso, Italy

Dr Mathews George, World Council of Churches, Switzerland

Dr Reena Mary George, Christian Medical College, India

Dr Samuel George, Ecumenical Disability Advocates Network, India

Rev. Dr Prof. Kondothra M. George, Orthodox Theological Seminary, India

Mr Peter Gerber, Reformed Churches Berne - Jura - Solothurn, Switzerland

Dr Joseph Gerson, American Friends Service Committee, United States of America

Mr Emanuele Gervasoni, Gen Rosso, Italy

Ms Tsovinar Ghazaryan, Armenia Inter-Church Charitable Round Table Foundation

Rev. Nilton Giese, Consejo Latinoamericano de Iglesias, Ecuador

Mr Miles Boudewijn Giljam, African Enterprise South Africa, South Africa

Rev. Theodore Gill, World Council of Churches, Switzerland

Mr Longgena Ginting, Vereinte Evangelische Mission, Indonesia

Ms Maria Rosina Girotti, Assisi Pax International, Italy

Rev. Dr Barbara Glasson, Methodist Church, United Kingdom

Ms Beth Godfrey, World Council of Churches, Switzerland

Ms Angela Godfrey-Goldstein, Grassroots Jerusalem, Israel

Dr. Nafisa Goga D'Souza, Laya, India

Mr Rodolfo José Gomez Moreno, Foro de Género y Lucha contra la Violencia, Paraguay

Mrs Moraima González Ortiz, Christian Institute of Studies of Gender, Cuba

Ms Maike Gorsboth, World Council of Churches, Switzerland

Rev. Krise Anki Gosal, Communion of Churches in Indonesia (PGI)

Archpriest Mikhail Goundiaev, Moscow Patriarchate (Russian Orthodox Church), Switzerland

Mrs Nakka Victoria Grace, United Evangelical Lutheran Churches in India

Ms Julie Grace, Seminarian, United States of America

Mr Rémond Graf, EAPPI, Switzerland

Rev. Mark Graham, Church of Melanesia, Solomon Islands

Ms Marcia Graham, Local Volunteer, Jamaica

Mr Gerard Granado, Caribbean Conference of Churches, Trinidad and Tobago

Ms Margareta Grape, World Council of Churches, Sweden

Ms Tamara Grdzelidze, World Council of Churches, Switzerland

Mr Omar Green, Media, Jamaica

Rev. Dr. Devorah Greenstein, Ecumenical Disability Advocates Network, United States of America

Mrs. Shaya Gregory, Presbyterian Church (USA)

Rev. Olaf Grobleben, EKD-Evangelical Lutheran Church in Oldenburg, Germany

Mrs Adriana Groenewegen, Ecumenical Disability Advocates Network, Netherlands

Fr Dr Daniel G. Groody, Notre Dame University, United States of America

Mrs Claudia Grosdidier Schibli, Interpreter, France

Mr Martin Gück, Kairos Europa, Germany

Mr Thomas Guisy, Visitor, Germany

Rev. Gomar Gultom, Huria Kristen Batak Protestan (HKBP), Indonesia

Dr Sybille Gundert-Hock, EKD-Evangelical Lutheran Church of Mecklenburg, Germany

Rev. Mechthild Gunkel, Evangelische Kirche in Hessen und Nassau (EKHN), Germany

Mr Sebastian Gunkel, EKD-Evangelisch-Lutherische Landeskirche Sachsens, Germany

Rev. Hartmut Haas, Evangelische Brüder-Unität, Switzerland

Bishop Gregorios Hadjiouraniou, Church of Cyprus

Prof. Heidi Hadsell, Hartford Seminary, United States of America

Mr Bill Hagarty, MFMci Conference Interpretation, United States of America

Ms Sepiuta Hala'api'api, Anglican Church in Aotearoa, New Zealand and Polynesia, Fiji

Ms Adele Halliday, United Church of Canada

Ms Karin Hallin, EAPPI, Sweden

Rev. Dr. Carlos Ham, World Council of Churches, Switzerland

Most Rev. Dr K.G. Hammar, Church of Sweden, Sweden

Rev. Dr Kook Il Han, Presbyterian Church of Korea, Republic of Korea

Mr Jerico Hanson, Church of God of Prophecy, Jamaica

Ms Ann Hanson, United Church of Christ, United States of America

Dr Yanike Hanson, Seminario Evangélico de Teología, Cuba

Mr Alexander Harang, Peace for Life, Norway

Mr Michiel Hardon, Oikos, Netherlands

Rev. Alice Harper-Jones, United Church of Christ, United States of America

Prof. Anthony Harriott, Violence Prevention Alliance, Jamaica

Rev. Gary Harriott, Jamaica Council of Churches, Jamaica

Mr Mark Harrison, United Methodist Church, United States of America

Ms Katrin Hatzinger, EKD-Evangelical Church in Germany, Belgium

Rev Reinhard Hauff, Visitor, Germany

Mr Tyler Hauger, Evangelical Lutheran Church in America, Norway

Mr Rob Hay, Redcliffe College, United Kingdom

Ms Jelise Hayden, Local Volunteer, Jamaica

Ms Florella Hannah Adelaide Hazeley, Sierra Leone Action Network on Small Arms (SLANSA)

Mr Lefrank Hedghill, Local Volunteer, Jamaica

Rev. Andrew Hefkie, Methodist Church of Southern Africa, South Africa

Mr Klaus Heidel, Evangelische Kirche in Deutschland, Kirchenamt der EKD, Germany

Mr Marc-Henri Heiniger, World Council of Churches, Switzerland

Dr Wolfgang Heinrich, Church Development Service, Germany

Rev. Anne Heitmann, EKD-Evangelical Church in Baden, Germany

Mr Michael Held, EKD-Evangelical Church of Kurhessen Waldeck, Germany

Mr Raymond Helmick, Seminarian - Mentor, United States of America

Rev. Dr Margaretha M. Hendriks-Ririmasse, Gereja Protestan Maluku (GPM), Indonesia

Rev. Sarah Henken, Presbyterian Church (USA), Bolivia

Ms Caroline Hennessy, World Council of Churches, Switzerland

Rev. Dr. Roy Henry, Jamaica Baptist Union

Mr Arlene Henry, Local Volunteer, Jamaica

Mrs Mauleen Henry, United Church in Jamaica and the Cayman Islands, Jamaica

Mr Anthony Henry, Media, Jamaica

Rev Susan Henry-Crowe, United Methodist Church, United States of America

Mrs Rusheyne Henry-Ferguson, Jamaica Council of Churches

Ms Winsome Heslop, Violence Prevention Alliance, Jamaica

Ms Angela Hesse, EKD-Evangelical Church of Bremen, Germany

Rev. Izaac Hendry Hetharie, Gereja Protestan Maluku (GPM), Indonesia

Mr Shir Hever, The Alternative Information Center, Germany

Rev. Dr. Roderick Hewitt, Council for World Mission - CWM, South Africa

Rev. Edgar Hewry, Jamaica Baptist Union

H.E. Metropolitan Hilarion of Volokolamsk, Russian Orthodox Church (Moscow Patriarchate), Russian Federation

Mr Michael Hiller, EAPPI, Germany

Mrs Ruth Hilton, Touchstone, United Kingdom

Rev. Sylvan Hinds, United Church in Jamaica and the Cayman Islands, Jamaica

Dr Elizabeth Hinson-Hasty, St Andrews Presbyterian College, United States of America

Ms Almut Hinz, EKD-Evangelical Church of Bremen, Germany

Rev. Rudolf Hinz, Theological Faculty of the University of Kiel, Germany

Mr Ashley Wesley Hodgson Rios, Iglesia Morava en Nicaragua

Rev. Verena Hoff, EKD-Evangelical Reformed Church Bavaria and Northwestern Germany

Mrs Christine Hoffmann, Deutsche Kommission Justitia et Pax, Germany

Ms Rhian Holder, Christian Aid, Jamaica

Rev. Dr. Professor Scott Holland, Bethany Theological Seminary, United States of America

Dr Trevor Hope, Local Volunteer, Jamaica

Ms Anna Hopfer-Wola, Evangelical Church of the Augsburg Confession in Poland

Ms Christine Housel, World Student Christian Federation - WSCF, Switzerland

Ms Kristine Hofseth Hovland, Christian Council of Norway

Rev. Dr. Ralph Hoyte, United Church in Jamaica and the Cayman Islands, Jamaica

Rev. Hong-Chi Hu, Presbyterian Church in Taiwan

Mr Steve Hucklesby, Methodist Church, United Kingdom

Sr. Bernadette Hughes, Roman Catholic Archdiocese of Kingston, Jamaica

Rev. Greg Hughson, Methodist Church of New Zealand

Rev. Chun Jung Huh, Presbyterian Church of Korea, Thailand

Mrs. Marilyn Hull, Methodist Church, United Kingdom

Prof. John Hull, Methodist Church, United Kingdom

Mrs Ana Huml-Zontar, Taizé Community, Bosnia Herzegovina

Rev. Abraham L. Hutasoit, Christian Protestant Angkola Church (GKPA), Indonesia

Mr Yhomo Hutchinson, Media, Jamaica

Mr Winston Hutchinson, Local Volunteer, Jamaica

Mr Merlyn Hyde-Riley, Local Committee Seminarian, Jamaica

Ms Laura Tuulikki Hytti, Evangelical Lutheran Church of Finland

Ms. Anna Hyvärinen, Finnish Ecumenical Council

Venerable Dr John Olusola Igbari, Church of Nigeria (Anglican Communion)

Mr Daniel Infanger, Seminarian, Switzerland

Ms Margareta Ingelstam, Mission Covenant Church of Sweden

Rev. Neila Ingram, African Methodist Episcopal Church, Jamaica

Rev. Dr Carlos Intipampa Aliaga, Instituto Superior Ecuménico Andino de Teología - ISEAT, Bolivia

Mr Eric Mwangi Irungu, Gen Rosso, Italy

Rev. Endre Iszlai, Reformed Church in Hungary

Rev. Daniel Izquierdo Hernández, Iglesia Presbiteriana-Reformada en Cuba

Ms Kati Jääskeläinen, Evangelical Lutheran Church of Finland

Ms Maryse Jackman, Medical team, Jamaica

Ms Amber Jackson, Seminarian, Jamaica

Ms Susan Jacob, Malankara Orthodox Syrian Church, India

Mr Vonnie E.L. James, Seminarian, Jamaica

Rev. Ioan Livius Jebelean, Polish Catholic Church in Poland, Switzerland

Ms Janice Jenner, Eastern Mennonite University, United States of America

Ms Jagbir Jhutti-Johal, University of Birmingham, United Kingdom

Dr Ruthann K. Johansen, Church of the Brethren, United States of America

Prof. Robert Johansen, Church of the Brethren, United States of America

Ms Mari Johansen Aune, Changemaker, Norway

Mrs Dawn Johns-Gordon, Anglican Diocese of Jamaica

Mr Victor Johnson, Media, Jamaica

Mr Anthony Johnson, Media, Jamaica

Ms Claude Johnson, Media, Jamaica

The Rt. Rev Dr S. Tilewa Johnson, Anglican Diocese of Gambia, Gambia

Rev. Karl Johnson, Jamaica Baptist Union

Ms Kelli Jolly, Methodist Church in the Caribbean and the Americas, Jamaica

Rev. Kjell Jonasson, Jerusalem Inter-Church Centre (JIC), Palestine

Mr Wendell Jones, Seminarian, Jamaica

Mr John Y. Jones, Networkers SouthNorth, Norway

Mr Bernt Jonsson, Media, Sweden

Mr Jason Jordan, Emmanuel Apostolic Church, Jamaica

Ms Iselin Jørgensen, Christian Council of Norway

Rev. Svein G. Josefsen, Visitor, Norway

Mr Rastko Jovic, Pedagogical-Catechetical Institute of Theological Faculty, Serbia

Dr Samuel Njuguna Kabue, Ecumenical Disability Advocates Network, Kenya

Mrs Nancy Mugure Kabue, Ecumenical Disability Advocates Network, Kenya

Ms Anne-Kathrin Kaiser, Gen Rosso, Germany

Rev. Canon Grace Clement Kaiso Isabirye, Council of Anglican Provinces of Africa (CAPA), Kenya

Dr Pantelis Kalaitzidis, Volos Academy for Theological Studies, Greece

Rev. Micheline Kamba Kasongo, Église du Christ au Congo - Communauté presbytérienne de Kinshasa, South Africa

Ms Desiree' Kameka, World Student Christian Federation - WSCF, United States of America

Mrs Jenitha Abela Kameli, Evangelical Lutheran Church in Tanzania

Ms Melissa Kaminker, Christian Health Association Platform (ACHAP), Kenya

Mr Victor Kaonga, Trans World Radio, Malawi

Ms Annegret Kapp, World Council of Churches, Switzerland

Mr Mathias Kaps, Gen Rosso, Germany

Ms Carmencita Karagdag, Peace for Life, Philippines

Dr Camillus Kassala, The Standing Interfaith Committee on Socio-economic Justice and Integrity of Creation, Tanzania

Prof Dr. Margot Kässmann, EKD-Evangelical Lutheran Church of Hanover, Germany

Mr Anthony Kelly, Media, Jamaica

Dr Konstantinos Kenanidis, Ecumenical Patriarchate, Greece

Ms Joy Kennedy, United Church of Canada

Bp William Kenney, Gothenburg Process, United Kingdom

Dr Guillermo Kerber, World Council of Churches, Switzerland

Mr Michael Kerr, Media, Jamaica

Rev. Dr Jooseop Keum, World Council of Churches, Switzerland

Colonel Oral Khan, Violence Prevention Alliance, Jamaica

Mr Kom Khandech, Ecumenical Disability Advocates Network, Thailand

Mr Wassim H. Khazmo, Palestinian Negotiations Support Unit, Palestine

Ms Tamar Khositashvili, Georgian Orthodox Church

Mr Yohannes Ogubamichel Kidane, Connection e.V. - Internationale Arbeit für Kriegsdienstverweigerer und Deserteure, Germany

Ms Marianne Kilchenmann, Reformierte Kirchen Bern-Jura-Solothurn, Switzerland

Ms Susan Kim, United Methodist Church, United States of America

Rev. Munkee Kim, Asia Pacific Center for Integral Study of Life & Asia Pacific Graduate School for the Study of Life, Republic of Korea

Prof. Yong-Bock Kim, Advanced Institute for Integral Study of Life & Asia Pacific Graduate School for the Study of Life, Republic of Korea

Rev. Kyung In Kim, Presbyterian Church of Korea, Republic of Korea

Dr Kirsteen Kim, Leeds Trinity University College, United Kingdom

Dr Martin Luther King III, The King Center, Untied States of America

Mrs Mbari Kioni, All Africa Conference of Churches, Kenya

Mr Vakhtang V. Kipshidze, Russian Orthodox Church (Moscow Patriarchate), Russian Federation

Mrs Marina Kiroudi, Arbeitsgemeinschaft Christlicher Kirchen in Deutschland e.V., Germany

Ms Kanan Kitani, United Church of Christ in Japan

Rev. Charles Klagba-Kuadjovi, Eglise méthodiste du Togo

Bishop Milos Klátik, Evangelical Church of the Augsburg Confession in Slovakia

Mr Michael Klatt, EKD-Nordelbische Evangelisch-Lutherische Kirche, Germany

Mrs Gitta Klein, Visitor, Germany

Ms Natasha Klukach, World Council of Churches, Switzerland

Ms Marcia Knight, Local Volunteer, Jamaica

Rev. Detlev Knoche, Zentrum Oekumene der EKHN, Germany

Mr Senaid Kobilica, Islamic Council of Norway

Ms Julika Koch, EKD-North Elbian Evangelical Lutheran Church, Germany

Rev William M. Koenig, Presbyterian Church (USA) - World Mission

Mr Kensuke Koito, Seminarian, Japan

Mr Toreon Albert Kong, Blessings and Deliverance Church of God, Jamaica

Mrs Judith Königsdörfer, Protestant Church in Central Germany

Mrs Susan Koshy, Advanced Institute for Integral Study of Life & Asia Pacific Graduate School for the Study of Life, Korea

Dr Ninan Koshy, Advanced Institute for Integral Study of Life & Asia Pacific Graduate School for the Study of Life – Korea

Mr Nikos Kosmidis, World Council of Churches, Greece

Mrs Arpi Kouzouian, Armenian Apostolic Church (Mother See of Holy Etchmiadzin)

Ms Asha Kowtal, NCDHR, India

Ms Marie Ann Krahn, Evangelical Church of the Lutheran Confession in Brazil

Ms Joy Faith Kronenberg, South African Council of Churches

Rev. Claudia Kuchenbauer, EKD-Evangelical Lutheran Church in Bavaria, Germany

Mr Masimba Lovemore Kuchera, Students Solidarity Trust, Zimbabwe

Mrs Regula Kummer, Federation of Swiss Protestant Churches, Switzerland

Mrs Heidi Kusmin-Bergenstad, World YWCA, Finland

Rev. Lorenst Kuzatjike, EKD-Evangelical Church in Rhineland, Germany

Rev. Andrzej Kuzma, Polish Autocephalous Orthodox Church

H. E. Seraphim Kykkotis, Greek Orthodox Patriarchate of Alexandria and All Africa, Zimbabwe

Mr Jorge Laffite, American Friends Serivice Committee (AFSC), Brazil

Ms Leslene Laing, Local Volunteer, Jamaica

Mr Glenroy Lalor, Seminarian - Mentor, Jamaica

Rev. Holger Lam, Baptist Union of Denmark

Ms Sacha Lambert, Local Volunteer, Jamaica

Ms Willemijn Lammers, ICCO & Kerk in Actie, Netherlands

Mr Rainer Lang, Visitor, Germany

Rev. Paul Lansu, Pax Christi International, Belgium

Father Michael Lapsley, Institute for Healing of Memories, South Africa

Mr Shane Lawrence, Local Volunteer, Jamaica

Mr Dane Lawrence, Local Volunteer, Jamaica

Bishop Nathanael Lazaro, Evangelical Methodist Church in the Philippines

Rev. Hum-Sam Lee, National Council of Churches in Korea

Rev. Dr. Hong Jung Lee, Presbyterian Church of Korea, Republic of Korea

Ms Ye Ja Lee, Ecumenical Disability Advocates Network, Republic of Korea

Mr Yun Hee Lee, National Council of YMCAs of Korea Life-Peace Center, Republic of Korea

Prof. Dr Lee Samuel Lee, National Council of Churches in Korea, Republic of Korea

Mr Ha Jung Lee, Seminarian, Republic of Korea

Mr Philip Lee, World Association for Christian Communication - WACC, Canada

Dr Nigussu Legesse, World Council of Churches, Switzerland

Mr Daniel Legutke, Deutsche Kommission Justitia et Pax, Germany

Mr Marcelo Leites, Federación Universal de Movimientos Estudiantiles Cristianos (FUMEC), Argentina

Prof. Puleng Lenka Bula, College of Human Sciences, South Africa

Mr Horace Levy, Violence Prevention Alliance, Jamaica

Rev Marjorie Lewis, United Theological College of the West Indies, Jamaica

Dr Patricia Lewis, Center for Nonproliferation Studies Monterey Institute of International Studies, United States of America

Mr Jason Lewis, Providence Methodist Church, Jamaica

Ms. Lichiou Li, Seminarian, United States of America

Mr Joshua Lian, Seminarian, Taiwan

Ms Amica Liburd, Seminarian, Jamaica

Rev. Dr Swee Hong Lim, United Methodist Church, United States of America

Ms Alcris Limongi, United Church of Canada

Dr Rommel F. Linatoc, National Council of Churches in the Philippines

Ms Melissa Lindo, Medical team, Jamaica

Ms Latonya Linton, Media, Jamaica

Mr Oliver Livingston, United Church in Jamaica and the Cayman Islands, Jamaica

Rev. Anna Ljung, Swedish Mission Council

Mr Jorge Lockward, United Methodist Church, United States of America

Rev. Tristan Bernard Lola Pulumba, Church of Christ in Congo - Mennonite Community in Congo

Ms Peta-Ann Long, Portmore Gospel Chapel, Jamaica

Rev. Dr. A. Wati Longchar, Senate of Serampore College, India

Mr Yuri Gala Lopez, Cuban Embassy, Cuba

Sr Ernestina Lopez Bac, Roman Catholic Bishops' Conference of Guatemala

Dr Janice Love, Candler School of Theology, Emory University, United States of America

Mrs Alix Lozano Forero, Iglesia Cristiana Menonita de Colombia

Mrs Betty Ruth Lozano Lerma, Fundacion Akina Saji Sauda - Conexión de Mujeres Negras y de Tradición Bautista y Ecuménica por conv., Colombia

Rev. Nicta M. Lubaale, Organisation of African Instituted Churches, Kenya

Ms Esther Lubunga Kenge, Circle of Concerned African Women Theologians, South Africa

Mrs Monika Lude, EMS - Evangelisches Missionswerk in Südwestdeutschland e.V., Germany

Rev. Tafue M. Lusama, Ekalesia Kelisiano Tuvalu E.

Ms Ruut Luukkonen, Changemaker, Finland

Mr Bongani Luvalo, Uniting Presbyterian Church in Southern Africa, South Africa

Rev. Hong-Tiong Lyim, Presbyterian Church in Taiwan

Mr Stefan Maass, EKD-Evangelische Landeskirche in Baden, Germany

Mrs Ana Pickering Macanawai, Ecumenical Disability Advocates Network, Fiji

Mr Setareki Seru Macanawai, Ecumenical Disability Advocates Network, Fiji

Rev. Peter Macdonald, Iona Community, United Kingdom

Miss Christine MacMillan, The Salvation Army, United States of America

Mr Richard Madete, Vereinte Evangelische Mission, Tanzania

Mr Enoch Magala, Greek Orthodox Patriarchate of Alexandria and All Africa, Uganda

Mr Sanju Maharaj, Medical team, Jamaica

Rev. Elizabeth Christina Mailoa-Marantika, Gereja Protestan Maluku (GPM), Indonesia

Mr Justin Makaruse, Seminarian, Jamaica

Ms Daneillia Malcolm, Local Volunteer, Jamaica

Ms Mae Maureen Malecdan, Episcopal Church in the Philippines

Mrs Vicenta Mamani Bernabe, Red Internacional de Derechos Humanos (RIDH), Bolivia

Rev. Dr Deenabandhu Manchala, World Council of Churches, Switzerland

Ms Gladys Mangiduyos, Seminarian, Philippines

Rev. Dr. Varghese Manimala, Henry Martyn Institute of Islamic Studies, India

Rt. Rev. Dr Philip Phembuar Marandi, Church of North India, India

Mrs Seta Margossian-Hadeshian, Middle East Council of Churches, Lebanon

Rev. Hugo Marillán Millavil, Iglesia Metodista de Chile

Rev. Chandran Paul Martin, Lutheran World Federation, Switzerland

Ms Eileen Tamara Martinez Lewis, Iglesia Morava en Nicaragua,

Rev. Christopher Mason, United Church in Jamaica and the Cayman Islands, Jamaica

Mr Ntsikelelo Mateta, Institute for Healing of Memories, South Africa

Mr Gordon Matthews, Friends World Committee for Consultation, United Kingdom

Rev. Edward M. Matuvhunye, United Church of Christ in Zimbabwe

Mr Jeremy Maxwell, Medical team, Jamaica

Dr Fulata Mbano-Moyo, World Council of Churches, Switzerland

Rev. Dr Johnson Apenad Mbillah, Programme for Christian-Muslim Relations in Africa (Procmura), Kenya

Mr Ryan McGregor, Methodist (Inter-denominational), Jamaica

Mr Gregg McCalla, Media, Jamaica

Mr Kerron McCalla, Media, Jamaica

Ms Mikka McCracken, Lutheran World Federation, United States of America

Ms Joan McDonald, Anglican Diocese of Jamaica

Ms Sheldon McIntosh, Medical team, Jamaica

Rev. Brian McIntosh, United Church of Canada

Mr Leon McPherson, Media, Jamaica

Mr Craig Mears, Anglican (Episcopal) Diocese of Jamaica

Mr Johannes Meier, Media, Germany

Mr Marcial Melian, Cuban Embassy, Cuba

Mr John Mendez, Progressive National Baptist Church, Inc., United States of America

Ms Sarah Mendez, Progressive National Baptist Church USA, Jamaica

Mrs Alexandra Monica Meneses Andrade, Ecumenical Disability Advocates Network, Kenya

Ms Beatrice Merahi, World Council of Churches, Switzerland

Ms Senwelo Erica Mere, Methodist Church of Southern Africa, South Africa

Mr Alain Meuwly, World Council of Churches, Switzerland

Ms Jéruscha Vasti Michel, World Association for Christian Communication (WACC), Haiti

Mr Matti Michelmann, European Forum of Lesbian, Gay, Bisexual and Transgender Christian Groups, Latvia

Mr Tomasz Mikusinski, Gen Rosso, Italy

Mrs Maha Milki Wehbe, Middle East Council of Churches, Lebanon

Ms Grace Miller, Methodist Church, Jamaica

Prof. Michael Miller, Christian Theological Seminary, United States of America

Ms Afesha Millette, Methodist Church in the Caribbean and the Americas, Jamaica

Mr Donurine Mills, Local Volunteer, Jamaica

Ms Marlene Milner, Stitching Peace, United Kingdom

Mr Stanley Milner, Stitching Peace, United Kingdom

Dr Keisha Mitchell, Methodist (Saxphorpe-Western St. Andrew Circuit), Jamaica

Rt. Rev. Valentine Mokiwa, Anglican Church of Tanzania

Rev. Dr Lennart Molin, Christian Council of Sweden

Rev. Subodh Chandra Mondal, Methodist Church in India

Ms Greta Montoya, Presbyterian Reformed Church of Cuba

Mr Bevar Moodie, Society of Friends (Quakers), Jamaica

Rev. Christopher Robert Morck, Consejo Latinoamericano de Iglesias, Ecuador

Ms Sylvia Morrison, Christian Peacemaker Teams, Canada

Rev. Sunitha Mortha, Evangelical Lutheran Church in America

Ms Cathleen Moss, Ecumenical Network for Youth Action, Czechoslovak Hussite Church, Czech Republic

Sr Mary Motte, Mission Resource Center, Franciscan Missionaries of Mary, United States of America

Rev. Dr Jochen Motte, Vereinte Evangelische Mission, Germany

Ms Amohelang Mpiriane, Methodist Church of Southern Africa, South Africa

Dr Rogate Mshana, World Council of Churches, Switzerland

Mr Nader Muaddi, EAPPI, Palestine

Mrs Josephine Bwalya Muchelemba, United Church of Zambia

Mr Paul Edward Muego, Oikos, Philippines

Rev Joachim Mukambu Ya'Namwisi, Church of Christ in Congo - Mennonite Community in Congo

Dr Eberhard Müller, Visitor, Germany

Dr Geiko Müller-Fahrenholz, United Lutheran Church of Germany

Mgr Bernard Munono Muyembe, Roman Catholic Church - Official Delegation, Vatican City

Mr Ivan Murray, Spiritual Prayer Deliverance, Jamaica

Bishop Julio E. Murray, Consejo Latinoamericano de Iglesias, Panama

Rev. Dr. Ezamo Murry, Ecumenical Disability Advocates Network, India

Dr Muna Mushahwar, Arab Orthodox Union Club, Palestine

Mr Zejnulla Mustafa, World Council of Churches, Switzerland

Ms Clara Minoo Muthuka, All Africa Conference of Churches, Kenya

Rev Istvan Muzsnai, Ecumenical Disability Advocates Network, Hungary

Dr Samuel Mwenda, Christian Health Association Platform (ACHAP), Kenya

Chairwoman Jang Myungsook, Ecumenical Disability Advocates Network, Republic of Korea

Mrs Alida Nababan, Huria Kristen Batak Protestan (HKBP), Indonesia

Dr Soritua Albert Ernst Nababan, Huria Kristen Batak Protestan (HKBP), Indonesia

Prof Sarojini Nadar, University of KwaZulu-Natal School of Religion and Theology, South Africa

Rev John Donald Naudé, Ecumenical Disability Advocates Network, United Kingdom

Mr Lukasz Nazarko, Polish Autocephalous Orthodox Church

Dr Karen Nazaryan, Armenian Apostolic Church (Mother See of Holy Etchmiadzin)

Rev. Notsen Ncube, Brethren in Christ Church Zimbabwe

Rev. Olivier Ndayizeye Munyansanga, Presbyterian Church of Rwanda

Rev. Thulani Ndlazi, Church Land Programme, South Africa

Mr Joseph Nelson, Local Volunteer, Jamaica

Mrs Margarita B. Nelyubova, Russian Orthodox Church (Moscow Patriarchate), Russian Federation

Ms Binalakshmi Nepram, Control Arms Foundation of India & Manipur Women Gun Survivors Network, India

Rev. Johannes Neudeck, EKD-Evangelical Lutheran Church of Saxony, Germany

Mr Michael Neuroth, United Church of Christ, United States of America

Rev. Senoro Newell, African Methodist Episcopal Church, Jamaica

Ms Beverly Newell, Anglican Diocese of Jamaica, Jamaica

Mrs Sarah Newland-Martin, Ecumenical Disability Advocates Network, Jamaica

Mr Dennis Ng Rosales, Gen Rosso, Italy

Mr Kees Nieuwerth, Religious Society of Friends (Quakers), Netherlands

Ms Anna Malin Nilsson, Church of Sweden

Canon Joyce Nima, Uganda Joint Christian Council

Rev. Weldon Nisly, Seattle Mennonite Church, United States of America

Ms Chrisida Nithyakalyani, Tamil Evangelical Lutheran Church, India

Mr Stanley Noffsinger, Church of the Brethren, United States of America

Lic Ormara Alicia Nolla, Ecumenical Disability Advocates Network, Cuba

Rev. James Noonan, Maryknoll Office for Global Concerns, United States of America

Ms Cvijeta Novakovic, CCPN-Centar za Kulturu Mira i Nenasilja, Bosnia Herzegovina

Mr Giovanni Novelli, Media, Italy

Mr Gianni Novello, Pax Christi Italy

Mr Michel Nseir, World Council of Churches, Switzerland

Ms Utelene Nugent, Media, Jamaica

Pfarrerin Dr. Gerdi Nützel, EKD-Evangelical Church in Berlin-Brandenburg-Silesian Oberlausitz, Germany

Rev. Léon Halo Nyikeine, Eglise évangélique en Nouvelle-Calédonie et aux Iles Loyauté, New Caledonia

Rev Gerardo Carlos Cristian Oberman, Iglesias Reformadas en Argentina

Mr Carlos Ocampo, Christian Conference of Asia, Thailand

Brother Clive Ocnacuwenga, Moravian Church in Jamaica

Ms Cynthia Odera, Ecumenical Disability Advocates Network, Kenya

Dr. Ulrich Oelschläger, EKD-Evangelical Church in Hesse and Nassau, Germany

Canon Dr Paul Oestreicher, British Yearly Meeting, Religious Society of Friends, United Kingdom

Rev. Pernille Oestrem, Evangelical Lutheran Church in Denmark

Mr Jussi Ojala, FinnChurchAid, Finland

Ms Abigail Okyere, Presbyterian Church of Ghana

Archbishop Orlando Oliveira, Igreja Episcopal Anglicana do Brasil, Brazil

Ms Harriett Jane Olson, United Methodist Church, United States of America

Mr Oluremi Omotoso, Methodist Church Nigeria

Bishop Sunday Ndukwo Onuoha, Methodist Church Nigeria

Rev. Dr Ofelia Ortega Suárez, Iglesia Presbiteriana-Reformada en Cuba

Archbishop Dr Rufus Ositelu, Church of the Lord (Aladura) Worldwide, Nigeria

Ms Deri Ann Palmer, Jamaica Baptist Union

Rev. Harry R. Panjaitan, Indonesian Christian Church (HKI)

Ms Pauline Pannell, Seminarian, Jamaica

Ms Christina Papazoglou, World Council of Churches, Switzerland

Ms Marlin Junita Paranggai, Gereja Toraja, Indonesia

Mr Jean-Michel Paris, World Council of Churches, Switzerland

Rev. Prof. Dr Seong-Won Park, Young Nam Theological University and Seminary, Republic of Korea

Ms Janet Parkinson, Local Volunteer, Jamaica

Reverend Evalina Pasaribu, Indonesian Christian Church (HKI)

Ms Margaret A. Pater, Interpreter, Germany

Mr Alexander Patico, Orthodox Peace Fellowship North America, United States of America

Mr Chris Patterson, Media, Jamaica

Rev. Dr. Peter Pavlovic, Conference of European Churches, Church and Society Commission, Belgium

Rev. Dr. Philip Vinod Peacock, Church of North India

His Grace Athenagoras Peckstadt, Ecumenical Patriarchate, Belgium

Rev. Dr Jayasiri Peiris, Church of Ceylon, Sri Lanka

Ms Aikaterini Pekridou, Volos Academy for Theological Studies, Ireland

Ms Athena Peralta, World Council of Churches, Philippines

Dr Mindawati Perangin-angin, Karo Batak Protestant Church (GBKP), Indonesia

Mrs Adriana Perez, Cuban Embassy, Consejo de Iglesias de Cuba

Mr Ray Perez, MFMci Conference Interpretation, United States of America

Dr Anna Perkins, Roman Catholic Church, Jamaica

Mr Ferdinando Perna, Gen Rosso, Italy

Rev. Lennart Persson, The Church Resource Centre Against Violence and Sexual Abuse, Norway

Rev. Rodney Petersen, Boston Theological Institute, United States of America

Mr Hung Pham, Roman Catholic Church, Vatican City

Mrs Anila Philip, Church of South India

Rev Bijesh Philip, Malankara Orthodox Syrian Church, India

Mr Modayil Mani Philip, Church of South India

Ms Phillipia Phillips, Media, Jamaica

Bishop Dr Isaac Mar Philoxenos, Mar Thoma Syrian Church of Malabar, India

Prof Alison Phipps, Iona Community/Scottish Episcopal Church, United Kingdom

Prof. Isabel Apawo Phiri, University of Kwazulu-Natal, South Africa

Rev. Dr Larry Pickens, United Methodist Church, United States of America

Mrs Iulia Picu, Oikos, Romania

Rev. Garland Pierce, World Council of Churches, United States of America

Dr Matti Pikkarainen, Evangelical Lutheran Church of Finland

Mrs Claudette Pious, Violence Prevention Alliance, Jamaica

Dr. Kathryn Poethig, Seminarian, United States of America

Ms Annette Poitier, Fellowship of the Least Coin, Bahamas

Ms Alexandra Pomezny, World Council of Churches, Switzerland

Mrs Johanna Simone Poortman, Protestant Church in the Netherlands

Rev. Thomas Porter, Seminarian - Mentor, United States of America

Mr Ralf-Erik Posselt, Evangelische Kirche in Deutschland, Kirchenamt der EKD, Germany

Ds Janna Postma, Mennonite Church in the Netherlands

Mr Mano Pottinger, Media, Jamaica

Rev. Dr Bernice Powell Jackson, United Church of Christ, United States of America

Dr Joseph Prabhakar Dayam, United Theological College, India

Rev. Dr Shanta Premawardhana, United Church of Canada, United States of America

Rev Thomas Prieto Peral, Foundation Wings of Hope, Germany

Ms Olvi Prihutami, Communion of Churches in Indonesia (PGI)

Dr. Elizabeth H. Prodromou, Ecumenical Patriarchate, United States of America

Mr Jean Charles Puippe, Raptim Travel, Switzerland

Prof. Ram Puniyani, All India Secular Forum, India

Rev. Nigel Pusey, United Church in Jamaica and the Cayman Islands, Jamaica

Dr Martin Quack, Brot für die Welt, Germany

Dr Audeh B. Quawas, Greek Orthodox Patriarchate of Jerusalem, Jordan

Mr Manuel Quintero Perez, World Council of Churches, Switzerland

Mr Dirk Rademacher, Evangelische Kirche in Deutschland, Kirchenamt der EKD, Germany

Rev. Dr Konrad Raiser, EKD-Evangelische Kirche in Deutschland, Germany

Rev. Dr Peniel Jesudason Rufus Rajkumar, United Theological College, India

Mr Christopher Rajkumar, National Council of Churches in India

Dr Modeste Rakoto Endor, Malagasy Lutheran Church, Madagascar

Ms Micaela Ramirez, Cuban Embassy, Cuba

Mrs Mireya Ramirez Marquez, Swiss Interchurch Aid, Colombia

Ms Amy Ramiro-Calumpag, United Church of Christ in the Philippines

Mr Jean Denys Louisy Rano, Russian Orthodox Church (Moscow Patriarchate)

Ms Ruth Rapp, Visitor, Germany

Ms Siham Rashid, Ecumenical Accompaniment Program in Palestine and Israel, Palestine

Dr Theodor Rathgeber, Vereinte Evangelische Mission, Germany

Ms Ralphine Razaka Manantenasoa, Ecumenical Disability Advocates Network, Madagascar

Most Rev. Donald J. Reece, Caribbean Conference of Churches, Jamaica

Rev Kathy Nadine Reeves, United Methodist Church, United States of America

Rev. Jürgen Reichel, EKD-Evangelical Church in Germany, Germany

Ms Imogene Reid, Local Volunteer, Jamaica

Mrs Paulette Reid, Mother's Union, Jamaica

Rev. Dr Delroy Reid-Salmon, Oxford Centre for Christianity and Culture, United States of America

Mr Adelson Jorge Reis de Oliveira, Gen Rosso, Italy

Rev. Mark Reisinger, United Methodist Church, United States of America

Ms. Regina Reuschle, Interpreter, Switzerland

Rev. Fr Rex R.B. Reyes, Jr., National Council of Churches in the Philippines

Ms Lisa Rheinheimer, EKD-Evangelical Church of the Palatinate, Germany

Ms Ellen Ribeiro, Church of Norway

Mr L. Seaton Richards, Media, Jamaica

Rev. Msgr. Kenneth Richards, Roman Catholic Church - Official Delegation, Jamaica

Rev Dr Tony Richie, Church of God, United States of America

Mrs Sue Richie, Church of God, United States of America

Rev. Klaus Rieth, EKD-Evangelical Church in Württemberg, Germany

Rev. Father Martin Ritsi, Orthodox Autocephalous Church of Albania, United States of America

Mrs Ruby Robertson-McGhie, Methodist Church in the Caribbean and the Americas, Antigua and Barbuda

Mr Cory Robinson, Media, Jamaica

Ms Heather Robinson, Moravian Church in Jamaica

Mrs Marjorie Robotham, Interpreter, Jamaica

Rev. Dr Martin W. H. Robra, World Council of Churches, Switzerland

Mr Carlton Rodney, United Church in Jamaica and the Cayman Islands, Jamaica

Ms Norva Rodney, Jamaica Baptist Union

Rev. Dushantha Lakshman Rodrigo, Church of Ceylon, Sri Lanka

Ms Marta T. Rodriguez, Presbyterian Church (USA)

Mrs Martha-Inés Romero, Pax Christi International, Colombia

Dr Birgit Rommel, Visitor, Germany

Rev. Dr. Pascale Rondez Drammeh, Federation of Swiss Protestant Churches

Rev. Garnett Roper, Jamaica Theological Seminary

Mr Mario Rose, Local Volunteer, Jamaica

Don Adriano Rosso, Media, Italy

Rev. Eilert Rostrup, Church of Norway

Ms Donna-Marie Rowe, Media, Jamaica

Rev. Barbara Rudolph, EKD-Evangelical Church in Rhineland, Germany

Dr. Victoria Rue, Seminarian, United States of America

Mrs Marietta Ruhland, World Council of Churches, Switzerland

Ms Katrin Rux, EKD-Evangelical Church in Central Germany

Mrs Olga Salanueva, Cuban Embassy, Consejo de Iglesias de Cuba

Ms Jutta Salzmann, EKD-Evangelical Lutheran Church in Brunswick, Germany

Rev. Izett Samá Hernández, Iglesia Presbiteriana-Reformada en Cuba

Rev. Georges Samoela, Malagasy Lutheran Church, Madagascar

Mr Keith Samuda, Local Volunteer, Jamaica

Ms Jacqueline Samuda, Local Volunteer, Jamaica

Fr. Gebre Selessie Eric Samuels, Ethiopian Orthodox Church, Jamaica

Mrs Sara San Martín, Centro de Estudios Ecuménicos, Mexico

Mrs Noeline Sanders, Church of England, United Kingdom

Revd. Samuel Azeem Sandhu, Church of Pakistan

Mr Luigi Sandri, Media, Italy

Rev. Dr Dan Sandu, Romanian Orthodox Church

Rev Eunice Santana, Christian Church (Disciples of Christ) in the United States of America, Puerto Rico

Ms June Saunders, Local Volunteer, Jamaica

Ms Maxine Savage, Local Volunteer, Jamaica

Mrs Anne-Marie Saxer-Steinlin, Reformierte Kirchen Bern-Jura-Solothurn, Switzerland

Mrs Renate Sbeghen, World Council of Churches, Switzerland

Mr Gerard Scarff, World Council of Churches, Switzerland

Ms Lena Schaefer, Evangelische Kirchengemeinde Oer-Erkenschwick, Germany

Bishop Martin Schindehütte, EKD-Evangelical Church in Germany

Ms Lisa Schirch, Eastern Mennonite University, United States of America

Ms Miranda Schirch Goldberg, Visitor, United States of America

Ms Hannelore Schmid, World Council of Churches, Switzerland

Ms Daniele Schmidt Peter, Igreja Evangélica de Confissão Luterana no Brasil, Brazil

Rev. Ulrike Schmidt-Hesse, Association of Churches and Missions in South Western Germany (EMS)

Dr Marcelo Schneider, Evangelical Church of Lutheran Confession in Brazil

Mrs Barbara Schneider, Evangelischer Pressedienst epd-Zentralredaktion, Germany

Rev Friedhelm Schneider, EKD-Evangelical Church of the Palatinate, Germany

Mr Peter Schönhöffer, Ecumenical Network in Germany

Rev Michael Schuenemeyer, United Church of Christ, United States of America

Rev. Christoph Schuler, Old-Catholic Church of Switzerland

Rev. Frank Schürer-Behrmann, EKD-Evangelical Church in Berlin-Brandenburg-Silesian Oberlausitz, Germany

Mr Michael Schut, Episcopal Church in the USA

Mr Henry Schwier, EKD-Evangelical Lutheran Church of Hanover, Germany

Mrs Marcia Scott, United Church in Jamaica and the Cayman Islands, Jamaica

Mr Timothy Seidel, Mennonite Central Committee, United States of America

Dr Erlinda Senturias, Christian Conference of Asia, Thailand

Mr Kumala Setiabrata, Gereja Kristen Indonesia (GKI), Indonesia

Rev. Dr Hermen Shastri, Council of Churches of Malaysia

Mr Adrian Shaw, Church of Scotland, United Kingdom

Mr Michael Shaw, Media, Jamaica

Ambassador Elenor Sherlock, Office of the Prime Minister of Jamaica

Mr Michael Shim-Hue, Jamaica Baptist Union

Ms Yasuko Shimizu, Japanese Catholic Council for Justice and Peace (JCCJP)

Rev. Bog Hyun Shin, Korean Methodist Church, Republic of Korea

Archdeacon Mark Shirin, Armenian Apostolic Church (Holy See of Cilicia), United States of America

Mr Ek-Hong Sia, Presbyterian Church in Taiwan

Mr Ariel Siagan, Iglesia Evangelica Metodista En Las Islas Filipinas, Philippines

Mr Joseph Raphael Panlaque Siason, Gen Rosso, Italy

Mr Renato Sicoli, MFMci Conference Interpretation, Canada

Rev. Dr Stephen J. Sidorak, Jr., United Methodist Church, United States of America

Mr John Siebert, United Church of Canada

Rev. Jose Simeon, Convention baptiste de Haïti

Mr Marian Simion, Institute for Peace Studies in Eastern Christianity (IPSEC), United States of America

Ms Doneida Simpson, Local Volunteer, Jamaica

Mr Mark Simpson, Media, Jamaica

Rev. Marlon Simpson, United Church in Jamaica and the Cayman Islands, Jamaica

Mr Chola Simwanza, Salvation Army, Zambia

Ms Udith Sinclair, Methodist Church in the Caribbean and the Americas, Jamaica

Ms Simone Singh, Presbyterian Church in Trinidad and Tobago

Rev. Carlos Alberto Sintado, Interpreter, Switzerland

The Rev. Ilkka Sipiläinen, Evangelical Lutheran Church of Finland

Mr Zisis Siskos, Ecumenical Patriarchate, Greece

Ms Elizabeth J.A. Siwo-Okundi, Seminarian, United States of America

Rev. Dimitry Sizonenko, Russian Orthodox Church (Moscow Patriarchate), Russian Federation

Ms Natalia Skakun, Lutheran Church in Belarus

Rev. Sonia Skupch, Evangelical Church of the River Plate, Argentina

Dr,MD,PhD. Larisa Skuratovskaya, Academy of the Medical Sciences of Russia, Russian Federation

Mr Pillin Slater, Visitor, Jamaica

Rev. Robert O. Smith, Evangelical Lutheran Church in America

Mrs Shernette Smith, United Church in Jamaica and the Cayman Islands, Jamaica

Ms Susan L. Smith, First Congregational Church, UCC Salem, United States of America

Ms Julia Smucker, Seminarian, United States of America

Rev. Marsha Snulligan Haney Dr., Seminarian - Mentor, United States of America

Fr. Basilios Sobhy, Coptic Orthodox Church, Egypt

Ms Kerstin Söderblom, European Forum of Lesbian, Gay, Bisexual and Transgender

Christian Groups, Germany

Prof. Lilia Solano Ramirez, Justicia y Vida, Colombia

Ms Randi Solberg, European Forum of Lesbian, Gay, Bisexual and Transgender

Christian Groups, Norway

Rev. William Somplatsky-Jarman, Presbyterian Church (USA)

Ms Mary Sorum, United Theological College of the West Indies, Jamaica

Rev. Oliver Spies, EKD-Nordelbische Evangelisch-Lutherische Kirche, Germany

Ms Miriam Spies, United Church of Canada

Mr Michael Spyrou, Church of Cyprus

Mr Adrian St. Louis, Local Volunteer, Jamaica

Ms Rachel Stacy, Religious Society of Friends, United States of America

Rev. Alexander Stahlhoefer, Missão Evangélica União Cristã, Brazil

Mr Melroy Sterling, Media, Jamaica

Ms Khaliah Stewart, Moravian Church in Jamaica

Mr Rainer Stiehl, EKD-Evangelical Church of Kurhessen Waldeck, Germany

Rev. Jane Stranz, World Council of Churches, Switzerland

Rev. Peter Stucky, Colombian Council of Protestant and Evangelical Churches

Mrs Silke Stürmer, Visitor, Germany

Rev. Dr. Solomon Sumani Sule-Saa, Presbyterian Church of Ghana

Mr Sumardijana, East Java Christian Church (GKJW), Indonesia

Rev. Krisna Ludia Suryadi, Pasundan Christian Church (GKP), Indonesia

Rev Esther R. Suter, Media, Switzerland

Ms Veronica Sutherland-Ocnacuwenga, Moravian Church in Jamaica

Ms Jenny Svensson, Life and Peace Institute, Sweden

Mr Wilhelm Swan, Medical team, Jamaica

Mr Daniel Szadvari, Evangelical Church of the Augsburg Confession in Slovakia

Mr Elías Claudio Szczytnicki Broutman, Religions for Peace Latin America and the Caribbean, Peru

Ms Denise Tait, Media, Jamaica

Ms Faautu Talapusi, World Council of Churches, Switzerland

Rev.Dr. Yak-Hwee Tan, Council for World Mission, Taiwan

His Grace Bishop Anoushavan Tanielian, Armenian Apostolic Church (Holy See of Cilicia), United States of America

Ms Tara Tautari, World Council of Churches, Switzerland

Prof. Dr Wedad Abbas Tawfik, Coptic Orthodox Church, Egypt

Rev. Dr. Burchell Taylor, Baptist World Alliance, United States of America

Mr Okirua Teokoitu, Cook Islands Christian Church

Mr Emmanuel Kwame Tettey, Presbyterian Church of Ghana

Ms Natoya Thomas, Seminarian, Jamaica

Ms Aleyamma Thomas, Mar Thoma Syrian Church of Malabar, India

Rev. Ursula Thomé, Evangelical Church in the Rhineland, Germany

Ms Carolyn Thompson, Ecumenical Disability Advocates Network, United States of America

Rev. Karen Georgia Thompson, United Church of Christ, United States of America

Dr. med. Wolfgang Thon, Friedensinitiative, ACK, Martinskirche, Germany

Mrs Monica Thon, Friedensinitiative Bad Herdfeld - Rotenburg, Germany

Rev. Dr Michael Tita, Romanian Orthodox Church

Ms Erlini Tola Medina, Yatiyawi, Bolivia

Rev Letizia Tomassone, Waldensian Church, Italy

Mr Andrew Tomlinson, Quaker United Nations Office (QUNO), United States of America

Rev. José Miguel Torres Pérez, Instituto Martin Luther, Nicaragua

Mr Bernardo Toscano Sardinãs, Cuban Embassy

Ms Tarah Towler, Medical team, Jamaica

Dr Michael Reid Trice, Evangelical Lutheran Church in America

Rev. Deacon Nephon Tsimalis, Ecumenical Patriarchate, Turkey

Mr Siobhan Tuitt, Medical team, Jamaica

Mr Wessley Tukana Vatanitawake, Methodist Church in Fiji and Rotuma, Fiji

Rev. Dr Olav Fykse Tveit, World Council of Churches, Switzerland

Rev Jeanne Tyler, Ecumenical Disability Advocates Network, United States of America

Ms Sini Tyvi, Seminarian, Finland

Rev. Sabine Udodesku, World Council of Churches, Switzerland

Rev Hiroko Ueda, National Christian Council in Japan

Rev. Prof. Dr. Bernard Ugeux, Roman Catholic Church, Democratic Republic of Congo

Rev. Ukoha Ngwobia Ukoha, Presbyterian Church of Nigeria

Rev. Jonathan R. Ulanday, United Methodist Church, Philippines

Mr Misa Ulise Pilima, Ecumenical Disability Advocates Network, Tonga

Venerable (Archdeacon) Lawrence Ngozi Umar, Church of Nigeria (Anglican Communion)

Mr Noel Jose Unson, Gen Rosso, Italy

Rev. Edelberto Juan Valdés Fleites, Iglesia Presbiteriana-Reformada en Cuba

H.E. Bishop Rodolfo Valenzuela Núñez, Roman Catholic Church - Official Delegation, Guatemala

Ms Marijke van Duin, Media, Netherlands

Rev. Lisa Vander Wal, Reformed Church in America

Mr Ram Madhav Varanasi, Bharat Prakashan, New Delhi, India

Ms Laura Vargas, Pax Christi International, Peru

Dr. Saramma Varghese, Malankara Orthodox Syrian Church, India

Mr Liju Varghese, Malankara Orthodox Syrian Church, India

Rev Viji Varghese Eapen, Church of South India

Prof. Mammen Varkey, People's Reporter, India

Mr Milton Vassall, Methodist (Inter-denominational), Jamaica

Mrs Linnette Vassell, United Church in Jamaica and the Cayman Islands, Jamaica

Prof. Dr Petros Vassiliadis, Society for Ecumenical Studies and Inter-Orthodox Relations, Greece

Rev. Alexander Vasyutin, Russian Orthodox Church (Moscow Patriarchate), Russian Federation

Dr. C. Rosalee Velloso-Ewell, World Evangelical Alliance Theological Commission, United Kingdom

Archbishop Dr Joris Vercammen, International Old Catholic Bishops Conference, Netherlands

Mr Damien Vercauteren, World Council of Churches, Switzerland

Mr Rolando Maura Verdecia Avila, Consejo de Iglesias de Cuba

Rev. Peter Verhoeff, Protestant Church in the Netherlands

Mr Job Gleeson Vernon, Young Mens Christian Association, Trinidad and Tobago

Dr Tânia Mara Vieira Sampaio, Universidade Católica de Brasilia, Brazil

Rev. Felix Villanueva, United Church of Christ, United States of America

Ms Yasmina Visinand, World Council of Churches, Switzerland

Mr Ivan Vivas, United Evangelical Lutheran Church, Argentina

Mr Dmitry Vlasov, Russian Orthodox Church

Ms Jane Vogt Evensen, Norwegian Church Aid, Tanzania

Mr Wolf von Marschall, EKD-Evangelical Church in Central Germany

Ms Tanja von Rüsten, EKD-Evangelical Lutheran Church of Hanover, Germany

Mr Stephan von Twardowski, Evangelisch-methodistsche Kirche (United Methodist Church), Germany

Bishop Bärbel von Wartenberg-Potter, EKD-Nordelbische Evangelisch-Lutherische Kirche, Germany

Mrs Anne-Marie Vuignier-James, World Council of Churches, Switzerland

Dr Rachel Wagner, Ithaca College, United States of America

Rev. Dr. Christopher Walker, Uniting Church in Australia

Ms Althea Walker, United Church in Jamaica and the Cayman Islands, Jamaica

Rev. Dr. Angelique Walker-Smith, National Baptist Convention USA, Inc.

Dr Beverly Wallace, Seminarian, United States of America

Ms Shaniel Walters, Medical team, Jamaica

Ms Maria Luise Walz, Visitor, Germany

Mrs Margaret Wambui Mwaura, Ruiru East Jirani Pamoja, Kenya

Mrs Liv Hukset Wang, Norwegian Church Aid

Dr Elizabeth Ward, Violence Prevention Alliance, Jamaica

Mr Ashley-Jo Watson, Local Volunteer, Jamaica

Ms Yachelle Watson, Portmore Methodist Church, Jamaica

Rev. Dr. Craig Watts, Christian Church (Disciples of Christ) Disciples Peace Fellowship, United States of America

Rev. Prof. Dr. Gerhard Wegner, EKD-Evangelical Church in Germany

Ms Mary Wehbeh, Greek Orthodox Patriarchate of Antioch and All the East, Syrian Arab Republic

Mr Peter Weiderud, Church of Sweden

Mr Jörg Weisshaupt, Kirche und Jugend, Switzerland

Dr Deborah Weissman, International Council of Christians and Jews, Israel

Dr. Emily Elisabeth Welty, Presbyterian Church (USA)

Mr Stefan Wenger, Kirche und Jugend, Switzerland

Mrs Ricarda Wenzel, EKD-Evangelical Lutheran Church of Mecklenburg, Germany

Mrs Claudette Werleigh, Pax Christi International, Belgium

Rev. Dr Dietrich Werner, World Council of Churches, Switzerland

Mr Clifford Barrington White, Seminarian, Jamaica

Rev. Dr Paulus Sugeng Widjaja, Mennonite World Conference, Indonesia

Mr David Wildman, United Methodist Church General Board of Global Ministries, United States of America

Mr Kerone William, Media, Jamaica

Dr Stanley William, Integrated Rural Development of Weaker Sections in India

Mrs Enith M. Williams, Holy Trinity Cathedral, Jamaica

Mr Dewayne Williams, Seminarian, Jamaica

Mr John Williams, Media, Jamaica

Ms Danique Williams, Salem Baptist Church, Bahamas

Mr Peter Williams, World Council of Churches, Switzerland

Ms Nadine Wilson, Media, Jamaica

Rev. Lois M. Wilson, United Church of Canada

Ms Sophia Wilson, Local Volunteer, Jamaica

Mr Richard Wilson, Methodist (Saxthorpe Church), Jamaica

Mr Marvin Lance Wiser, Seminarian, United States of America

Mr Frank Witte, Media, Germany

The Hon. Mr Justice Lensley Wolfe, United Church in Jamaica and the Cayman Islands, Jamaica

Mr Lyndale Woolcock, Media, Jamaica

Mr Charles Wright, Media, Jamaica

Mr Fritz Wunderli, Federation of Swiss Protestant Churches

Ms Doreen Wynter, Jamaica Baptist Union

Ms Phoebe Yang, Seminarian, Jamaica

Ms Janelle Colleen Yanishewski, Presbyterian Church in Canada

Mr Brad Yoder, Church of the Brethren, Jamaica

Mr SANTINO ZACCHETTI, Gen Rosso, Italy

Rev. Dr. Elga Zachau, EKD-Evangelical Church of Westphalia, Germany

Rev. Dr. Hesdie Zamuel, Moravian Church in Suriname

Rev. Dr U Zaw Win, Myanmar Baptist Convention

Mr BARTLOMIEJ Zielinski, Gen Rosso, Italy

Mr Coetzee Zietsman, Dutch Reformed Church in South Africa

Mr Mark Johnson

Dr Guillermo Kerber Mas

Dr Deenabandhu Manchala

Dr Fulata Mbano-Moyo

Dr Rogate Mshana

Ms Alexandra Pomezny

Ms Tara Tautari

Ms Sabine Udodesku

IEPC Staff Group: Content Coordination

Dr Mathews George (*Overall Coordination*)

Ms Nan Braunschweiger (*Coordination*)

Ms Sabine Udodesku (*Spiritual Life*)

Mr Doug Chial (*Opening and Closing Plenaries*)

Dr Tamara Grzdelidze (*Bible Studies*)

Dr Guillermo Kerber Mas (*Plenaries*)

Ms Tara Tautari (*Workshops*)

Dr Fulata Mbano-Moyo (*Seminars*)

Ms Segma Asfaw (*Just Peace Companion*)

Mr Jonathan Frerichs (*Just Peace Companion*)

Mr Theodore Gill (*IEPC Message*)

Mr Mark Beach (*Communication*)

Appendix 8. IEPC Planning and Preparatory Committees and Staff Groups

DOV Reference Group and IEPC Planning Committee

Prof. Dr Fernando Enns, Germany (Moderator)

Ms Violet Al Raheb, Palestine

Rev. Omar Cortes-Gaibur, Chile

Ms Koila Costello-Olsson, Fiji

Rev. Dr Emmanuel Claspsis, USA,

Mr Ashley Hodgson, Nicaragua

Ms Tale Hungnes, Norway

Rev. Canon Grace Kaiso Isabirye, Uganda

Rev. Micheline Kamba Kasongo, South Africa

Mgr Bernard Munono Muyembe, Vatican City

Rev Dr Jayasiri Peiris, Sri Lanka

Mr Rodney Peterson, USA

Rev. Peter Stucky, Colombia

Rev. Angelique Walker-Smith, USA

IEPC Planning Sub-Committee

Mag. Viola Al Raheb, Palestine

Dr Oluwakemi Linda Banks, West Indies

Rev. Dr Emmanuel Clapsis, USA

Prof. Dr Fernando Enns, Germany

Rev. Gary Harriott, Jamaica

Rev. Canon Grace Clement, Uganda

Mr Jussi Ojala, Finland

Rev. Dr Jayasiri Peiris, Sri Lanka

Prof. Alison Phipps, U.K

Mr Joel Richards, Caribbean Conference of Churches

Members of the IEPC Spiritual Life Committee:

Rev. Fritz Baltruweit, Evangelical Lutheran Church of Hanover, Germany

Rev. Georgis Dimtsu, Ethiopian Orthodox Tewahedo Church, England

Rev. Susan Henry-Crowe, United Methodist Church, USA

Rev. Dr Swee Hong Lim, United Methodist Church, Singapore

Rev. Dr Ralph Hoyte, United Church of Jamaica and the Cayman Islands

Ms Jenitha Kameli, Evangelical Lutheran Church of Tanzania

Dr Moisés Mayordomo, Mennonite Church, Switzerland

Rev. Gerardo Oberman, Reformed Church of Rio de la Plata, Argentina

Prof. Dr Alison Phipps, Iona Community, Scotland

Ms Rima Tarazi, Episcopal Church, Ramallah, Palestine

Fr. Alexander Vasyutin, Russian Orthodox Church, Russia

Ms Simei Monteiro, WCC staff

Ms Hannelore Schmid, WCC staff

Rev. Sabine Udodesku, WCC staff

IEPC Host Committee in Jamaica

Rev. Dr Lenworth Anglin, Jamaica Umbrella Groups of Churches

Dr Deanna Ashley, Violence Prevention Alliance

Major Desmond Brown,Jamaica Baptist Union

Mrs. Shirley Carby,Jamaica Methodist District

Dr Byron Chambers, United Theological College of the West Indies

Mrs. Elaine Commissiong United Church in Jamaica and the Cayman Islands

Ms Myrtha Deslume Haitian/ Jamaican Society

Ms Fae Ellington, United Church in Jamaica and the Cayman Islands

Rev. Fr. Michael Elliott, Anglican Diocese of Jamaica

Mr Dwayne Fagan, United Church in Jamaica and the Cayman Islands

Rev. Gary Harriott (Chairperson), Jamaica Council of Churches

Rev. Dr Roy Henry, Jamaica Baptist Union

Rev. Dr Ralph Hoyte, United Church in Jamaica and the Cayman Islands

Mrs. Dawn Johns-Gordon, Anglican Diocese of Jamaica

Colonel Oral Khan, Violence Prevention Alliance

Rev. Marjorie Lewis, United Theological College of the West Indies

Rev. Christopher Mason, United Church in Jamaica and the Cayman Islands

Ms Joan McDonald (Local Coordinator), Anglican Diocese of Jamaica

Mr Bevar Moodie, Society of Friends (Quakers)

Ms Beverly Newell, Anglican Diocese of Jamaica

Dr Anna Perkins, Catholic Church

Mrs. MarciaScott, United Church in Jamaica and the Cayman Islands

AmbassadorElenorSherlock, Office of the Prime Minister, Jamaica

Mrs. Shernette Smith, United Church in Jamaica and the Cayman Islands

Ms Mary Sorum, United Theological College of the West Indies

Ms VeronicaSutherland-Ocnacuwenga, Moravian Church in Jamaica

Dr ElizabethWard,Violence Prevention Alliance

First Drafting Group of Ecumenical Call to Just Peace (ECJP)

Dr Daniel Benga, Romanian Orthodox Church

Dr Wanda Deifelt, Evangliecal Church of the Lutheran Confession in Brazil

Fr. Jacob Kurian, Malankara Orthodox Syrian Church

Dr Hong-Hsin Lin, Presbyterian Church Taiwan

Dr . Loreen Iminza Maseno, Deliverence Church in Kenya

Dr Muriel Orevillo-Montenegro, Siliman University Divinity School

Prof. Larry Rasmussen, Evangelical Lutheran Church in America

Prof. Robert Schreiter, Roman Catholic Church

Dr Geiko Müller-Farenholz , Germany

Second Drafting Group of Ecumenical Call to Just Peace

Rev. Dr Konrad Raiser, Germany (Moderator), Germany

Mrs. Alba Arrieta Seminario Teológico Presbiteriano de la Gran Colombia - STPRG

Mr Jione Havea, United Theological College

Mr Scott Holland, Bethany Theological Seminary

Ms Susan Jacob, Malankara Orthodox Syrian Church, India

Ms Iselin Jørgensen, Church of Norway, Norway

Dr Anna Kasafi Perkins, University of the West Indies, Jamaica

Prof. Dr Assaad Elias Kattan Centrum für Religiöse Studien - Westfälische Wilhelms- Universität Münster

Mrs. Joyce Nima, Uganda Joint Christian Council, Uganda

Rev. Peter Stucky, Iglesia Cristiana Menonita de Colombia, Colombia

IEPC Message Drafting Committee

Bishop Ivan Manuel Abrahams, Methodist Church, South Africa (Moderator)

H.E. Archbishop Narag Alemezian, Armenian Apostolic Church (Holy See of Cilicia), Lebanon

Rt. Rev. Duleep Kamil De Chickera, Church of Ceylon, Sri Lanka

Prof. Dr Heinrich Bedford-Strohm, EKD-Evangelical Church, Germany

Ms Meredith Coleman-Tobias, Lutheran Theological Seminary, Chicago, USA

Rev. Marjorie Lewis, Princip United Theological College, Kingston / Local Committee Jamaica

Mrs. Margarita B. Nelyubova Russian Orthodox Church (Patriarchate), Russia

Rev. Theodore Gill, World C of Churches, Geneva, Switze

IEPC Follow-up Reference

Bishop Ivan Manuel Abrahar South Africa

Dr Nora Bayrakdarian-Kabal Lebanon

Bishop Duleep Kamil De Chi Sri Lanka

Rev. Shirley Elaine DeWolf, Zimbabwe

Bishop Sally Dyck, United Methodist Church, USA

Prof. Dr Fernando Enns, Ger

Mrs Margarita Nelyubova, Ru

Dr Audeh B. Quawas, Jordan

Rev. Dr Dan Sandu, Romania

Ms Meredith Coleman-Tobia

IEPC Staff Group: Planning Preparation

Dr Mathews George (Moderat

Ms Nan Braunschweiger

Mr Mark Beach

Dr Daniel Buda

Mr Doug Chial

Ms Segma Asfaw

Mr Jonathan Frerichs

Dr Tamara Grdzelidze

Dr Carlos Ham